Sci

D0956055

2/18 3/00 8/10

10/9-97

JUL 16 1996

The Shoulders of
Giants

A HISTORY OF HUMAN FLIGHT
TO 1919

Phil Scott

Helix Books

Addison-Wesley Publishing Company
Reading, Massachusetts   Menlo Park, California   New York
Don Mills, Ontario   Wokingham, England   Amsterdam   Bonn
Sydney   Singapore   Tokyo   Madrid   San Jaun
Paris   Seoul   Milan   Mexico City   Taipei

Library of Congress Cataloging-in-Publication Data
Scott, Phil, 1961–
    The shoulders of giants : a history of human flight to 1919 / Phil
Scott.
      p. cm.
    Includes bibliographical references and index.
    ISBN 0-201-62722-1
    1. Aeronautics—History.   I. Title.
    TL515.S412   1995
    629.13'09—dc20   94-45977
                                CIP

Jacket design by Lynne Reed
Text design by Janis Owens
Set in 11.5-point Bembo by Compset, Inc.

1 2 3 4 5 6 7 8 9 10-MA-98979695
First Printing, May 1995

To Hope

"The bulk of mankind is as well equipped for flying as thinking."

—*Jonathan Swift*

"—which is now a more hopeful statement than Swift intended it to be."

—*Will Durant*

CONTENTS

PART TWO

Après Moi

Chapter Eight: 1904 to 1908

Chapter Nine: 1908 to 1909

Preface and Acknowledgments

As well as I can remember, this book began in my second year of college, during one of those beer-sodden conversations with a friend, Peter Engelman.

"Something is invented because *its time has come*," Engelman blurted out while cooking dinner.

"You have finally mastered the statement of the obvious," I said.

"No—I mean, take, for example . . ." He thought for a moment. "Take *the airplane,* for example. You had to develop all its various components first, like engines, and then develop the science of aeronautics, et cetera, and when all of those things could come together, you had *the airplane. Its time had come,*" he said, flourishing a spatula.

I winced. "That doesn't mean we were ready for it," I said, but then I started getting into the spirit of it. "You know, the first one could barely get off the ground," I continued. "It had taken twenty-five hundred years to get to that point, and in two decades they're flying one across the Atlantic. Its invention seemed to proceed at a mathematical rate, while its development happened geometrically. I wonder. . . ."

"Its time had come," he shrugged, getting bored with my rambling. He changed the subject by citing his new favorite quote, "You must lead the lemmings to the sea," which came from a TV sitcom, and he feigned surprise that high art might come from lowbrow entertainment.

While we watched TV and gorged ourselves on his cooking and cheap beer that night, I kept thinking about why the airplane's time had come when it had and what the ramifications of that were, and I probably returned to ponder the subject about once a month until just over a year ago, when a conversation with Jack Repcheck, an editor at Addison-Wesley's Helix Books, gave me the opportunity to become truly obsessed with the details.

I want to thank Jack, of course, for starting this whole project, and for seeing it most of the way through, and for being pretty darned encouraging, too. I hope I didn't slip any four-letter words past you, Jack, even though I really tried. Thanks to my other editor at Helix, Heather Mimnaugh, who saw it at its dirtiest and grittiest, Janet Biehl, the copyeditor, and Lynne Reed, who saw it the rest of the way through.

I am greatly indebted to the world's two greatest libraries, without whose assistance this volume would not have been possible. The first, the New York Public Library, provided what seemed like hundreds of rolls of turn-of-the-century newspaper microfilm, along with dusty, ancient, often obsolete volumes from its science and technology branch. The second is the Paola Free Library, where my research actually began years ago. I still can't believe there are places where someone will hand you, no questions asked, a rare and priceless manuscript for your viewing pleasure.

I also want to thank the staffs of the Library of Congress, the National Air and Space Museum archives, and the Royal Aeronautical Society of Great Britain for providing materials and papers relating to this volume. Also thanks to Tom Crouch of the National Air and Space Museum, for initial guidance on the project; Ronald G. Marweg of NCR Corporation (which now owns the Wright mansion, Hawthorn Hill) for giving me a private tour of this private building;

Lindsley A. Dunn, curator of the Glenn Curtiss Museum, for sending along research materials vital to the AEA and Curtiss sections; Edward L. Leiser of the San Diego Air Museum, for the information and photos on the Cayley glider reproduction there; and Crawford-Peters Aeronautica, whose assistance in obtaining some important articles and manuscripts kept me from moving into the New York Public Library for weeks at a stretch.

Since you never know when your first book is also your last, you feel inclined to take the opportunity to thank your every influence and mentor. Therefore, my thanks to the *Flying* magazine gang: Bill Garvey, Mary McDonnell, Amy Harr, Len Morgan, Gordon Baxter, and especially Dick Collins, for his firsthand account of flying with the Langley aerodrome squadron in the battle of Campho-Phenique during the Spanish-American War. Also thanks to Pat Luebke, who kept me in touch with the outer world, and whom I promised to mention before Charles Manson. Thanks to the entire staff of *Air & Space/Smithsonian* magazine, but most of all Pat Trenner, for research items, coddling, a crash pad, assignments when I really needed them most (truthfully, though, you cut it a little too close to the bone sometimes, Pat), and for buying me that model of the Wright Flyer, which sat upon my word processor throughout this project, and which, now, sadly, only the Silver Hill staff could possibly restore to pristine condition. And naturally thanks to the dear departed *Omni* gang: Sandy Fritz, Kellee Monahan, Ed "Willy" Gutman, Beth Howard, Rob "Gettysburg" Killheffer, Lambeth Hochwald, Shari Rudavsky, Rani Levy, and Jack Rosenberger, and most of all Ben Spier and Teresa Allee, my Copy Department Commandos. We had some fun, eh?

Also I want to express my deepest and sincerest appreciation to my parents, Mary and R. S. Scott, and my sister Sherry Hoover, all of Paola, Kansas, for putting up with me and my obsessions while I lived with them; to Kevin Gray, my high school journalism instructor, for putting up with me in his class; and to Brian Chisam, Jim

Norris, James Chancellor, and Brian Nash, at one time or another the best friends I ever had. And, naturally, thanks to Yashi and Kitty, who contributed as only cats can.

Thanks especially to Hope Edelman, who read most of the rough manuscript, offered just enough advice, and always had time for encouragement and support.

Finally, thanks to Peter Engelman, wherever life has taken him, and who unbeknownst to him somehow started all this. You led the lemming to the sea, Pete.

PART ONE

They Might Be Giants

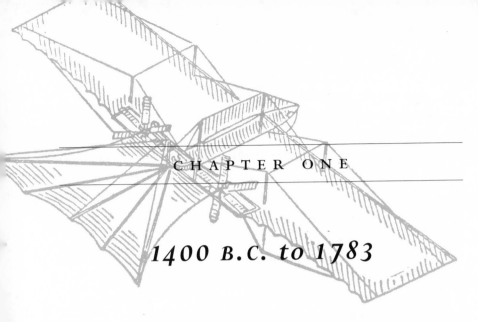

CHAPTER ONE

1400 B.C. to 1783

Preamble: Stranger on a Train

He told the regular customers back home that he was going camping. But no one came to the Outer Banks for that then; they came for the same reason most go anywhere: to be born, wrestle an existence from the landscape or the sea, then go on meekly to their reward. Back then, Elizabeth City was the end of the rail line, and it had taken the thin stranger two days on a train to get there.

He waited silently in the shadow of the small red-brick station, sweat trickling in tiny rivers from beneath his celluloid collar down his wool suit. Railroad hands unloaded his trunk and the long pine boards from the baggage car onto a wagon he had hired. When the men were finished, he carefully made sure of their work, then he climbed up beside the driver, and they started toward the waterfront, a mile or two away. He put in for the night at a respectable hotel.

In the morning the man walked the docks asking about passage to a settlement across Albemarle Sound, but no boatman or fisherman had heard of the place, let alone knew how to reach it. He persisted for three long days before he finally met Israel Perry, who had not only heard of the settlement, he could also take the man there in his fishing boat, anchored three miles down the river that flowed into the Sound.

In a skiff loaded to the gunwales with the trunk and lumber, and with a light breeze blowing from the west, the stranger, the fisherman, and his cabin boy set out down the river. Right away the skiff dipped water and began leaking. The man and the cabin boy started bailing and kept it up until they reached Perry's fishing schooner. A flat-bottomed vessel with a large cabin, the schooner, too, was in rough shape—even worse than the skiff. Upon boarding, the man spied frayed lines and rotted sails and a half-eaten rudderpost. He ducked into the cabin, found it filthy and ridden with vermin, and backed out, disgusted.

His hired crew unfurled the sails and pulled up anchor, but the light wind soon died out. Hours later, at dusk, the schooner finally floated from the river's mouth and reached the Sound. The water felt rough for such a light wind, and in the gathering darkness the man sensed Captain Perry's unease. As the wind grew stronger it shifted to the southeast: a headwind. With its big cabin, flat bottom, and light load, the schooner had trouble sailing against it; waves hit high on the sides while the boat rolled and pitched. One wave slammed into it from below and lifted it off the water. The boat landed hard and began taking on water.

And the stranger and the cabin boy bailed.

Gale-force winds drove the schooner closer to the north shore. Any attempt to turn the boat about would capsize it, but Perry thought he could try to round the light that marked the mouth of the North River and take refuge behind the point. He aimed for the light.

The foresail broke loose from the boom, roaring as it whipped about. The man and the cabin boy fought it in while the boat rolled. Whipping canvas roared again. This time it was the mainsail that tore loose, leaving only a jib sail. Now the captain couldn't make it around the light.

He knew it sat on a little finger of land pointing out a quarter mile from the shore. If they could make a straight run over the bar with just the jib—

He had to swing the schooner's stern around into the wind without capsizing it and go straight over the bar. It was their only chance.

The man and the cabin boy fought down the mainsail, then braced themselves as the ride began. Waves flew high over the bar and crashed over the schooner's stern. But in seconds it was over: They had made it.

Over his passenger's protest, the captain refused to make landfall for the night, and he set anchor. The man stretched out on the deck in the dark, spooning jelly from a jar his sister had thought to pack in his suitcase. As he ate, he laughed to himself. *The captain has been so long a stranger to the touch of water on his skin that it affects him very much,* he thought—much more than their recent adventure. Then the man fell asleep.

The next day they waited till the afternoon for the wind to shift before they set sail; by night, they had finally reached that fishing settlement on the Outer Bank. It was late, so once again the man dined on jelly, slept on deck, and fought off mosquitoes. When he awoke the next morning, he stood and took a good look around. Beyond a few pine trees in the bay stood some scattered houses, then sand dunes, then nothing but ocean and sea gulls. And sky and wind.

It had taken him a week to get there. But as far as he knew, there was no more perfect spot on earth to do what he'd set out to accomplish.

"For some years I have been afflicted with the belief that flight is possible to man," he had written to the greatest living expert in the field earlier that year, an aging engineer musically named Octave Chanute. "My disease has increased in severity and I feel that it will soon cost me an increased amount of money if not my life. I have been trying to arrange my affairs in such a way that I can devote my entire time for a few months to experiment in this field."

And so Wilbur Wright was about to set foot for the first time on the sands of Kitty Hawk.

Daedalus Takes Flight

Wright was well-versed on his subject. He knew that at the dawn of history, only birds and the gods held the power of flight. Apollo drove the horses and chariot of Helios, the sun, across the sky every day; Hermes, the divine messenger, was borne aloft by wings on his sandals. The gods might occasionally allow mortals to borrow this power, but the results were usually tragic. Thus when Poseidon and Athena allowed Bellerophon to ride the winged horse Pegasus: "Mounting it straightway he brandished his arms, himself in armor of bronze; with it he slew the archer army of women, the Amazons, shooting them from the unpeopled bosom of the cold upper air," the Greek poet Pindar wrote. Now believing himself worthy of the company of the gods, Bellerophon tried to fly to their palaces on Mount Olympus, but Pegasus threw him from a great height. "If any man sets his eye on a distant target, he is too short to reach the brass-paved home of the gods," warned the poet.

Sometime before 1400 B.C. lived Daedalus; he could trace his ancestry to Hephaestus, the god of fiery arts who hammered Zeus' thunderbolts. Daedalus came from Athens, where his clever inventions heaped fame on his name. But when his gifted nephew and protégé, Talus, invented the saw and the potter's wheel, Daedalus grew jealous. In a fit of rage one night he threw Talus from the

Acropolis. He then fled across the Aegean Sea to the island of Crete, ruled by the tyrannical King Minos. Minos was thrilled to have an engineer with the reputation of Daedalus, even if he was Athenian, and put him to work.

Powerful people tend to have embarrassing offspring, and Minos was no exception. His wife had had a night of passion with a bull, and Minos wished to conceal the result: a sulky man-beast called the Minotaur. He took Daedalus to a spot just beyond the royal palace and ordered him to build there an arbor maze with blind walls. This Daedalus did to perfection, for, wrote the Roman poet Ovid centuries later, "as one entered it only a wary mind could find an exit to the world again." There were no blueprints, no plans, and though only Daedalus had such a wary mind, even he couldn't remember how to get out of the place.

As one condition of a peace treaty, every nine years Athens sent Crete its fourteen best young people, whom cruel Minos shoved into the Labyrinth to wander in panic and confusion—until they were hunted down, murdered, and devoured by the Minotaur. When the third group of Athenian youths arrived, Daedalus, hoping to buy back some goodwill with Athens, smuggled a sword to the cleverest youth, Theseus, with which to kill the Minotaur. Theseus then asked for a powerful device to lead the other Athenian youths from the maze.

Daedalus thought and then held out a ball of thread. Theseus could tie one end to the Labyrinth's entrance, unroll the ball until he came upon the man-beast, slay him, and follow the thread back to the entrance. This Theseus did, and sailed back to Athens, though without Daedalus or his son Icarus. King Minos was not amused, however; he locked the pair inside the Labyrinth—and threw away their string.

Daedalus took to wandering the maze, wondering how to escape its walls, and Minos' grasp. "Though earth and water in subjection laid, O cruel Minos, thy dominion be," he said, "We'll go through air; for sure the air is free." And so Daedalus studied the birds that flew overhead. When he finally learned their secret, he and Icarus collected feathers from the floor of the maze. Then, according to Ovid,

> *A row of quills in gradual order placed,*
> *Rise by degrees in length from first to last. . .*
> *Along the middle runs a twine of flax,*
> *The bottom stems are joined by plant wax:*
> *Thus, well compact, a hollow bonding brings*
> *The fine composure into real wings.*

When Daedalus finished the wings, he strapped them across his shoulders and began flapping. His feet left the ground, and briefly he glided through the air.

He built another set of wings for Icarus and gave his son a lecture on their art, and a lesson in moderation: "My boy, take care," he said, "If low, the surges wet your flagging plumes; If high, the sun the melting wax consumes. . . . But follow me: Let me before you lay Rules for the Flight, and mark the pathless way."

Icarus, however, was a teenager.

The pair took off, with Daedalus leading the way, and flew high over the heads of many—a fisherman, a farmer, a shepherd all saw the pair and mistook them for gods. As Icarus grew more accustomed to wings, his boldness grew godlike. He flew far ahead of his father, swooping and diving, then climbing higher and higher toward the gods. But the higher he went, the closer he flew to Helios' chariot, melting the wax on his wings. It ran off in thick streams; single feathers peeled off, then clumps. Soon Icarus was beating only his naked arms in the air. He plunged into the sea, screaming Daedalus' name.

His father arrived and found nothing but feathers floating on the waves. Legend says he flew on to Sicily, a Greek colony, where he received asylum from both Crete and Athens. He cursed his art and crushed the wings and threw the wreckage into the sea. Soon thereafter he died, taking the secret of the birds with him.

Archimedes, Nero, and Hero

Whether a man named Daedalus existed is disputable, but from the east Greek culture did indeed fly west, to not one but a thousand places; for centuries the fractious city-states and their likewise fractious colonies ruled the Mediterranean. As in every great civilization, evil coexisted with good: For every Minos, a democratic Pericles ruled, then a warlike Alexander. The health and stability of the time fed humanity's hunger for knowledge, which gave rise to Western science, both theoretical and practical. Of the second branch, the science of mechanics was the homely stepchild. The Greeks had little need for labor-saving devices; to do work, they had slaves or their own backs.

Yet Archimedes, born in 287 B.C. in Sicily, devoted much of his research to mechanics. He refined the Egyptian water screw, a helix within a cylinder that raised water from lower to higher levels. And everyone knows the story of how King Hieron charged Archimedes with finding whether a metalsmith had corrupted the king's gold crown with a base metal, and how, while considering the problem in the baths, Archimedes realized something that caused him to leap up and run naked in the street shouting "Eureka!" It was the principle of hydrostatics—in a fluid a body loses weight equal to the weight of the fluid it replaces. Archimedes lived until 212 B.C., long enough to see the flame of Greek enlightenment begin to dim. During the conquest of Sicily, a Roman soldier, part of an invasion fleet, took Archimedes' life.

The Romans, too, relied on slave labor and so left mechanics to ceremony. As Rome turned from Republic to Empire and decay set in, a slave might be offered his freedom if he could fly; to add suspense, the wings were to be built in front of an audience at the Colosseum—before the release of hungry wild animals. Prisoners were usually torn to shreds before they could pass on their aerodynamic research to the next round of contestants.

Nero, who reigned as emperor from A.D. 54 to 68, seemed especially interested in human flight: Before his suicide, he grew to believe himself so powerful and divine that he could will his subjects to fly. According to Suetonius in *The Twelve Caesars,* during a performance of the ballet *Daedalus and Icarus,* "the actor who played Icarus, while attempting his first flight, fell beside Nero's couch and splattered him with blood."

Amidst the cruelty of the ancient world, man continued to pursue knowledge. Hero of Alexandria, a Greek said to have lived between the first and third century A.D., studied the power of air pressure; he built a boiler that fed steam through a curved arm and issued forth from the tail of a toy wooden dove, spinning it in circles. Hero saw his device's power to amuse yet seemed blind to its potential for flight.

So during the next few centuries, men who believed human flight possible thought only of following Daedalus' lead of imitating birds. The legend, after all, said he was successful (and as if to concur, the philosophers of the time said man is but a featherless biped). Thus would an intrepid birdman convince himself that he, too, might fly like a bird. Around A.D. 852 the Moor Armen Firman clad himself in canvas and leaped from a tower in Cordoba, Spain. He reached the ground safely, for air filled the cloak and allowed him to float to the ground. Just twenty-three years later, a similarly named Spaniard, Abbas b. Firnas, built wings and covered them and himself in feathers, assuming they carried the magic that helped birds defy gravity. According to a contemporary account by the historian al-Makkari, "he flew to a considerable distance . . . but in alighting again . . . his back was very much hurt, for not knowing that birds when they alight come down upon their tails, he forgot to provide himself with one."

Wayland the Smith, Bread from Windmills, and the Flying Monk

With the slow decline of Rome's power, barbaric hordes from the north ransacked the Empire's ragged fringes. Around their campfires these Norsemen told their own legends, how their hero Wayland the Smith stole a Valkyrie's swan plumage and with it learned to fly. After nine years the Valkyrie stole the wings back and allowed an enemy king to imprison Wayland on an island. To escape, Wayland made his own wings and enlisted his brother Egil to test them, though Egil protested he had no knowledge in the field.

"Against the wind shalt thou rise easily," Wayland instructed, "Then when thou wouldst descend, fly with the wind." Egil took off and flew indeed, but on landing he was swiftly thrown headfirst into the ground. Shocked at the wings' sudden failure, he confessed, "If they were really good, I would have kept them."

Wayland said, "When I bade that thou shouldst with the wind make thy descent I told thee wrong. . . . I did not trust thee quite. Remember this, that every bird that flies rises against the wind and so alights."

Norsemen gradually overran the Roman Empire, often bearing the blame for Western Civilization's collapse into the Dark Ages, but for the mass of men things were just as dark as they had always been. The people spent their days toiling in the fields, and fighting off wild animals and conscription parties for the Crusades, and they spent their nights collapsed exhausted on a bed of straw. Everything was still powered by human muscle, or animal muscle, if one were rich enough to buy a horse or oxen. "Is not every man born to labour as a bird in flight?" wrote Saint Anselm in 1081.

But those to the manor born still had servants to do chores, like grow wheat, grind it, then bake bread. The eldest son eventually inherited the estate; the second would enter the clergy. Life wasn't dark for everyone in the Dark Ages.

The Church kept society from breaking down after the Roman Empire collapsed. It also kept alive the ancient wisdom that had survived, for monks copied, translated, and studied the ancient texts of poets like Ovid, and philosophers like Plato, and scientists like Archimedes and Hero. They also recorded history as it had been passed down through the ages. One monk, Geoffrey of Monmouth, wrote the history of the kings of England until his time; he told of Bladud, who ruled for twenty years during the ninth century before Christ. Bladud is best known for giving the world his son Leir, the tenth king of Britain, but he also put the baths in Bath, and Geoffrey records that Bladud was enlightened, having encouraged the study of "Neckromantick Art"—magic—throughout his kingdom. His own experiments culminated in the construction of a pair of wings, with which he proposed to fly.

King Bladud proved as adept at flight as King Lear was at judging daughters. "He came down on top of the Temple of Apollo in the town of Trinovantum," writes Geoffrey, "and was dashed to countless fragments."

Slowly though, life was improving. A clever individual, whose name is lost to history, took a cross of wood and fashioned on it angled blades like those found on a sycamore seed. He mounted that on a shaft with gears, which meshed with gears from a shaft protruding from a millstone. When wind blew against the blades, it turned the millstone and ground grain. Thus, the windmill, which by the year 1200 dotted the countryside and began appearing in the illuminated manuscripts drawn by monks.

Monks also observed and recorded a peculiar phenomenon: The windmill's fan was held in place by front and back stops; normally the pressure of wind against the fan blades would wear down the back stop and it would have to be replaced. But on some windmills the front stop wore down—the blades were actually *advancing* into the wind. No one could explain it, though perhaps the phenomenon inspired the eleventh-century Benedictine monk Oliver, when he sought to fly like a bird. In a stained-glass window at Malmesbury Abbey, a tonsured Oliver holds a small replica of his flying machine with its two of white, batlike wings shaped like windmill fans, a heavy wooden frame, and a rope harness. His chronicler Bescherelle wrote: "[Oliver] sprang from the top of a tower against the wind. He succeeded in sailing a distance of 125 paces; but either through the impetuosity or whirling of the wind, or through nervousness resulting from his audacious enterprise, he fell to the earth and broke his legs."

Echoing the unlucky lesson of the Spaniard Firnas, Bescherelle says, "Henceforth [Oliver] dragged a miserable, languishing existence, attributing his misfortune to his having failed to attach a tail to his feet."

Some two centuries later, man's feet still stood fixed firmly on the ground, though he might allow his mind to soar. Another English monk, Roger Bacon, foretold of "the fabrication of instruments of wonderfully excellent usefulness, such as machines for flying, or for moving in vehicles without animals and yet with incomparable speed. . . . Flying machines can be made, and a man sitting in the middle of the machine may revolve some ingenious device by which artificial wings may beat the air in the manner of a flying bird."

Perhaps Bacon had heard of Brother Oliver, for he wrote: "And it is certain that there is an instrument to fly with, which I never saw, nor know any man that has seen it, but I full well know by name the learned man that invented the same."

He may have known the man's name, but Bacon neglected to write it down.

Tall Tales from Marco Polo;
Leonardo da Vinci's Great Bird

In 1298 a Venetian merchant was captured during battle with Gen-
oese forces and thrown in prison for one year. From his cell Marco
Polo dictated to a fellow prisoner fantastic stories from his youth: of
his travels to the Far East, of his observations as an ambassador for
the great Kublai Khan. Of the many strange stories he told, one
stands out: "When any ship must go on a voyage . . . [the Chinese]
will find some fool or drunkard and lash him to [a wicker frame-
work], for no one in his right mind or with his wits about him
would expose himself to that peril. Then they raise the framework
into the teeth of the wind and the wind lifts up the framework and
carries it aloft, and the men hold it aloft by [a] long rope." So, while
the medieval Europeans dressed as birds and flung themselves from
towers, Polo watched the Chinese lift a man into the air with a kite.
For years, though, no one believed a word of Polo's adventures in
"the Gorgeous East"—they were simply too fantastic, the fabrica-
tions of an overly active imagination.*

The combined wealth of Polo's merchant class and the Church
provided medieval Italy with artistic excellence and intellectual
power unsurpassed by other countries, unmatched even by the ancients. Italy gave the world the politics of Machiavelli, the heavenly
order of Galileo, and the mind of Leonardo da Vinci. Leonardo's
swift pen outran his age's ability to set his ideas in concrete: He lived
from 1452 to 1519 and left the world *The Last Supper* and the *Mona
Lisa,* as well as a legacy of sculpture, architecture, and engineering.
Giorgio Vasari attributed his great and vast talents to his lovable disposition; he wrote that when Leonardo visited the marketplace, he

---

*The Chinese had a fantastic tale of their own: Legend said that as a boy, Emperor
Shun, who lived from 2258 to 2208 B.C., was captured by his father's enemies but es-
caped by donning "the work clothes of a bird" and flying away.

would buy caged birds for the pleasure of setting them free. "In return he was so favored by nature that to whatever he turned his mind or thoughts the results were always inspired and perfect; and his lively and delightful works were incomparably graceful and realistic," Vasari said.

It was in 1486, while in the service of Lodovico of Milan as military engineer—and court costume maker—that Leonardo became infatuated with flight. In one notebook alone Leonardo left some 35,000 words and 500 sketches describing birds in flight and a variety of machines designed to duplicate it: Screws with which to spin upward through the air, and wooden-framed parachutes with which to descend from it. Mostly, however, he sought to imitate nature.

"A bird is an instrument working according to mechanical law. This instrument it is within the power of man to reproduce with all its movements," he wrote, "but not with a corresponding degree of strength." A bird's most powerful muscles—the ones that drive its wings—are in its breast; in man the leg muscles are strongest. For the mechanical "great bird" he designed for Gianni Antonio di Mariolo, Leonardo sought to drive the wing-flapping mechanism with the power of the pilot's legs. His arms—and his head—would steer and control the great bird through a system of pulleys and lines leading to the wingtips. It would have a birch framework held together with leather thongs and raw silk joints, and starched linen-covered wings, solid like a bat's, "because its membranes serve as . . . a means of binding together the framework of the wings."* He advised "trial of the machine over water, so that if you fall you do not do yourself any harm."

Though no one knows for sure, he may have tried to build and test the great bird himself. There is this tantalizing reference from his journal: "Tomorrow morning, on the second day of January,

---

*A great bird recently constructed to Leonardo's written instructions, for display in the British Museum, weighed nearly five hundred pounds.

1496, I will make the thong and the attempt." If he did try, he certainly failed. No record exists of a successful test, and Leonardo clearly knew how the world would react if he succeeded. "The great bird will take its first flight . . . filling the whole world with amazement and all records with its fame; and it will bring eternal glory to the nest where it was born."

He seemed to conceive every method of conquering the air yet settled on none; to the end his energy remained diffused. Soon after he died, Leonardo's aeronautical notebooks went to his beneficiary, Francesco Melzi, who tucked them away in a library.

There they disappeared, lost until Napoleon's time.

While Sir Isaac Newton Considers Bodies in Fluid, Others Cast Doubts on Human Bodies in Air

Progress in human flight languished for nearly a century and a half after Leonardo's death, waiting for the Renaissance to bloom throughout the rest of Europe. And when the rebirth of knowledge spread north after the Reformation, men once again began practical as well as theoretical work toward flying—but not always together. Although Sir Isaac Newton did not know it, the theoretical research began with him. Newton, who said, "If I have seen farther . . . it is by standing on the shoulders of Giants," had been building upon the observations of Aristotle and Galileo to advance human understanding of a subject seemingly unrelated to flight: how solid bodies move through fluids.

When Aristotle made observations on the subject, he found force to always be pushing an object forward, yet he didn't conceive of one resisting the forward motion. When Galileo observed his pendulum, however, he had noted just such a resistance. Newton, in his *Philosophiae Naturalis Principia Mathematica,* sought formulas to measure those forces. He said, first, that the force acting on a body and a fluid are the same whether the body is moving through the fluid or the fluid is moving around the body.

He went on to calculate that, for a body exposed to a fluid stream of a given speed, the forces produced are proportional to the fluid's velocity squared, the square of the body's length, and the density of the fluid. Newton also said that air is a fluid, so his observations applied to it as well as to any other fluid—water, for instance; the force each fluid exerts is proportional to its density. Now informed practical experimenters might test their theories in one medium and rest assured that it applied to the other.

As for those practical experimenters: Unaided by the lost Leonardo notebooks, others began to conclude that man could not fly by arm power alone.

In 1660 English mathematician and Newtonian rival Robert Hooke disclosed to members of the Royal Society that he had built a spring-powered, wing-flapping model that took off and could generally support itself in the air, yet when he tried to make the design Hooke-size, it couldn't get off the ground.

"The way of flying in the air seems principally impracticable by reason of the want of strength in human Muscles," he wrote in his *Micrographia*. "If therefore that could be supplied, it were, I think, easier to make twenty contrivances to perform the offices of wings." And that was good enough for Hooke.

But it wasn't good enough for a French locksmith whose last name was Besnier (and whose first name is lost to time). Like Leonardo, Besnier built his device to incorporate the power of his legs. It functioned on the theory that a flying bird supports its entire weight by flapping its wings. The device consisted of two poles, one over each shoulder, with each pole having a hinged wing on each end. Besnier held on to the poles with each hand—he tied his legs to the aft ends—and as he proceeded to swim or climb through the air, the wings coming up would fold shut to lessen resistance, while

BESNIER, 1678: THE FRENCH LOCKSMITH
PLUNGED INTO HUMAN FLIGHT WITH A
SIMILAR DEVICE.

the wings coming down would snap open to provide support in the atmosphere. Had the air been nearly as thick a fluid as water, his apparatus might have succeeded. In truth, his 1678 flight was short—more of a plummet really. But like many shallow ideas its reach was deep, influencing schemes both serious and fantastic for more than a century.

The Fall of Barometric Pressure and the Rise of the Aerial Ship

Father Francisco de Lana Terzi, in 1670 a thirty-nine-year-old Jesuit science teacher, wasn't interested so much in how solid bodies react in fluid. Nor did he concern himself much with the difficulties inherent in muscle-powered flight. ("[It] may not . . . have been a myth what is related about Daedalus and Icarus," he allowed in his treatise titled *The Aerial Ship*, for de Lana himself had heard reports of a flight across the Lake of Perugia by the Italian mathematician J. B. Danti in an apparatus of otherwise unknown form.) The good

Jesuit was, however, interested in an entirely original idea: "No one has . . . deemed it possible so to construct a vessel that it would travel on the air as if it were supported on water, insomuch that it has not been thought practicable to make a machine lighter than the air itself."

Through his experiments with the newly discovered barometer, de Lana believed he had found a way to make a vessel lighter than air. He had measured atmospheric pressure at different elevations; the higher he went, the lighter was the air: It had weight. De Lana weighed a glass vessel first with air, then with the air evacuated, and from that he calculated that a cubic foot of air weighed an ounce. "[It] is certain that one can construct a vessel of glass or other material which could weigh less than the air contained therein," he said, and deemed it possible to construct what he called an aerial ship. It would be held aloft by four copper vacuum globes, each some 14 feet in diameter and weighing 154 pounds—yet according to his calculations each would displace a whopping 718 pounds of air. "From this it can be easily seen how it is possible to construct a machine which, fashioned like unto a ship, will float on the air." For propulsion he suggested a sail and oars, "to travel with great speed to any place at will," with sandbags to control its rate of ascent.

Pleading that his vow of poverty prohibited expending the hundred ducats it would cost to construct the machine, de Lana never built his aerial ship. Yet he fended off his critics by casually discounting all the various construction problems that he could foresee "save only one. . . .

"God would never surely allow such a machine to be successful, since it would create many disturbances in the civil and political government of mankind.

"Where is the man," he continued, "who can fail to see that no city would be proof against surprise, as the ship could at any time be steered over its squares, or even over the courtyards of dwelling-houses, and brought to earth for landing its crews? And in the case of ships that sail the seas, by allowing the aerial ship to descend from the high air to the level of their sails, their cordage could be cut; or even without descending so low iron weights could be hurled to wreck the ships and kill their crews, or they could be set upon by fireballs and bombs; not ships alone, but houses, fortresses, and cities could be destroyed, with the certainty that the air ship would come to no harm as the missiles could be hurled from a vast height."

Where, indeed, is the man who could not foresee such carnage? And where is that kind and just God who would never surely allow it to happen?

A decade later, Giovanni Alphonso Borelli, a professor of mathematics at Messina, published a manuscript partly to refute de Lana's scheme of the aerial ship. "This is to be a vain hope," Borelli wrote in a monograph published a year after his death in 1679, ". . . [because] if such a great vacuum were made the thin brass vessel could not resist the strong pressure of the air, which would break or crush it." But that was merely an aside, as the title of his monograph suggests: *De Motu Animalium,* the motion of animals. Borelli was concerned with the flight of birds, and in his work he sought to compare the muscles of birds to those of man. "When . . . it is asked whether man may be able to fly by their own strength . . . it is clear that the motive power of the pectoral muscles in men is much less than necessary for flight," he said, for he calculated that a bird's pectoral muscles make up more than a sixth of its weight, yet the pectorals are less than one hundreth of a man's. " Hence," he said, to the dismay of romantics everywhere, "it is deduced that the Icarian invention is entirely mythical because impossible." And, Borelli concluded, "Wherefore either the strength of the muscles ought to be increased, or the weight of the human body must be decreased, so that the same proportion obtains in it as exists in birds." That is a surgical atrocity made possible by modern medicine but as of yet prevented by its humanity.

Montgolfiers Invent the Aerostatic Globe

Nevertheless, Father de Lana's concept of lighter-than-air flight had made its way into humanity's collective consciousness. History only needed to wait more than a century for an accident.

Joseph and Étienne Montgolfier made their living as papermakers in the French town of Annonay, outside of Lyon. Details are sketchy about how they stumbled into aeronautics sometime in 1782. One account says they saw paper ashes rise in a column of smoke; another account says the ascending object was a shirt hung to dry over a fire; a picturesque third account, no doubt apocryphal, says it was the drying, billowing petticoats of Joseph Montgolfier's wife (though the legend does not say whether she was in them at the time).

According to *The Air Balloon,* an uncredited treatise written the following year, the Montgolfiers found that smoke, "which being specifically lighter than the atmospheric air, is carried up the chimney and only settles when it gets to that height which is equal to its own levity." If the brothers could only capture enough of it in a bag, the smoke might lift that bag; and given a large enough bag—

It might lift a person as well.

Ignoring the paper business momentarily, the Montgolfiers sewed a small silk bag, held it over an especially smoky fire of wool and straw, and then let the bag go. It bobbed heavenward, and so elevated were the brothers by the sight that they began constructing a series of ever larger spherical bags, which they inflated with their special fire, which continued to launch the bags skyward.

They were ready to show the public.

On June 4, 1783, before a large crowd that had assembled in the marketplace of Annonay, the Montgolfiers put the torch to a pile of wool and straw and inflated a 110-foot-circumference envelope of paper-lined linen. They set it free, and to the crowd's—and the brothers'—great delight, the balloon ascended to an estimated altitude of 6,500 feet.

They were ready to take their show on the road.

In Versailles that September, before 130,000 spectators—including Louis XVI, Marie Antoinette, and the entire royal court—the brothers inflated a more elaborate, decorated balloon. This time they had attached a wicker basket and placed in it a sheep, a cock, and a duck. Since no one knew how far above the ground the air would be too light to breathe, it was thought wiser to first asphyxiate a few farm animals before moving on to a farmer.

But the launch went well, and the trio of aeronauts managed to cover a distance of two miles in eight minutes, then land on earth, scared but still breathing.

The Montgolfiers were ready for the next step.

They constructed a balloon of blue cotton cloth 70 feet high and 46 feet in diameter, "elegantly decorated and painted on the outside with the signs of the zodiac, and the monogram of the king, fleur-de-lys, etc." said a contemporary account written by one Tiberio Cavallo. "The lower opening of the aerostat was encircled by a wickerwork gallery which was about three feet high. The inside diameter of this gallery and of the opening of the balloon (the neck of which was surrounded by the gallery) was almost 16 feet. There was an iron grate or brasier in the middle of this opening secured by chains to the sides of the craft . . . for members of the crew to stoke a fire which had been lit on this grate . . . keeping hot air flowing into the opening of the balloon." All told, the "aerostatic globe" weighed 1,600 pounds and had a volume of 60,000 cubic feet.

Now that they were ready to take that first dangerous ascent into the heavens—inside a combustible, fragile cloth bag that no one knew how high it might go—which of them would actually become the very first human to fly aloft? The Montgolfiers looked at one another and made a bold decision.

They needed a volunteer.

CHAPTER TWO

1783 to 1812

Mankind's First Flight

While the Montgolfiers finished preparing their balloon, King Louis XVI himself contemplated the candidates for first aeronaut. Following Nero's lead, Louis ordered that condemned prisoners be the first to try flying, but one Pilatre de Rozier stepped forth and announced his intentions to be first. King Louis would not hear of de Rozier risking his life—until the Marquis d'Arlandes went to Louis and told him the vehicle was so safe that the marquis himself would be happy to accompany de Rozier. His Royal Highness bestowed His Royal Blessing on the pair.

The aeronauts first went aloft quietly in a tethered trial ascent on October 19, 1783, and the aerostat held up well. One month later the pair went to the grounds of the Chateau la Muette in Paris, where another huge crowd had gathered, this time including the royal family. For one final time the aeronauts climbed the launch platform stairs and boarded the inflated balloon. That afternoon at two, with the smoking balloon straining against the tethers and the wind out of the northeast, de Rozier and d'Arlandes were cut loose.

The aerostat rose and slowly drifted over a stand of trees; when they had reached a height of about 300 feet, the aeronauts doffed their hats to the delight of the amazed crowd.

As the Marquis d'Arlandes later wrote to a friend, "I was surprised at the silence and absence of movement which our departure caused among the spectators, and believed them to be astonished and perhaps awed at the strange spectacle." The marquis himself was awed, too, and forgot his assigned duties.

"You are doing nothing, and the balloon is scarcely rising a fathom," de Rozier said to him, so the marquis tossed a bundle of straw on the fire, then promptly lost himself identifying the bends of the River Oise, below.

"If you look at the river in that fashion you will be likely to bathe in it soon," de Rozier said. "Some fire, my dear friend, some fire!"

"The river is very difficult to cross," the marquis said to de Rozier, who continued his nervous lecturing. So d'Arlandes threw more straw on the fire and stirred it, and felt the balloon begin to rise. "For once we move," he said.

At that moment he heard a sharp crack from the top of the envelope, but he saw nothing. He felt a shock, and for a moment he thought the balloon had burst.

"What are you doing?" he asked de Rozier, who had gone into the interior. "Are you having a dance to yourself?"

"I'm not moving," de Rozier replied.

They heard another loud report; overhead, another cord had cracked. The marquis looked inside the balloon and saw several holes had burned in the envelope.

"It must descend," he cried.

"Why?"

"Look," d'Arlandes said, pointing at the holes. He sponged water on ones still burning. "We must descend."

"We are upon Paris."

"It does not matter," he answered. "Only look! Is there no danger? Are you holding on well?"

"Yes," de Rozier said.

"We can cross Paris," the marquis decreed.

And so they kept on floating gently. They floated near the towers of St. Sulpice, where observers calculated they had reached an altitude of 1,650 feet; then the balloon gradually sank toward the ground. The marquis climbed on top of the gallery, and as they touched down, he felt the balloon press softly against his head. He pushed it back and jumped off. In an instant the envelope collapsed—on top of de Rozier, who crawled out from under the mass of balloon fabric, smoky and dusty but unharmed. They had flown.

Neither reported having had trouble breathing the thin air, and at the rarefied altitude they could see places forty-eight miles away. "The grounds about Paris appeared to them like bouquets," reported *The Air Balloon,* "and the people passing and repassing (according to the expression of Monf. Rozier) 'like so many mites in a cheese'—no bad situation to humble the pride of man."

The aerostatic globe worked by Archimedes' principle, the law of hydrostatics: a body in a fluid loses weight equal to the weight of the fluid it replaces. When filled with heated air, the balloon's envelope displaced so much air that it weighed less than the cool air it had displaced—it was lighter than air. Other than the fact that it was hot, the smoke from burning wool and straw had no mystical properties, nor did it produce a strange new gas—though the excited, smoke-blackened aeronauts did not yet understand that.

But they did understand one thing: They had become the first humans to actually fly.

Eureka!

Complications Arise with
Newcomen's Steam Engine

The world that floated serenely below while the Marquis d'Arlandes clung to the railing, transfixed, was nonetheless revolving at a sometimes violent pace. Across the English channel, Adam Smith's *The Wealth of Nations* was spreading the concept of laissez-faire economics throughout the British Empire and thus the globe. In d'Arlandes's own country a revolution was fomenting between the happy crowd and the monarchs who came together to watch the launch: In a few short years it would see Louis XVI and Marie Antoinette guillotined, along with most of the ruling class. *"Après moi le déluge,"* Louis's grandfather had predicted. Swept along by the deluge, nationalism would soon spread from France through Europe and to the rest of the world.

Change was not limited to economics and politics; science had been revolutionized by Newton a century before.

New labor-saving machines meant that, instead of toiling in fields, the mass of men would soon toil in factories. For industry, which previously relied on windmills and waterwheels and muscle to propel the machines that produced the grain, a revolution began when Hero's children's toy started working for adults.

Ironically, some excess water fired the development of the steam engine. As British miners dug ever deeper for coal, groundwater would stream in and fill the mine's lower levels. Around the year 1700, miners began using a simple device to pull this water up to the surface and out of their way. They called it a "steam fountain." Perfected by civil engineer John Smeaton, it consisted of a pair of cylindrical vessels fed with mine water from a string of pipe leading into the bottom of the mine. By producing a vacuum in alternate cylinders, then emptying each cylinder with a high-pressure blast of steam from a nearby boiler, water was continuously stepped up through the pipe; while one cylinder emptied, the other filled.

Then a British inventor named Thomas Newcomen looked at the steam fountain and, to the dismay of the mechanically disinclined ever since, he saw that what it needed was more moving parts. Newcomen took the fountain's cylinder and inserted a piston into it, which he attached to a rod, which he attached to a beam resting like a teeter-totter on a fulcrum. The opposite end of the beam attached to the string of pipe, culminating in a pump mechanism in the mine's depths.

When a cold-water jet shot inside the cylinder, it cooled and condensed everything, including the steam, which secured a partial vacuum and pulled the piston, rod, and beam downward, lifting the pipe up, letting the water level rise inside the pump. Then a blast of steam pushed the piston up, shoving the pipe down.

More efficient than the steam fountain, though correspondingly heavier, this engine would rock on as long as it had enough coal fuel to turn water into steam—all to pull water from the mine to get more coal.

It was a vicious circle.

In 1774 Scottish engineer James Watt started making a fortune and a name for himself by analyzing the Newcomen engine. He found that when the jet of water cooled and condensed the steam and the cylinder as well, it wasted a lot of steam. Watt remedied all that by adding still more parts: He built a separate condenser that kept the cylinder operating at a constant temperature. Since all these iron parts were no longer expanding and contracting haphazardly, Watt found he could make his engine even more efficient with airtight, finely machined cylinders. So while it was even more complex and heavier than the Newcomen engine, the new Watt steam engine could operate two-thirds more efficiently than the Newcomen engine. Watt was pumping water out of mines almost as fast as it could pour in.

Then, in 1781, Watt's assistant William Murdock added a planetary gear system at the point where they once attached the water pipe, changing the engine's vertical motion into rotary motion. Now the steam engine could spin the machinery that rolled out iron and steel, as well as the looms used to weave delicate lace; factories could start up virtually wherever enough fuel existed to fire the boilers. By 1804, England's Richard Treuithick had even mounted a steam engine on a carriage placed on rails in South Wales; it could move ten tons at five miles per hour. The industrial revolution was speeding along at a furious clip.

The Aerostation's World Tour

But all of Watt's steam engines together weren't powerful enough to propel through the air a single *montgolfière,* as the French called hot-air balloons. Around the time of the first manned flight, Joseph Montgolfier tried to give ballooning a little direction, if not some additional speed. He equipped the envelope of one balloon with vents; in theory, when he opened a vent opposite the direction he wanted to fly, escaping hot air would blow the balloon in the desired course. It didn't work, though: *montgolfières* lacked enough internal pressure to overcome the mildest summer breeze. In a second attempt at reaction propulsion, the aerostat even failed to rise from the launch pad. The crowd that had gathered grew violent and set upon the balloon, destroying it.

Aeronauts seemed the first to learn the folly of enraging French peasants.

Even for the day, ballooning developed at a phenomenal rate. Just ten days after de Rozier's first ascent, Professor J.A.C. Charles flew aloft with a passenger in a silk- and rubber-coated balloon filled with newly discovered hydrogen gas—dubbed a *charlière* by the crowd. Launching before 400,000 spectators, Charles managed a two-hour flight covering 27 miles; at dusk the same day he launched again, alone, rose to an altitude of 9,000 feet, and got to watch the sunset a second time.

During one early ascent a French officer leaned over to a foreign dignitary in attendance and asked, "But of what use is it?"

"Of what use is a newborn baby?" replied Benjamin Franklin.

Echoing Father Francisco de Lana Terzi, English author Horace Walpole said, "I hope these new mechanic meteors will prove only playthings for the learned or the idle, and not be converted into engines of destruction to the human race, as is so often the case of refinements or discoveries in science." But they would not remain adult toys; in 1794, during the Battle of Maubeuge in the French revolutionary wars, aeronauts were sent aloft in a tethered hydrogen balloon to observe enemy movements and to direct artillery. The infant had quickly lost its innocence.

But of what use was it, really? It was huge, unwieldy, at the mercy of the shifting wind, and it could only launch in the mild breeze of morning or sunset. It lacked the power over direction and control inherent in the meanest crow. There had to be a better way to fly.

Nevertheless, nothing could halt the spread of balloon fever from France throughout Europe and the Western world. In less than two years, Jean-Pierre Blanchard would cross the English Channel in a balloon; within a decade Blanchard would also make the first American ascent while he made the first airmail delivery—a letter from George Washington. Nothing was safe from this airborne plague: Balloons became a popular motif in every art from the decorative to the satirical; plates and snuff-boxes and women's dresses contained balloons, while political cartoonists and caricaturists embraced the balloon's abundant metaphoric images of hot air, gas, and yes, even wind. "You will observe," wrote Samuel Johnson, "that the balloon engages all mankind."

Sir George Cayley's Quiet Life

One member of the human race thus engaged was an English boy, not yet ten years old, but born as curious as he was privileged. George Cayley entered the world in a house named Paradise and spent most of his days living at the ancestral family estate of Brompton Hall, in Yorkshire. Instead of ruminating on the nuances of etiquette or horsemanship, young George preferred daydreams of floating along in an aerostat, while learning mechanics at the village watchmaker's.

When Cayley was seventeen, his father sent him to study with a noted scholar, Reverend George Walker at Nottingham. At twenty-two he married his teacher's daughter, Sarah. (She was also, surprisingly for the day, a fellow student.) By now the sixth Baronet of Brompton, Sir George threw aside his childish interest in balloons but kept the dream of flying, for "an uninterrupted navigable ocean that comes to the threshold of every man's door ought not to be neglected as a source of human gratification and advantage," he wrote.

Like everyone else so inclined, he analyzed the flight of birds—and also flying models. In 1796, at the age of twenty-three, he constructed a small toy popularly known as a Chinese top. It looked like a drawn bow, with a cross of feathers stuck perpendicularly into either end of the arrow. The arrow was actually a rotating shaft; the device shot upward by the action of the unwinding drawstring spinning the shaft—and thus the feathers—as the flexed bow unflexed. But all that was still child's play. Cayley set about turning Brompton Hall into a laboratory to study controlled, heavier-than-air flight.

Encouraged by his mother, Cayley had for a long time kept a notebook in which he recorded the minutiae of his country squire's life: Everything from the growth of his thumbnail (exactly half an inch on the hundred days before April 9, 1799), the weight of eggs (on average, four duck eggs weigh five hen eggs), and the nature of democratic government ("a nation is made up of men not competent to decide on the simplest political questions, & therefore the will of such a majority would probably be wrong . . . the collective *wisdom* of a nation is the only . . . body corporate whose will ought to decide."). Upon weighing different steam engines and different types of coal, he calculated how long one would run on how little of the other.

Amidst these entries Sir George sprinkled hundreds of observations related to flight: the velocity of crow flight on a calm day (23 miles per hour), a drawing of a solid of least resistance (the streamlined body of a trout), and a rumination on a seed:

"I was much struck with the beautiful contrivance of the chat of the sycamore tree . . . an oval seed furnished with one thin wing. [The seed] is so formed and balanced that it no sooner is blown from the tree than it instantly creates a rotative force preserving the seed for the centre, and the centrifugal force of the wing keeps it nearly horizontal, meeting the air in a very small angle like the bird's wing." In an inspired act of propagation, nature had created a device that harnessed the essence of aerodynamics.

It was in this notebook that Cayley first perched on the shoulders of Newton, defining the principles of aerodynamics based upon minor passages in the philosopher's *Principia*. Cayley began with a cognitive leap greater than de Lana's vision of lighter-than-air flight: he ignored the conventional belief that a bird held itself aloft with flapping wings and concentrated on when "in the act of flying, which may well be called skimming," the bird extends its wings in a single plane and flies in a straight line. He theorized that its wing, like that of the sycamore seed, always remains slightly inclined to the forward flow of air—he called this the angle of incidence. Air striking the inclined wing produced a force perpendicular to the wing and held it aloft, he said.

He sought to measure that force through principles derived from Newton's research on the resistance of solid bodies in fluid, and he formulated what is now mistakenly known as Newton's sine-square law of air resistance. Cayley drew a triangle based upon the angle of the wing to the forward flow of air, then took the sine, the ratio between the opposite and the hypotenuse of that triangle, then squared that, then multiplied it by the density of the air times the wing area times the speed of the wing, squared. That gave him the amount of force that held the bird aloft. From that he also calculated the amount of resistance produced by the air against the bird in its flight and thus how much power it used to stay airborne.

In 1799, at the age of twenty-six, he had a small silver medallion engraved with the diagram of those three forces used in flight: lift; resistance or drift, later called drag; and power, or thrust. On the opposite side he had engraved his design for a craft that would apply those theories and perhaps become the first powered vehicle to fly through the air. Its wing was squarish and covered with cloth stretched between two longitudinal spars. Beneath the wing, the pilot sat in a canoe-shaped cockpit, from which protruded a tail made up of at least three surfaces, and a pair of flappers to help sweep the tiny craft along through the air. Its prime mover was apparently the pilot's muscle power.

Sir George made a few technical drawings of the craft, then returned to more theoretical research: testing how much weight a given flat surface area would support against the resistance of air. To get a steady stream of air moving against said surface, Cayley constructed an ingenious but simple whirling arm device. The flat surface (actually paper tightly stretched over a frame) and arm were balanced by a counterweight over a pivot. Around this pivot Cayley wound a cord, which went over a pulley and then down a stairwell at Brompton Hall. He put a bag on the end of the cord to hold weights; letting the bag drop down the stairwell would make the arm spin like a bad yarn, while varying the weight would change the arm's velocity. Once he had calculated the velocity of the plate, Cayley could measure how much weight it could lift at various angles and at various speeds, and so he derived tables of lift.

His next act, also in 1804, was a touch inspired. He took a common paper kite (common since contemporary European traders returned from China with them, confirming Marco Polo's fantastic tales), and attached it to a long pole at an angle of six degrees, the angle that on Cayley's whirling arm produced the most lift with the least resistance. On the pole's aft end he attached a cross-shaped (or cruciform) tail not unlike that of an arrow, except that it could be set to any angle to the pole. On the pole's forward end he placed a movable weight to control the device's balance, or center of gravity. Cayley took the whole apparatus outside and gave it a heave.

"If a velocity of 15 feet per second was given to it in an horizontal direction, it would skim for 20 or 30 yards supporting its weight," he wrote in his *Note-Book*. "It was very pretty to see it sail down a steep hill, & it gave the idea that a larger instrument would be a better and safer conveyance down the Alps than even the surefooted mule, let him meditate his track ever so intensely. The least inclination of the tail towards the right or left made it shape its course like a ship by the rudder."

In one fell swoop, Sir George had quietly launched the first controllable gliding machine.

Jacob Degen Announces His Flight

Five years later, while Cayley privately scribbled away in his journal, European newspapers began publishing accounts of a flying Viennese watchmaker. Before a number of observers in Vienna, the papers said, Jacob Degen rose to a height of 54 feet by rapidly beating the wings of a craft of his own design.

What Degen called his *Flugmaschine* weighed just 20 pounds. It had two heavily wired teardrop-shaped umbrellas, with a total of 130 square feet of sustaining surface, which Degen flapped while standing on a perch between them. With the watchmaker onboard,

JACOB DEGEN, 1812: HE COULDN'T RISE
ABOVE THE HOSTILITY.

each square foot of wing would be lifting more than one pound of weight. The umbrellas were of taffeta strips designed to close on the downstroke and open on the upstroke, the same sort of valvular action pioneered by the French locksmith Besnier more than a century earlier.

The newspapers' accounts included woodcut prints of Degen swooping gracefully through the sky. This was it: After centuries of trying, a man had finally flown like a bird, unaided by a balloon.

Cayley on Aerial Navigation

When a newspaper account of Degen's success landed on the door of Brompton Hall, Sir George Cayley paused, and decided that it was time to publish the results of his aeronautical research and receive some credit before it was too late.

From the start, though, he wanted to distance his work from that of the mountebank arm-flappers and the country showmen in their colored gasbags. The very term *flying* itself had taken on negative connotations, he felt, so "for the sake of giving a little more dignity to a subject rather ludicrous in the public's estimation," Sir George chose a phrase with gravity: *aerial navigation*. To further show he wasn't joking about being serious, Cayley turned his back on newspapers and instead chose to publish (beginning in 1809) his three-part series *On Aerial Navigation* in a ponderous-sounding scientific magazine, *Nicholson's Journal of Natural Philosophy, Chemistry and the Arts.*

He began with a bow to Degen and a snub to Borelli: Cayley asserted that there is no substantial proof that a man is comparably weaker than a bird, and he said it was probable that first forays into the air would be human-powered. Then he borrowed a page from de Lana: "I feel perfectly confident . . . ," he wrote, "that this noble art will soon be brought home to man's general convenience, and that we shall be able to transport ourselves and families, and their goods and chattels, more securely by air than by water, and with a velocity of from 20 to 100 miles per hour. To produce this effect it is only necessary to have a first mover, which will generate more power in a given time, in proportion to its weight, than the animal system of muscles."

Watt's steam engines were too heavy at the moment, he said, though he added that new steam engines that operated by expansion only might soon be built light enough for an aerial transport. And he even looked beyond steam power.

"It may seem superfluous to enquire further relative to a first mover for aerial navigation," he wrote, "but lightness is of so much value in this instance that it is proper to notice the probability that exists of using the expansion of air, by the sudden combustion of inflammable powders of fluids, with great advantage."

He mentioned experiments by the French on inflammable powder engines, and English work on an engine powered by the combustion of spirit of tar that he predicted could soon produce one horsepower at a weight of 50 pounds, although with its rate of combustion, carrying the necessary fuel might prohibitively weigh down a craft. He even mused about an illuminating-gas-powered engine, in which case the inflammable air would weigh nothing at all. Nonetheless, one point remained in focus: "Upon some of these principles it is perfectly clear that force can be obtained by a much lighter apparatus than the muscles of animals or birds," he wrote.

He then described in detail his analysis of bird flight—his breakdown of forces into lift, thrust, and drag. And with uncharacteristic pith he added, "The whole problem is confined within these limits . . . To make a surface support a given weight by the application of power to the resistance of air." He told about his experiments with the whirling-arm apparatus, and the tables he had derived from them, and how he had applied them to achieve actual flight with the kite-skimmer: "It was beautiful to see this noble white bird sail majestically from the top of a hill to any given point of the plane below it with perfect steadiness and safety, according to the set of its rudder."

Cayley even told his readers how they, too, could build their very own Chinese top with a few common household items, and he promised that larger versions were possible with adequate power behind them.

From there he went on to describe the theory behind "the alternative motion of surfaces backward and forward," by which Besnier and Degen had been reported to propel themselves through the air; along with an inverted parachute design for evacuating balloons, which should be more stable than umbrellalike ones that were just then being used by aeronauts to make crowd-thrilling leaps from their aerostats. Then, for a grand finale, Sir George slyly segued into a description of a skimming machine he had constructed from the sum of his knowledge of aerial navigation.

Like an inverted cone parachute, the skimming wing would be inherently stable. Looking down its nose, the wing, or sail as he called it, angled upward in a wide V—otherwise known as dihedral. "This angular form, with the apex downward, is the chief basis of stability in aerial navigation . . . and this most effectively prevents any rolling of the machine from side-to-side." Stability was increased by putting the pilot's carriage beneath it, below the point of suspension and the center of gravity.

"The stability in this position . . . is added by a remarkable circumstance that experiments alone could point out": He had found that when the machine flew into the wind at extremely acute angles, the wing's center of pressure resistance was not at the center of the wing; it was well in front. But as the wing's angle moved to become perpendicular to the wind, the center of pressure merged and united with the center of the wing.

What did all this mean? When the machine tilted forward or backward, the center of support shifted behind or before the point of suspension and operated to restore the machine to its original position. Confirming the instinct of Abbas b. Firnas and Oliver the Flying Monk, Cayley wrote, "To render the machine perfectly steady, and likewise to enable it to ascend and descend in its path, it becomes necessary to add a rudder in a similar position to the tail in the bird." If the powers exerted on the plane are in balance, then the least pressure into the airstream from the upper or lower surface of the rudder, "according to the will of the aeronaut . . . will cause the machine to rise or fall in its path so long as the propelling force is continued with sufficient energy."

Cayley also found that when he propelled the machine forward rapidly, it wanted to rise farther into the air, so depressing this horizontal rudder downward would force the machine to fly level. In order to keep it sinking too quickly as it slowed, "as in the act of alighting," the operator depressed the rudder less, until it was horizontal, then eventually elevated into the airstream "for the purpose of preventing the machine from sinking too much in front, owing to the combined effect of the want of projectile force sufficient to sustain the center of gravity in its usual position, and the center of support approaching the center of the tail."

Now that he could control the machine's rise and fall with the tail, "the appendage must be furnished with a vertical sail and be capable of turning from side to side in addition to its other movements, which effects the complete steerage of the vehicle."

He assured his readers that he had tested each principle on crafts both large and small, including one with a sustaining surface of three hundred square feet, "which was accidentally broken before there was an opportunity of trying the effect of the propelling apparatus, but its steerage and steadiness were perfectly proved, and it would sail obliquely downwards in any direction according to the set of the rudder." The machine weighed 56 pounds empty and was loaded to 140 pounds, which meant about two square feet of wing supported each pound.

"Even in this state," he said, "when any person ran forward in it with his full speed, taking advantage of a gentle breeze in front, it would bear upward so strongly as scarcely to allow him to touch the ground, and would frequently lift him up and convey him several yards together."

Just one piece of the puzzle was missing: "The best mode of producing the propelling power is the only thing that remains yet untried towards the completion of the invention." If the solution were to be found in nature, propulsion might not be a big problem: in aerial navigation man may successfully imitate a bird's "oblique wafting of the wing" while gliding along; "when we consider the many hundred miles of continued flight exerted by birds of passage, the idea of its being only a small effort is greatly corroborated."

But that solution itself had additional problems. Consider "the great power that must be exerted previous to the machine's acquiring that velocity which gives support on the principle of the inclined plane," but then consider how the big birds get into the air—by running and flapping their wings for yards—"yet they . . . can fly with great power when they have acquired this full velocity."

"The large surfaces that aerial navigation will probably require, though necessarily moved with the same velocity, will have a proportionately longer duration both of the beat and return of the wing, and hence a greater descent will take place during the latter action than can be overcome by the former." In other words, a man would never have the power and strength to initially overcome gravity by wing-flapping alone. Though to get up enough speed for takeoff, he wrote, "there appear to be several ways of obviating this difficulty," like a two-surfaced flapping mechanism of the Besnier-Degen camp; oblique action, "as in rotative flyers"—based upon the Chinese top; "a number of small wings in lieu of larger ones," like the bird's feathered wingtips; and "by making use of light wheels to preserve the propelling power." Finally, he advised "making choice of a descending ground like the swift." That is, by running downhill. Among the ways to overcome the wing's equal and opposite reaction to manual flapping—for nature's was the best propulsion he could find—Cayley offered "using the continued action of oblique horizontal flyers."

And then he moved on to practical construction. "The general difficulties of structure in aerial vehicles (arising from the extension, lightness, and strength required in them, together with great firmness in the working parts, and at the same time such an arrangement as exposes no unnecessary obstacles to the current) I cannot better explain than by describing a wing which has been constructed with a view to overcome them."

This wing, smaller than the one on the 300-square-foot machine, "exemplifies almost all the principles that can be resorted to in the construction of surfaces for aerial navigation." It is shaped essentially by a pair of crossed bows, like a kite, upon which a cloth covering "is stretched with perfect tightness," he said, the bows "being couched within the cloth so as to avoid resistance." Diagonal braces produce "strength without accumulating weight . . . and produces but a trifling resistance in the air." Since the "hollow form of the quill in birds is a very admirable structure for lightness combined with strength where external bracing cannot be had," Cayley used light tubing for the bows, such as tubular bamboo cane; when that was combined with bracing, "surfaces might be constructed with a greater degree of strength and lightness than any made use of in birds." His calculations seemed to bear this out: The wings contained 54 square feet of surface and weighed 11 pounds. "Although both these wings together did not compose more than half the surface necessary for the support of a man in the air"—he had them built, he said, to experiment with propelling power—"yet during their waft they lifted the weight of nine stone [126 pounds]." By comparison, if the wings of a heron were 54 square feet, they would weigh just under eight pounds; the wings of your everyday waterfowl likewise proportioned would weigh under 19 pounds. Thus Cayley's wings "may therefore be considered as nearly of the same weight in proportion to its bulk as that of most birds."

Interestingly enough, these wings weren't meant to be flapped as if attached to a person's arms; they were meant to be rowed. "[A] footboard in front enables a man to exert his full force in this position," he wrote. (If Waterloo was to be won on the playing fields of Eton, then the air might be conquered on its waters.)

Above all, as a craft moved through the ocean of air, it must avoid upsetting the air currents. "Let it be remembered, as a maxim in the art of aerial navigation, that every lb. of direct resistance that is done away will support 30 lbs. of additional weight without additional power." Therefore, "It is of great importance to this art to ascertain the real solid of least resistance."

He said Sir Isaac Newton's theorem on the subject was "of no practical use" because under it each particle that strikes the solid has "free egress, making the angles of incidence and reflection equal. Light seems to behave in this manner, but not air; it acts as though

the particles accumulate "rushing up against each other in consequence of those in contact with the body being retarded."

Furthermore, Cayley noted an interesting phenomenon: "It has
been found by experiment that the shape of the hinder part of [a
solid] is of as much importance as that of the front in diminishing
resistance . . . [arising] from the partial vacuity created behind the
obstructing body. If there be no solid to fill up this space a defi-
ciency of hydrostatic pressure exists within it, and is transferred to
the [solid]. This is seen distinctly near the rudder of a ship in full sail,
where the water is much below the level of the surrounding sea. . . .
I fear, however, that the whole of this subject is of so dark a nature as
to be more usefully investigated by experiments than by reasoning,
and in the absence of any conclusive evidence from either, the only
way that presents itself is to copy Nature."

And thus concluded *On Aerial Navigation*.

Disappointingly, Cayley included no accompanying illustration of
the skimming machine that could lift a man, an unusual fact when
you consider Sir George's penchant for illustration. In *Aerial Navigation* alone he had included thirteen figures: drawings for a wing-
flapping device, his inverted parachute, Degen's wing-flapper, the
Chinese top, plus the forces of flight, which he'd also sketched
in his *Note-Book* (along with everything including the whirling-
arm device and the kite-glider), and which he had left engraved
for future generations on a silver disk—backed with a design he
had never constructed. Was it an enlarged kite-skimmer? Was he
merely trying to protect his work from being copied? Did it even
exist, or was it an imaginary defense against Degen's aeronautical
assault?

In any case, here was man's—and Cayley's—accumulated aeronautical knowledge published in three parts, the astonishingly accurate, enlightened path to successful, controlled, heavier-than-air
flight. Cayley is said to have hoped it would lure many others great

and small to stand on his shoulders, though ultimately no serious climbers stepped forward.

In Cayley himself, however, nearly every quality was in place. He could build a skimming machine based upon proven scientific principles, with control surfaces on a stabilizing tail, capable of steering the machine up or down and left or right. He had the free time and the finances as well; the price of admission into the air was always high. All Cayley believed he lacked for having a powered, controllable, heavier-than-air aerial navigator was a prime mover more powerful yet lighter than a man.

Sir George Cayley was just thirty-six years old in 1809. He would live to be eighty-four. Yet after the publication of *On Aerial Navigation,* Cayley's pen was at rest—save for a few articles about aerostations in the next decade. Instead, he resumed the country life of an English baronet, concentrated on administering his land scientifically, and joined Parliament as a liberal and active member.

As for aerial navigation, Cayley sank from view.

Degen Meets His Match

Jacob Degen, on the other hand, continued his ascents. In 1812, two years after *Nicholson's Journal* concluded the *Aerial Navigation* series, a Parisian crowd assembled for the third time to watch Degen attempt to fly his *Flugmaschine.* Two previous attempts had failed due to high winds.

The crowd was growing cranky.

After further delays that day, the flying clockmaker finally alighted in his usual manner—with a *charlière* attached above his machine, of course. It stayed attached throughout the erratic flight, until he steered the craft to a landing.

While he demonstrated more control over the aerostat than even the mighty Montgolfiers, there was no mention of hydrogen balloons in the newspaper accounts, nor in the engraved illustration that Degen himself provided.

The crowd did not approve. When Degen landed, they set upon him and beat him without mercy.

From that day on, Degen was nothing more than an airborne joke.

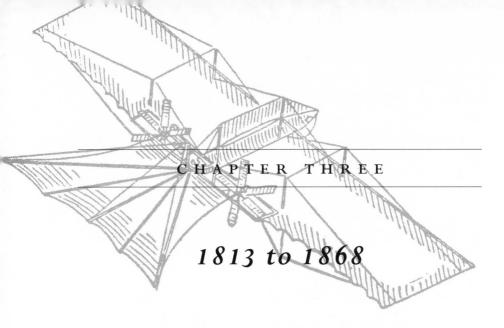

CHAPTER THREE

1813 to 1868

Stringfellow of Chard Meets Henson

One year after Jacob Degen's plunge into ridicule, a fourteen-year-old named John Stringfellow was working as an apprentice to a Nottingham lace manufacturer. During his time there, Stringfellow became acquainted with a family of lacemakers, the Hensons, and also with the workings of the new steam engines.

The dark-eyed, mutton-chopped Stringfellow eventually proved himself a gifted bobbin- and carriage-maker as well as mechanic. To expand their business, his grateful employers moved him to Chard, in southern England. There he grew interested in balloons and, beginning in 1831, usually launched one publicly during local festivals. The Henson family moved to Chard as well; by 1835, Stringfellow and the younger William Henson, thirteen years his junior, had grown close through their shared interest in the mechanics of flight. They would hunt birds of all species, then weigh them and measure their wings; "but no law or line could be found as to the shape and size of wings from the flight of birds," goes a contemporary account, "so they endeavoured to make movable wings of various designs." After Henson moved to London, they also began designing an aerial vehicle. To test the air resistance of various wing sections, Stringfellow held them at varying angles from the window of the express train speeding him to London.

Soon the younger man began to take the lead. In September 1842 Henson, now thirty years old, filled out the patent application for a "Locomotive Apparatus for Air, Land and Water," which was "for conveying letters, goods and passengers from place to place through the air," though the technology could be applied to "other machinery to be used on water or on land."

As soon as he received the provisional patent, Henson formed the Aerial Transit Company to help raise the £2,000 he calculated would cover the expense of completing and testing this Locomotive Apparatus for Air. According to the published proposal, "An invention has recently been discovered, which if ultimately successful will be without parallel even in the age which introduced the world to the wonderful effects of gas and steam. This work, the result of years of labor and study, presents a wonderful instance of the adaptation of laws long since proved to the scientific world. . . . The Invention has been subjected to several tests and examinations and the results are most satisfactory, so much so that nothing but the completion of the undertaking is required to determine its practical operation, which being once established, its utility is undoubted, as it would be a necessary possession of every Empire, and it is hardly too much to say of every individual of competent means in the civilised world. . . . Patents will be immediately obtained in every country where the protection to the first discovery of an Invention is granted."

To get in on the ground floor, the company was offering twenty shares of £100 each, with a guarantee of a threefold return in one year, and it was giving investors the satisfaction of helping launch the aerial transit business. Here's what they would actually be putting their money up for:

Henson's patent proposal called for a vehicle with a 4,500-square-foot, double-surface, rectangular wing of canvas or oiled silk; its span

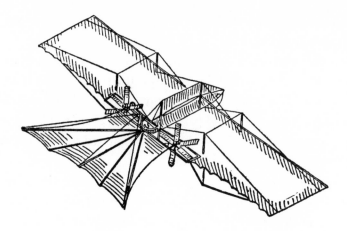

HENSON, 1842: LAUGHED ALL THE WAY TO
BANKRUPTCY—ALMOST.

140 feet, its width 32 feet. Kept rigid with three longitudinal spars, the wing was given form with 26 wooden ribs and braced against its own weight with a series of wires running over pylons like a suspension bridge. An enclosed windowed carriage, mounted beneath the center of the wing, curved gracefully inward and culminated in three wheels: one large one in front, and two on an axle in the rear. An adjustable, 1,500-square-foot triangular tail fanned outward from the carriage on the same plane as the wing; beneath it, parallel with the carriage, was a vertical rudder. Turning Cayley's Chinese top on its side, the 25- to 30-horsepower steam engine would drive twin six-bladed fans, a Henson-Stringfellow innovation for mechanical flight. "From the various experiments I have been enabled to make," Henson wrote, "there should be about one square foot for each half pound of weight of the machine . . . [therefore] . . . The machine I am making will weigh about 3,000 pounds." Estimating its speed at 50 miles per hour, Henson said the vehicle could fly 500 miles. He called it the "aerial steam carriage."

In England's political, scientific, and social circles, hell was about to break loose.

Henson Goes Public with the Aerial Transit Company

A few interested investors stepped forward, so in accordance with the law, Henson's lawyer presented the Aerial Transit Company's incorporation papers to the House of Commons for approval. MPs, however, looked upon the proposed aerial steam carriage with scorn and ridicule. They were quick to refuse the bill—and were slow to stop laughing about it.

So was the public, with all the unexpected publicity generated by the proposal. It was satirized in song and in print: Based upon Henson's accompanying illustration, caricaturists drew skies filled with aerial steam carriages big enough to support castles, hotels, and mission houses on their wings.

But others took the aerial steam carriage seriously—and not just the company's would-be backers. *The Times* of London declared Henson's research sound: "[We] are compelled, by careful inquiry, to profess our belief . . . that the earlier, if not immediate, possession of the long-coveted power of flight may now be safely anticipated."

A popular engineering journal, *Mechanics Magazine,* also took a great deal of interest in the aerial steam carriage and began a series of articles debating its validity. In its April 1843 issue the magazine published an analysis of the machine, written by the age's greatest living expert on aerial navigation: Sir George Cayley.

While Cayley found Henson's science sound—after all, it was based upon much of his own—he was fairly critical of the machine's engineering. "The extent of leverage," he wrote, "however well guarded by additional braces, is in this necessarily light structure, terrific. For though the wings are not intended to be wafted up and down, the atmosphere even in moderately calm weather near the earth, is subject to eddies; and the weight of the engine and cargo etc., in the central part of this vast extent of surface, would in the case of any sudden check, operate an enormous power to break the slender fabric."

So how could someone build an aerial carriage that could lift a rational load but without increasing the weight of the wing—because that would mean increasing the wing area even more? Cayley offered a simple solution to break the cycle: by stacking shorter wings. Instead of a single-winged monoplane, build a two-winged biplane, or a three-winged triplane. "Would it not be more likely to answer the purpose to compact the surface into the form of a three decker, each deck being 8 to 10 feet from each to give free room for the passage of air between them?" he asked.

For the next few months, while several journals attacked and defended the aerial steam carriage in their pages, Henson quietly prepared his own answer to end the controversy. It was a scaled-down model of the aerial steam carriage weighing 14 pounds, powered by a tiny six-pound steam engine, with an obstinate 40-square-foot monoplane wing. He called it *Ariel;* by July, it was ready for demonstrations at London's Adelaide Gallery.

Ariel was designed to be launched inside the gallery on an inclined plane, which ended in a wire net to catch the model if it refused to alight. And that was what it did on the first attempt—plunging safely into the wires and shearing its wing stays. A second attempt, with a second, more powerful steam engine, ended in the same way.

According to the August 4 *Morning Herald,* "A third, a fourth, and it is not likely known how many attempts were made, but with an invariable result. Directly the inclined plane was left the model came down flop. Up to the present time, therefore, the world is no nearer flying."

Discouraged by the relentless negative public reaction to his Aerial Transit Company, exacerbated by the abortive flight attempts at the Adelaide, Henson asked his attorney to abandon the formation of the company. Now broke as well as discouraged, he nonetheless held a glimmer of hope for the project and wrote to Stringfellow at Chard in November.

"I have been waiting for some time to come to Chard," he said, "but I could not think of allowing you to be at any expense without a chance of remuneration. . . . I am now enabled to offer you a repayment of five times for all money or moniesworth in workmanship or materials contributed by you to the amount of £200—or, in other words if you like to enter into an agreement to undertake to make a model with me in the way in which we talked about some time since, I am at liberty to offer you five fold to be paid before anything else out of the first profits arising from Exhibition. . . . I have not time to say more. Please send me an answer as early as possible."

Early in 1844, Henson moved back to Chard to begin experiments with Stringfellow.

Henson and Stringfellow's Model

To make things official, Henson and Stringfellow signed a joint agreement to "construct a model of an Aerial Machine." Henson was responsible for its framework, which was again based upon the patent drawings of his aerial steam carriage. He constructed a 20-foot-long by 3.5-foot-wide wing and covered it with silk. Including the tail, it had 80 square feet of sustaining surface.

Stringfellow naturally took on the power problem, building a tiny steam engine designed to fit inside the carriage nacelle and drive the model's pair of three-foot, four-bladed screw propellers at a rate of 300 revolutions per minute. The blades, which "occupied three quarters of the area of circumference, set at an angle of sixty degrees," turned in opposite directions to overcome the torque from both propellers turning the same direction.

They worked on the machine off and on until 1845, when Henson, probably exhausted by Stringfellow's irascible nature, moved back to London.

Stringfellow finished assembling the model—and then took it apart. Working by night to avoid notice, he and a few helpers loaded it on a haywain and drove it two miles up Snowdon Hill highway, to a tent erected upon the remote Bewley Downs. On the side of the hill facing the prevailing wind, Stringfellow set the model up on an inclined plane, "down which the machine would glide."

Still working nights to avoid public scrutiny—and to take advantage of the calm air—Stringfellow and his crew, including his fourteen-year-old son, Frederick John, prepared for the first launch.

"There stood our aerial protegee in all her purity—too delicate, too fragile, too beautiful for this rough world; at least those were my ideas at the time," said Stringfellow the Elder, "but little did I think how soon it would be realised. I soon found, before I had time to introduce the spark, a drooping of the wings[,] a flagging in all the parts. In less than 10 minutes the machine was saturated with wet from a deposit of dew, so that anything like a trial was not possible by night. I did not consider we could get the silk tight enough."

Less poetic perhaps, Stringfellow the Younger summed it up this way: "The machine could not support itself for any distance, but when launched off, gradually descended."

"Many trials by day, down inclined wide rails," said a magazine account two decades later, "showed a faulty construction, and its lightness proved an obstacle to its successfully contending with the ground currents." With no way to alter the angle of the tail, other than at the beginning of each flight, the experimentation could be brutal to the craft. Assessing it later, Stringfellow at last concurred with Cayley's analysis. "Indeed the framework was all too weak," he said, adding in his favor, "The steam engine was the best part."

After seven weeks, the Stringfellow contingent finally gave up and broke camp.

Henson Poses a Question of Cayley

William Henson still had one scheme left to raise money for the aerial steam carriage.

Although I am personally unknown to you I have taken the liberty of addressing you this letter upon Aerial Navigation. . . . You probably imagined that I had long since given it up as a failure, but you will be pleased to hear that I have in conjunction with my friend Mr Stringfellow been working more or less since 1843 towards the accomplishment of Aerial Navigation, and that we feel very sanguine as to the results of our endeavour and consider that we have arrived at that stage of proceedings which justifies us in obtaining that pecuniary assistance necessary to carry on our efforts upon an enlarged scale and with increased energy. We therefore resolved to apply to you as the Father of Aerial Navigation to ascertain whether you would like to have anything to do in the matter or not.

—William Henson, September 28, 1846.

I had thought that you had abandoned the subject, which tho' true in principle you had rushed upon with far too great confidence as to its practice some years ago. If you have been making experiments since that time you will have found how many difficulties you have to adjust and overcome before the results you wish can be accomplished. I think that Balloon Aerial Navigation can be done readily and will probably come into use before Mechanical Flight can be rendered sufficiently safe and efficient for ordinary use. . . . As to new principles, there are none. Of practical expedience there will soon be an endless variety, and to select the best is the point at issue . . . when if you can show me any

*experimental proof of mechanical flight maintainable for a sufficient time by me-
chanical power, I shall be much gratified. Though I have not the weight of capital to apply to such matters, I perhaps might be able to aid you in some measure
by my experience. . . . I do not however think that any money, except by exhibition of a novelty can be made by it.*

—Sir George Cayley, October 12, 1846.

At last, Henson had tried everything.

Within a year of his letter to Cayley, he married, patented a safety
razor, and boarded a square-rigger headed to America, where he had
business cards printed calling himself an engineer. He worked on
steam engines, but would work on aerial steam carriages no more.

Stringfellow Tests Powered Flight

Stringfellow, a successful businessman, still had the funds to keep
pressing forward. In his spare time he analyzed the machine, and
found that "our want of success was not for want of power or sustaining surface, but for want of proper adaptation of the means to
the end of the various parts." From 1846 to 1848 he concentrated on
the proper adaptation.

Its wing was ten feet long, half as long as the earlier model, and
measured two feet at the widest point. The wingtips tapered to a
point, like a sparrow's; its tail resembled a sparrow's as well. Altogether it had 18 feet of sustaining surface. The engine, tucked away
inside an *Ariel*-like nacelle, was an improved version of the previous
model. A full boiler and fuel brought its weight up to six pounds.

With its thin but deep nacelle slung beneath the wing, Stringfellow knew the configuration to be unstable in the turbulence of nor-
mal air, so he moved his experiments inside the longest room he
could find, one 66 feet long. There he set up a wire that inclined

downward, and he suspended the craft from a wheeled frame; a block would release the model after it had traveled down the wire several yards.

Stringfellow set the angle of the tail, fired the boiler, and got up steam. With the propellers spinning and its engine making a wild racket, he released the new aerial steam carriage.

It slid down the wire, hit the block, and shot toward the ceiling. Climbing a few yards, it hung on its nose in the air, then slid steeply backward, breaking its tail on impact.

Stringfellow quickly repaired the tail—but set it at a shallower angle—and started the engine again. Again, he released it.

This time it shot down the wire, slammed into the block, and rose gradually—it was flying!—at a speed later estimated to be 21 miles per hour—

smack into a canvas sheet meant to stop it on the opposite end of the room.

It was the first powered, heavier-than-air flight in history.

And it punched a hole in the canvas.

Cayley Tests Unpowered Flight

Yes, once again, circumstances had forced Sir George Cayley to take his views public on the subject of aerial navigation.

Though *On Aerial Navigation* had received a cool reception in 1810, public interest in the subject had heated in recent months due to the firestorm of publicity surrounding Henson's Aerial Transit Company. Suddenly Cayley found his expertise in demand. His reputation was sterling; his gentility trustworthy. The 1843 article in which he critiqued the aerial steam carriage was a new beginning: That year *Mechanics Magazine* also published new drawings and designs for "Sir George Cayley's Aerial Carriage," which had two pairs of stacked fans held above and outside what looked like a hollowed-out bird corpse. The fans were to lift the Cayley carriage to a proper altitude, where they would flatten into wings; then two rearward screws would take over and push the machine through the air.

He never built it. Not exactly. Successfully engineering those stacked fans would have taken him years. And unlike Henson and Stringfellow, Sir George preferred to work out the nuances of the machine's design before he added the motor. Then there was the problem Henson's aerial steam carriage posed; that of how to build a light wing strong enough to hold up to the oncoming air current and its own weight. Cayley's own thoughts on the matter—"to compact the surface into the form of a three decker"—provided the solution to his problem.

Working ever so slowly, by 1849 the man whom Henson christened the Father of Aerial Navigation had completed his "governable parachute." Its body resembled his aerial carriage's birdlike shape—well, perhaps the bird's form-fitting cage. The pilot sat inside the cage, atop a board. He held behind him a three-surface tail, which he would use to steer like a tiller on a small boat. For propulsion the governable parachute had the rowing wings described in *Aerial Navigation,* which the operator would somehow row along with both hands when he wasn't steering with the tiller. It rested upon three lightweight spoked wheels, one in back and two in front, that Cayley had designed before 1809.

Above all that, Cayley stacked three wings of 100 square feet each. They were squarish, as was Sir George's wont, and each was set at a small dihedral angle to give the craft some inherent stability. Yet another three-surface tail, this one unmovable, jutted behind the middle wing.

Cayley and his entourage rolled the governable parachute to a hillside on Brompton Hall, where "the balance and steerage were ascertained," and then Cayley placed in its pilot seat a ten-year-old boy, the son of a servant. They rolled him down the hill.

The boy "floated off the ground for several yards on descending [the] hill," Cayley reported, "and also for about the same space by some persons pulling the apparatus against a very slight breeze by a rope."

Cayley took all that he had learned from his boy-glider experiments and eventually went to work on a new governable parachute. This one had a covered bird-shaped body, a single 300-square-foot kite-shaped wing, and essentially the same two-tailed configuration of his earlier boy-glider. Since he was now getting to be seventy-nine years old, it was to be the culmination of his life's work in aerial navigation.

On a nice day in 1853, with a slight breeze and a few fluffy clouds, word spread through the village that Sir George was going to test this latest machine. Villagers began gathering at the gate of Brompton Hall. Cayley's servants rolled the governable parachute to the hillside as before, but this time Cayley told his fully grown coachman, John Appleby, to climb aboard, which he did.

Cayley examined the machine one last time and tested the wind with a wetted finger. Then, "drawn forward by an eager team of young Brompton men," the machine started down the hill, and as it rolled along, the machine picked up speed, then the wheels of the machine stopped making sound, and it began traveling along at a shallower angle while the ground dropped away. Cayley galloped slowly after the governable parachute, while, witnesses said, the gliding machine dipped, leveled, then bounced to a stop on the slope.

For the first time in recorded Western history, a man had flown in a heavier-than-air vehicle.

The coachman was shaking. To the elated master of Brompton Hall, he said, "Please, Sir George, I wish to give notice. I was hired to drive, not fly."

Cayley knew he could lift a man into the air. But he also knew he was still missing one important element in successful aerial navigation: propulsion, the very thing Stringfellow had been refining since his days with Henson.

Nevertheless, Cayley didn't live long enough to solve the propulsion problem for himself.

He died three years after losing the services of his coachman, and just days short of his eighty-fourth birthday.

He did live long enough, however, to see interest revived in his work—

Though they say no man is a prophet in his own home.

For one day sometime after his death, Sir George's only surviving son took the remains of one machine from its resting place on Brompton Hall's Low Garden and hauled the old hollowed-out bird corpse to a dilapidated barn—

Where it became a roost for chickens.

The Issue of Dirigibility, a Clockwork Bat, Plus the Rime of Le Bris

By this time, however, it seemed that no nation experimented in flight as broadly and as vigorously as did France. Having pioneered the aerostation, the French were determined to refine and perfect it for humanity, and for the glory of France.

The big hurdle with ballooning remained directional control, or dirigibility. To overcome the problem, engineer Henri Giffard fitted an aerodynamic—well, sausage-shaped—aerostation, made partially rigid from a framework, with a three-horsepower steam engine and a rudder. In September 1852 Giffard flew from the Hippodrome in Paris to Trappes, 17 miles away—although with its blistering 5.5-mile-per-hour pace, his dirigible balloon was easily outtrotted by a horse and carriage.

Later in the decade fellow Frenchman Félix Tournachon* chose to avoid dirigibles, but with his camera mounted on a tethered

* better known as Nadar

balloon he snapped the first aerial photograph, a serene portrait of Paris.

In warfare, though, the balloon was used elsewhere with increased frequency and cunning, though lacking French sophistication. Austrians in 1849 launched pilotless, bomb-carrying hot-air balloons against forces defending Venice, but to little strategic effect. During the U.S. Civil War, federal observation balloons revealed the ineptitude of the Union Army's commanding generals more than the position of enemy troops. Vague reports on Robert E. Lee's movements were issued from the hydrogen balloon *Intrepid* during the 1862 Peninsula Campaign, but they served only to panic the commanding Union general, George B. McClellan. McClellan withdrew his vastly superior forces and positioned just seven miles from Richmond, Virginia, instead of attacking the sparsely defended Confederate capital and ending the war three years and tens of thousands of lives sooner. In later eastern theater campaigns, Thaddeus Lowe, chief of aeronauts, Army of the Potomac, made ascents in a balloon linked to the ground with a tether and a telegraph wire, reporting on Confederate movements from the high ground. The Prussian army even sent Count Ferdinand von Zeppelin to learn what he could from this kind of warfare. But after General Joseph Hooker's disastrous showing during the Battle of Chancellorsville in 1863, Ulysses S. Grant took over and reorganized the Army of the Potomac. Preferring to rely more on attrition than intelligence, he disbanded the Balloon Corps.

Meanwhile, the French organized the world's first aeronautical society, the Société d'Aviation, and it seemed that their navy would lead the nation's efforts in heavier-than-air flight. As in England, experimenters aligned themselves into two camps. Members of the first camp preferred jumping right into powered machines from the start, as had Henson and Stringfellow; the second camp wanted to learn about controlling the flying machine first as an unpowered glider, as had Cayley.

In the power-first camp, a naval officer named Félix du Temple de la Croix began experiments in 1857 with small batlike models propelled by clockwork motors. Achieving flight quickly, he just as rapidly designed and patented a full-size machine. Building that machine, however, took much longer than he expected, because as the linear dimension of his machine increased arithmetically, the additional power it needed seemed to increase geometrically. Du Temple found he needed much time to work out this problem with the full-size machine. So while he remained land-bound, another sailor, but from the power-last camp, completed his machine.

Like Daedalus with his seagulls and Cayley with his crows, Captain Jean-Marie Le Bris was inspired by a particular species of bird and sought to capture its attributes. Le Bris was mesmerized by the albatross that soared tirelessly above his ship on its long voyages around the Cape of Good Hope, bringing the sailors good luck. And so, ignoring the warning of Coleridge's ancient mariner, our Captain Le Bris shot an albatross.

"I took the wing of the albatross," he said, "and exposed it to the breeze; and lo! in spite of me it drew forward into the wind; notwithstanding my resistance it tended to rise. Thus I had discovered the secret of the bird!"

His glider was a scaled-up version of the unlucky albatross. Like the bird, its wings were long, narrow, and graceful, and had a convex upper surface and a concave underside. Structurally the wings were nearly as complex as the bird's, too, since he hoped to imitate an albatross in the act of soaring: A system of levers, cords, and pulleys ran from a mast on the hood of the canoe-shaped body and would communicate a rotary motion to the leading edge of the wings, changing their angle of incidence to the oncoming wind. The wing spanned 50 feet and comprised 215 square feet of supporting surface; without Le Bris aboard, the albatross weighed just 92 pounds.

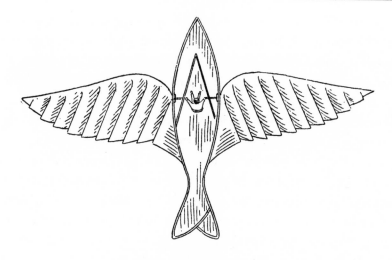

LE BRIS, 1857: THE HIGH
AND THE FLIGHTY.

The body was of light ash ribs and an impermeable cloth covering, 13.5 feet long and 4 feet at its widest point. A thin, spearlike bowsprit protruded sharply from the nose. Le Bris planned to stand inside the body, working the wing levers with his hands, while his feet on pedals would work the tail. The albatross had no undercarriage other than its belly for landing, and a horsecart that Le Bris would use for launch.

Testing commenced one windy Sunday morning in 1857, when albatross, captain, cart, and driver were all trudged by horse down a road aligned along the ten-knot breeze. With a safety rope in one hand tied around the cart in a slipknot, Le Bris told the driver to trot the horse, and he manipulated the levers so that the wind hit the top of the wings, which held the albatross on the ground. As the entourage gained speed the captain pressed on his levers, raising the wings' leading edges into the wind.

The albatross lifted off—and so Le Bris tugged the rope to separate bird from cart. But the slipknot refused to give, and the albatross dragged the cart into the air as well. Relieved of its burden, the horse began galloping, and the cart disintegrated. But the cart's driver had become entangled in the rope. Oblivious to all this action below, Le Bris and the albatross shot nearly 300 feet into the air—dragging the screaming and kicking driver aloft as well. Le Bris heard the commotion and descended slowly, placing his driver gently on the ground. Then he tried to climb once more. Without the driver along to balance his machine like a kite's tail, the albatross seemed to lose its equilibrium, having already lost much of its momentum. After rising briefly, Le Bris barely managed to control its descent. One wing hit the ground first and crumpled, but the rest of the albatross survived.

Elated nonetheless—his flight lasted 600 feet—the captain repaired his albatross and reconsidered his means of launch. This time he hoisted the bird up a mast erected upon the edge of a 100-foot-deep quarry, and climbed aboard. After waiting for a good breeze to blow over the bird's nose, Le Bris tripped a simple release hook and braced himself for the ride. The albatross flew ahead, over the middle of the quarry, then hit an updraft that pushed its tail high and its nose down. Le Bris quickly pressed on the levers to hold the wing's edges down, and his albatross flew up—but then it swooped again and crashed nose-first into the quarry.

Le Bris was pitched forward and thrown clear, though on his way out one of the levers slammed into his leg and broke it. This time the albatross was destroyed.

> *And I had done a hellish thing,*
> *And it would work 'em woe:*
> *For all averred I had killed the bird*
> *That made the breeze to blow.*

All's Well That Ends Well

Within a few years of the mariner's crash—1864 to be exact—one of his countrymen with a mouthful of names, Count Ferdinand Charles Honoré Phillipe d'Esterno, published a pamphlet titled "du Vol des Oiseaux." The culmination of his years of observation of bird flight, the pamphlet broke flapping flight down into seven laws, and soaring flight into eight. But most importantly, in it d'Esterno stated that flight had three distinct requirements: Equilibrium, guidance, and impulsion.

"[We] can derive from the wind, when it blows, an unlimited power, and thus dispense with any artificial motor," wrote the Count. He went on to predict, "In sailing (or soaring) flight, a man can handle an apparatus to carry 10 tons, just as well as one carrying his own weight."

Soon after, d'Esterno patented just such a vehicle, Le Bris *Albatross*-like in appearance, but designed to attempt to harness equilibrium, guidance, and impulsion. Whalebone-framed wings, controlled with a crude mechanism of ropes and drums, were to help the entire apparatus mimic the actions of a typical bird. Its wings would flap up and down, incline backward and forward, and twist; the broad tail would do the same. The operator would sit inside a cart equipped with a sliding seat, to help shift his weight, and thus change the machine's center of gravity to change its equilibrium.

Publicly, however, the Count was labeled a bit of a lunatic—it being supposed in more mainstream scientific circles that when not flapping, birds maybe used some unseen minor motions of their wings to keep them moving through the air—and perhaps because of the ridicule he left his apparatus on the drawing board.

That very same year, however, another Frenchman with a penchant for birdwatching and the belief that "Ascension is the result of the skillful use of the power of the wind, and no other force is

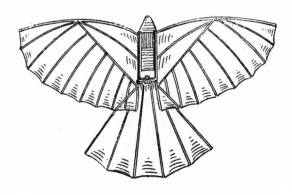

D'ESTERNO, 1864: IT FLAPPED,
INCLINED, TWISTED, AND REMAINED
ON THE DRAWING BOARD.

required," determined to attempt to fly himself. Since Pierre Mouillard lived outside of scientific circles, on his farm in Algeria, he could try his hastily built, disarmingly simple wing apparatus without much ridicule, though on the day he did he saw to it that he was all alone on the farm. Of African aloe wood and cloth, the wing was very light (33 pounds) and six times as long as it was wide. Mouillard stood in the center, and held the wing waist-high with straps.

"I strolled onto the prairie with my apparatus upon my shoulders," he wrote. "I ran against the air and studied its sustaining power. . . ." Close by lay a wagon road, with a ditch some 10 feet wide on either side. "I used to leap across [one ditch] easily without my apparatus," he said, "so I took a good run across the road, and jumped at the ditch as usual.

"But, oh horrors! once across the ditch my feet did not come down to earth; I was gliding on the air and making vain efforts to land, for my [apparatus] had set out on a cruise. I dangled only one foot from the soil, but, do what I would, I could not reach it and I was skimming along without the power to stop.

"At last my feet touched the earth. I fell forward on my hands, broke one of the wings, and all was over; but goodness! how frightened I had been. . . . All's well that ends well . . . I cannot say that on this occasion I appreciated the delights of traveling in the air. I was much too alarmed, and yet never will I forget the strange sensations produced by this gliding."

His main fear was that he would rise in the apparatus, tip over backward, and fall on his back. But before he could build a stronger, more complete apparatus with a tail to keep it balanced, Mouillard lost his farm and moved to Cairo, Egypt, where such experiments were not so easily performed out of view. Finally, he became chronically ill, and was no longer able to undergo the rigors of soaring.

Advances from the Aeronautical Society of Great Britain, and Its First Exposition

In London, January 1866, a handful of men filed into Argyll House—home of the family that unselfishly gave their socks to the world—and voted to form the Aeronautical Society of Great Britain. For their first chairman they elected the Eighth Duke of Argyll.

It was his house, after all.

In no time at all the Aeronautical Society had made some lasting contributions to the science. Presenting his paper *Aerial Locomotion* at the first meeting, charter member Francis Wenham revealed that in bird flight narrow wings lifted better than the squarish wings of Cayley's gliders. He even coined a new word in reference to the unflexing wings of beetles: *aeroplane*. And the Duke of Argyll himself was able to discount the popular theory that birds filled themselves with hot air and were thus made buoyant. If that were the case, he said, they wouldn't fall right from the sky when you shot them.

Yes, things were going along swimmingly at the Aeronautical Society.

In the June 1 issue of *Mechanics Magazine,* Wenham wrote, "I may state that the function of the Aeronautical Society has developed the fact, by the communications received, that many are now of the opinion that man may yet command the air as a medium of transport in any direction." But a year later, even after all those cards and letters came pouring in, the society was still having trouble attracting serious, legitimate support in scientific and political circles. What they needed was a little publicity.

Secretary Frederick Brearey suggested the society hold an exhibition of aeronautica at the Crystal Palace, a great hall of iron and glass four times the length of St. Paul's Cathedral. To encourage participation there would be prizes; the Shipwrecked Mariners Society, for example, offered to put up a £50 award for the best form of kite to communicate disaster from a ship. The Crystal Palace Company offered a small prize for any aerial machine that could stay aloft for 20 minutes (later reduced to five minutes) and offered a £5 prize for a light engine. The Aeronautical Society itself would offer a prize for best aircraft, plus a £100 prize for the engine with the lightest weight-to-power ratio.

Now all they needed was a few names. To that end, Brearey wrote to the now rheumatic sixty-eight-year-old John Stringfellow. "I hear you might perhaps have something to exhibit," he hinted.

Since his sparrow-winged steam-powered model shot into the sheet in 1848, Stringfellow had produced little for public consumption. His son Frederick John told an interviewer that "having now demonstrated the practicability of making a steam engine fly, and finding nothing but a pecuniary loss and little honour," his father chose to rest, satisfied with what little he'd been able to accomplish.

But over the intervening two decades, Stringfellow had still continued building and experimenting with flying steam-powered models, though without the ardor of his earlier years. He lacked the vast indoor space at Chard to properly test his large model aerial steam carriages—and the funds to acquire such space, "or I should not have kept my old models rotting for years," he wrote. He therefore concentrated on other interests: He patented a "galvanic battery" and established a successful photography studio in his hometown.

He had to be satisfied with taking but a small step. While the 1848 model represented the first successful powered flight, able to climb at an angle of one foot for every seven it covered, there was much Stringfellow needed to overcome. The craft could hold only enough water and fuel to power the engine for a brief flight, and its control surface—the tail—could not be adjusted during flight. Both of those facts together meant there was no safe way to land it without injury to either device or spectator. The model had enough power, after all, to punch a hole in fabric.

When he received the invitation from Brearey, Stringfellow first considered dusting off and patching up the old model. But with the success of Cayley's governable parachutes, Stringfellow decided that stacked wings might allow enough sustaining surface to lift a substantial steam engine and frame within the confines of the Crystal Palace at a low speed. He chose a configuration of three superposed planes, each successive plane measuring six, seven, and eight feet in span, for a total of 21 lineal feet—11 more than the 1848 monoplane model—and a total of 30 square feet of sustaining surface, 10 feet more than the earlier model. Its gross weight was but 12 pounds. He stayed with two propellers, each measuring 21 inches, blades angled at 60 degrees as always, and turning in opposite directions at a rate of 400 rpm via connecting rods by the dual-action piston of the engine, which Stringfellow estimated produced one-third of a horsepower.

He packed up the new model, then he and Frederick John boarded the steam locomotive for London.

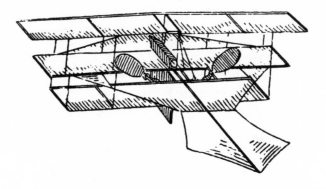

STRINGFELLOW, 1868: THE HIT OF
THE EXPOSITION.

The great eleven-day Exhibition of the Aeronautical Society of Great Britain opened on June 25, 1868. Brearey had managed to sign up seventy-seven exhibits. Charles Spencer was there with his 24-pound, 140-square-foot gliding machine, with which he said he could skim up to 130 feet; Mr. W. Gibson was in attendance, too, with his bi-wing flapping apparatus. Altogether the society had two machines based upon the Chinese top, two with fixed wings, and the rest with flapping wings of one type or another. There were eight steam engines as well, plus five engines powered by light-gas or oil and two fired by gun-cotton.

Stringfellow and son had arrived days earlier to set up the triplane, which they suspended on a wire run inside the Crystal Palace. On opening day they fired up the triplane's steam engine and sent the machine along its merry way. It performed well, lifting itself and its guidewire several feet toward the glass ceiling. This got the crowd's attention, and on each subsequent demonstration—two per day every day—they gathered in greater numbers to watch the triplane perform its high-wire act. Stringfellow was the hit of the show.

"It was a grand day for Uncle," wrote his niece Rose breathlessly to Mrs. Stringfellow back in Chard. "The Prince and Princess of Wales and Prince Alfred and several of the Princesses with their train of attendants was there. The Prince was so charmed with the Model that he sent the Duke of Sutherland to ask Uncle to go to the Royal Box. . . . Of course Uncle has won the prize."

That is, he had taken the coveted £100 steam engine prize. No one walked away with the Crystal Palace prize for having achieved five minutes' worth of flying. The jurors' committee did report, however, that "it was seen by several that after a certain velocity had been attained, the machine left the support of the wire and rose up. On one occasion the wire broke just after the start, but the buoyant power of the planes caused so light a descent that no damage occurred."

Stringfellow returned to Chard in quiet triumph. He vowed to continue his experiments, "with a view of ultimately constructing a larger machine that would be sufficient to carry a person to guide and conduct it."

CHAPTER FOUR

1868 to 1891

Le Bris Gets a Second Chance

Repairs from Jean-Marie Le Bris's first crash didn't quite empty his purse, but rebuilding from the second would have: Seafaring had only made him a naturalist, it hadn't made him rich. A decade passed before a public subscription in the coastal city of Brest allowed the good sea captain to build his second albatross.

It was much like the first; in the interim had nature improved upon the original? Actually, the new Le Bris albatross was somewhat lighter, and it incorporated a counterbalance mechanism intended to automatically overcome rapid changes in equilibrium.

Perhaps because of the subscription, or perhaps due to vanity, Le Bris displayed this new albatross publicly. We owe him for the first photograph taken of a heavier-than-air flying machine, showing a heavy-shouldered earthbound craft mounted backward on a cart, with light shining through translucent wings. The captain himself stood inside the albatross, poised behinds the levers, while sailors attended lines descending from each wingtip.

Le Bris began testing the new artificial bird in public as well, on the port levee, where a crowd gathered to watch him fly. Le Bris stood at his levers, waiting patiently for a good stiff breeze, but his

LE BRIS, 1867: IT WOULD WORK 'EM WOE.

public grew impatient. Why did the mechanical bird not take off and fly away like the real item? They grew vocal and demanding, so that when the next gust came, no matter how weak, Le Bris vowed he'd take it—and did.

The albatross took off, rose perhaps 36 feet into the air, flew forward twice as far, then settled gently to the ground. Anyone in the crowd could see that this was a pitiful display compared with what the real albatross could do, and Le Bris was so skewered that he conducted all further tests in private.

In these tests he damaged the bird slightly, though once, while flying it as a kite with only ballast aboard, the albatross rose 80 feet into the air, and—like the windmill fans of yore, like its smaller natural cousin slain by the captain—it *advanced* toward the breeze for nearly 600 feet, before settling again to earth.

Over the ensuing weeks further attempts resulted only in damage to the albatross. After repairing the machine, he determined to try again himself, once more from the levee. His backers instead convinced Le Bris to load the ballast in the bird, and watch from a safe distance.

And that's the way he launched the albatross into the gusty sea breeze. It rose initially, then twisted, then recovered briefly—then plunged headfirst into the ground. The albatross shattered, its bowsprit impaling the cockpit. The backers pointed to it and called Le Bris lucky: Had he been in the cockpit, *he* would have been impaled.

Lucky? His experience flying the machine taught him that the albatross was longitudinally unstable. If he had been operating the levers, he might have been able to fly the craft through the turbulence.

Lucky? Now he'd lost his albatross for good.

Le Bris was abandoned by his backers and his friends. Broke and ridiculed, he returned home, and when the war erupted between France and Prussia in 1870, Le Bris enlisted and served, we are told, with bravery and distinction.

Modern Warfare Leads to Stringfellow's Superfluous Steam Engine; and Francis Wenham's Little Black Box

That year, France had felt squeezed by a potential alliance between the German states and Spain, so it declared war against Prussia and struck first. But the Prussian army soon pushed the French army back to Paris and surrounded the capital.

On one side, a bright young German engineer named Otto Lilienthal amused, then bored, his fellow soldiers with tales of his experiments with feathered gliding machines. On the other side, a bright young Frenchman named Alphonse Pénaud, who had studied marine engineering and dreamed of becoming an officer in the navy like his father before him, was forced to sit out the siege inside Paris. Pénaud was stricken with a crippling bone disease and confined to crutches. Depressed, to distract himself he constructed a Chinese top like Sir George Cayley's, but much improved. Instead of a whalebone bow for power, Pénaud's flying screw used the stored energy of a twisted rubber band, which, when released, would propel the model an astonishing 50 feet into the air.

While Prussians surrounded Paris for four long winter months, famine was rampant, and conditions inside the city decayed to the point where Parisians could do little but starve, hope for relief, and

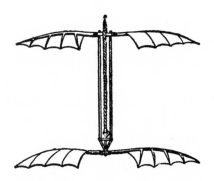

PÉNAUD, 1870: KIDS SIMPLY LOVED IT.

send off balloons to the outside world. In fact, they lofted a total of 65 balloons carrying 12 tons of mail, 164 people, 6 dogs, and 370 carrier pigeons with which allies sent messages back into the city.

As always during warfare, it was an opportune time for inventive nonparticipants to earn a living.

The aging John Stringfellow once again abandoned his flying steam models to develop an armored hand cart for protection on the battlefield. He also built a large, light, two-cylinder aerial steam engine intended to power a French dirigible over the heads of the Prussian besiegers. But Paris capitulated and France begged for an armistice before Stringfellow could sell his engines of war. Peace in Europe meant a minor setback for the armament industry, but the two seldom stroll hand-in-hand. And now Stringfellow's health declined along with his business fortunes; the elderly bobbin-maker found himself battling fits of neuralgia—a condition of acute pain radiating along nerve paths. He heard that the Aeronautical Society's Francis Wenham needed an engine, and with a superfluous aerial steam engine on his hands, he inquired of Mr. Wenham.

Wenham, however, had nearly completed building his own five-horsepower engine—which weighed nearly 700 pounds. He was unconcerned about heft, for his machine was bolted to the ground.

It was a ten-foot-long box with a fan.

Aerial navigation required power, lots of power, power that simply was not available in the era's finest, lightest steam engines. Even Stringfellow's triplane engine couldn't consistently generate enough energy long enough to sustain itself in the air. Wenham thought that given the low horsepower, endurance, and high weight of available engines, he might circumvent the problem by building a perfectly formed wing—a body of least resistance. The others before had experimented with shapes: Stringfellow by holding his flat plates from the window of the speeding London express train, even Cayley with his whirling-arm device. Both methods lacked precision: From similar experiments with other fluids, scientists knew that a whirling arm eventually spins fluid in the direction of the arm. Any tables of lift so derived would thus hold inaccuracies.

But Newton had stated that a solid body reacts the same whether it is moving through the fluid or the fluid is moving around the body. With his boxed fan, Wenham could place various forms inside and measure with a fair degree of accuracy the resistance each shape produced.

Wenham's tests with his box were "somewhat crude and incomplete," he said, though he did go on to design a glider in which the pilot lay prone and drove a pair of pusher propellers. It was a multiplane machine; in 1866 Wenham had advocated Cayley's theory of superposed planes so strongly that he even patented the concept for himself.

As for his own black box, he left it for the future to refine.

Alphonse Pénaud's Planophore

After the war was over, and flushed with the successful flights of his toy helicopter, Parisian Alphonse Pénaud continued working with rubber-band power. His later models resembled the kite-skimmer

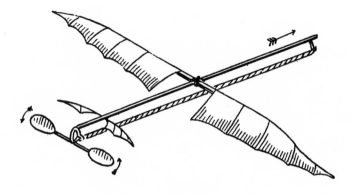

PÉNAUD, 1871: TAKING TURNS
AROUND A GARDEN.

of Cayley, but with the narrow, more efficient swallow wing of Stringfellow's 1848 model. Unlike Henson and Stringfellow, Pénaud didn't have to build huge models to contain the compact but heavy miniature steam engines; he could keep his models manageably small while he got the aerodynamics just right. In 1871 he built his *planophore,* a 20-inch-long model with 18-by-4-inch wings set at a stabilizing dihedral. An adjustable horizontal and vertical tail controlled its path, and a propeller on the end pushed it along.

That August, Pénaud hobbled to the garden of the Tuileries, and before members of the French Society of Aerial Navigation, he carefully wound the planophore's propeller 240 turns, pointed it skyward, and let go.

Several times it flew in a circle before the rubber band was exhausted, and it gently settled to the ground near where it started.

The members of the society were simply amazed and enthused at the prospect of overtaking their British rivals in heavier-than-air flight. And frankly, so was Pénaud. From that moment, he would dedicate his life to the construction of a powered, man-carrying planophore.

REAR VIEW

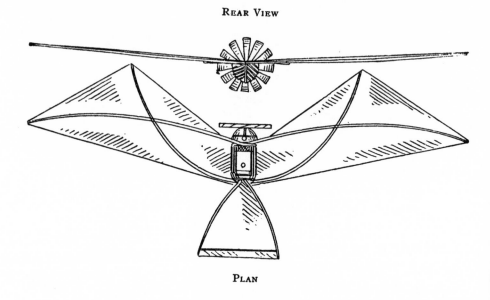

PLAN

DU TEMPLE, 1857 TO 1877: PRETTY IS AS
PRETTY DOES, WHATEVER THAT MEANS.

Hop Goes Du Temple

By 1874, seventeen years and one major war after his clockwork models, Félix Du Temple was finally ready to make tests in his full-size, steam-powered craft—in Brest, like Le Bris.

Its wing was silk-covered and delicately batlike, centered upon a barrel-shaped car of light wooden ribs, and it would have curved wooden spars set at a dihedral angle and a flexible trailing edge. It swept forward to surround the machine's multiple-bladed tractor propeller, which was mounted in the nose of the car and driven by a one-ton, six-horsepower steam engine. The pilot would sit behind it on a wicker chair. A horizontal tail followed, with a vertical rudder jutting below. The machine perched upon a triple-legged wheeled undercarriage so arranged as to present the craft to the on-coming air at an angle of 20 degrees. Through a system of springs the undercarriage would tuck up beneath the craft once it was airborne.

Engine aside, this final version weighed 160 pounds and had a wingspan of 40 feet; its final cost exceeded $6,000—"the workmanship being very fine," according to one chronicler.

Though reports are vague, either Du Temple or a sailor took the controls while the spindly-legged machine, its engine sputtering and its fan spinning, rolled down a ramp and—

It hopped—uncontrollably—for just a few feet. That was all.

Two years later, in 1876, Du Temple and his brother Louis patented a lightweight boiler in which rapidly circulating water was flashed by flame into steam. It weighed between just 39 and 44 pounds for every horsepower it would help generate. Recent developments by the enemy of France, however, rendered such advanced technology obsolete.

Nikolaus August Otto Builds the First Practical Four-Cycle Engine

The work was all stolen from a Frenchman, of course: He was Beau de Rochas, an engineer, who in 1862 published research showing that an engine generates more power more efficiently when combustion occurs under pressure.

De Rochas proposed a simple four-step process. First, his engine would compress an air and fuel mixture; second, a spark or flame would ignite the mixture while it was under pressure; third, the exploding gas would push a piston downward; and fourth, the exhaust gases would be allowed to escape. In this theoretical engine, the piston would travel up and down and up and down—four strokes, that is—to complete one cycle of combustion.

The parts for this new type of engine were essentially the same as those of the steam engine, except there was no heavy boiler, no condenser, no water to be converted to steam, and no constant external combustion to keep steam up. In de Rochas's engine, all combustion was internal, inside the engine itself.

One year before Beau de Rochas put all this in writing, a German engineer, Nikolaus August Otto, was actually building an internal combustion engine.

By 1867, he and German industrialist Eugen Langen formed a partnership, and together they developed an engine that took a gold medal at the Paris Exposition that year. Nine years later, 1876, Otto finished work on the four-stroke internal combustion engine envisioned by de Rochas, and he took out a patent on what came to be known as the Otto-cycle engine, which burned a coal gas and air mixture ignited with a flame. It would spin at only 150 to 200 revolutions per minute, but compared with steam engines, the new Otto engine was lighter, quieter, more efficient, and almost as reliable. A refinement in the ignition mechanism by the director of Otto's factory, Gottlieb Daimler, allowed the engines to reach speeds of up to 2,000 rpm.

In 1876, the same year that Nikolaus Otto built the first practical four-cycle engine, a Boston engineer named George Brayton exhibited at the Philadelphia Centennial Exposition another kind of engine, which burned a distillate of rock oil, or petroleum, popularly called gasoline.

Ultimately, the explosion wasn't contained within the Otto engine: More than thirty thousand units were built within the next decade alone, and Otto became a very wealthy man—until someone found out about the earlier patent of Beau de Rochas.

And so while the powder weapons of France and Germany had cooled, the legal guns were primed and leveled.

The Aerial Steamer Has Thomas Moy
Running in Circles, Declaring Flying
May Be Good for One's Health

While the gasoline internal combustion engine spread worldwide like a disease among a susceptible population, our would-be band of fliers seemed curiously immune to the infection. Many were unwilling to just up and abandon the centuries-old method of wing-flapping. Clément Ader, a French electrical engineer who had invented a variant of the telephone, began his experiments in flight in 1872 by building a 53-pound artificial bird with a wingspan of 26 feet, which Ader would drive by lying horizontally on the wing and driving a flapping mechanism with his feet; contracting elastic, mounted between wing and fuselage like muscle and sinew, would draw the wing back into position.

Restrained by ropes and in a high wind, the bird, Ader reported, would lift itself into the air. Yet finding himself unable to sustain the whole weight of the machine in calm air, he packed it into a crate and headed off to the birdcages of his local zoo to await further inspiration.*

Steam power was still the propellant of choice. Englishman Thomas Moy's 1875 aerial steamer used a three-horsepower engine that weighed 80 pounds (nearly 27 pounds per horse) and drove the steamer's twin six-foot-diameter, six-bladed "propelling aerial wheels." Resembling lath wired to a twisted wall, these blades changed their angle of incidence as they rotated, the hope being that they would simultaneously lift and propel. The steamer's sustaining surface consisted of two tandem planes of linen stretched on bamboo frames, each set at an angle of ten degrees to the oncoming wind, with the 64-square-foot rear plane set slightly higher than the 50-square-foot fore plane.

---

*We would hear from him again in the coming years.

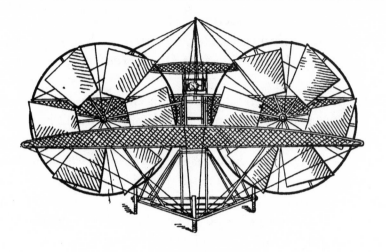

MOY, 1875: IN REALITY, LESS WAS MOY.

When he considered the various available methods of launching the craft, such as down a ramp, like Du Temple, or from a height, like Le Bris, Moy knew that in his steamer, "the traverse stability was better than the longitudinal stability, but both were bad," so he took the craft to the Crystal Palace, where he found a fountain centered upon a circular gravel path 300 feet in diameter. He placed a pole in the fountain's center, attached two cords from the pole to the steamer, and fired up the engine. On the first go-around, the gravel was too rough to let the machine pick up much speed, so he built a boardwalk over the path. On the next try, the steamer spun around the fountain at a speed of 12 miles per hour but remained adhered to terra firma. He tried larger propelling wheels, 12 feet in diameter, but that configuration failed, too.

"These experiments cost me many hundreds of pounds," he said before the Balloon Society a few years later, "and one of the experiments was witnessed by the Duke of Argyll . . . and others; to whom I explained that a 30-H.P. engine would do 10 times the work of a 3-H.P. engine, but would not weigh more than five times 80 lbs.

When this 3-H.P. engine lifted 120 lbs before their eyes, I thought that the results warranted raising funds for further experiments."

And that meant a larger aerial steamer powered by a 100-horse-power engine, for Moy was convinced he was on the right track, even though it was circular. But while he did receive "two chancery suits about shares in [my] patents," he got nothing in the way of financial support.

"Unless you can lift the last ounce of a model, the unscientific people call it a failure," he said elsewhere, "and few can appreciate that as size and weight increase, the relative hull resistance decreases, by reason of its diminished surface in proportion to its cubic contents."

After 1879 Thomas Moy abandoned his powered flight experiments, but he left behind an intriguing concept, "one which may be mastered by any intelligent man in a short time, and it is one which may be learned, in my judgment, with quite as much ease as bicycle riding."

All this intelligent man needed, Moy said, was a light sea anchor with a length of rope attached, a boat, and an inflatable Boynton dress attached to a pair of "stiff, immovable wings or aeroplanes" measuring 18 by 3 feet and able to hold three times the load to be imposed upon them (tested by balancing the aeroplane on its center and spreading 750 pounds worth of sandbags on it). When the next gale came along, the intelligent man would don the Boynton dress/wings combo, row out to sea, and hop in. When he crested with the next wave, he'd be flying.

Said Moy: "If you ask of what use is this? I say business, pleasure, healthful exercise, and the accomplishment of the initial step toward actual flight.

"If a man thus equipped can go in the teeth of a gale and carry a rope to a wreck, that is business.

"If a man thus equipped can travel at from 20 to 40 miles an hour over the waves, that is pleasure and healthful exercise.

"But it will also teach him the enormous sustaining power to be derived from swift motion, and it will also explode many of the silly, unmechanical notions which are now held upon the subject."

For in those days there were so many silly, unmechanical notions still afloat.

Pénaud's Manta Ray

In the years immediately following his planophore's successful spins around the gardens of the Tuileries in 1871, Alphonse Pénaud continued to recover from his hip disease; some thought his success in aeronautics helped fuel his recovery. His toy *hélicoptère* even made him a minor celebrity. Durable and cheap to manufacture, the toy helicopters swept the United States in the last years of the decade. They were such good, clean fun that a busy leader in the conservative United Brethren Church, Bishop Milton Wright, would gladly pick one up during a business trip as a present for his two youngest sons.

Like any proper American kids, they played with their toy for a while, and then took it apart to see how it worked. In a court deposition years later (responding to counsel's question, "Where and under what circumstances did you . . . first become interested in the problem of flight?"), the youngest son would recall, "We built a number of copies of this toy, which flew successfully. . . . But when we undertook to build the toy on a much larger scale it failed to work so well. The reason for this was not understood at the time, so we finally abandoned the experiments."

Meanwhile, Alphonse Pénaud's own investigations carried a broader range: with the planophore, he'd constructed the helicopter and a rubber-powered wing-flapper, along with a tailless kite; he contributed a number of valuable papers to the French journal *Aéronaute,* including one that explained updrafts as common atmospheric occurrences and thus helped account for what was known as "sailing flight"; he designed an internal combustion engine, as well as instruments to measure flight, such as a delicate barometer with which to measure altitude; and he made a balloon ascent in the name of science, being slightly injured in the descent. Pénaud was compared with Sir George Cayley and was said to tower intellectually above the elder members of the Société d'Aviation in debate—stirring up jealousies in the process.

Undaunted by criticism, he took a partner, Paul Gauchot, known for his mechanical prowess, and together they designed a manned flying machine that they patented in 1876.

Its most striking feature, when viewed from above, was its shape: It resembled a manta ray with a vestigial tail. Some 634 square feet of varnished silk covered its framework wing, with tips that either bent upward for stability or might even be flexed somehow. Two small, balanced horizontal rudders aft changed position automatically to adjust the machine's horizontal equilibrium, and a vertical rudder beneath and between them was for changing the craft's direction right or left.

An enclosed cabin for the machine's operator lay underneath the wing. The pilot steered the craft from there with a single lever that, when pulled or pushed, moved the horizontal surfaces; when twisted, it moved the vertical surface back and forth.

The operator's head was surrounded by a glass windscreen. On either side were counterrotating propellers, driven by a steam engine of 20 to 30 horsepower and weighing not more than 22 pounds per horse. It did not exist yet, nor did the partners know of any such steam engine with that power-to-weight ratio. That small detail aside, they would mount the 440- to 660-pound engine so as to bring the flying machine's center of gravity one-fifth of the wing's width from the leading edge, just behind the pilot. For its takeoff run it had wheeled appendages that would retract during flight.

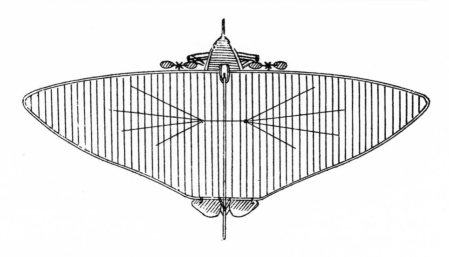

PÉNAUD AND GAUCHOT, 1876: DEAD FROM
LACK OF SUPPORT.

With a second crewman or passenger, its weight might total 2,640 pounds—0.24 square feet of sustaining surface per pound.

It was never built. Pénaud's detractors said the machine lacked longitudinal equilibrium because of its taillessness, that its sustaining surface was too small to hold such weight. After four years of effort, he failed to raise any funds for construction.

In despair, Pénaud committed suicide. He was thirty years old.

Stringfellow's End

Age and rheumatism, not despair, impeded John Stringfellow's ambition to build a man-carrying heavier-than-air powered flying machine.

He continued the long-running aeronautical dialogue with Frederick Brearey, now honorary secretary of the Aeronautical Society, and heard Brearey tell of lecturing to audiences as large as twelve

Woodcut of the Crystal Palace Exhibition of 1868. The focal point of the nearly 80 exhibits was Stringfellow's triplane, which made two runs per day. (Photograph courtesy of The Royal Aeronautical Society, London, England.)

Near Berlin, 1895: Otto Lilienthal stands at the foot of his
manmade hill holding the *No.
15 Biplane Glider.* Beneath the
dark cap of said hill is storage
space for various other gliders.

Lilienthal keeps his biplane on
an even keel by shifting his
body weight, no mean feat of
strength.

The Wrights' big 1901 glider, the largest flying machine ever flown up to that time. Here Bill and Dan Tate launch Wilbur from a dune at Kitty Hawk.

October 1903: Samuel Langley's *Great Aerodrome* is readied for its first launch on the Potomac.

December 17, 1903. First flight of the day. John T. Daniels, photographer.

Orville (left) and Wilbur, at Huffman Prairie, May 1904.

Summer, 1908: Glenn Curtiss kicks up a little dust in the AEA's *June Bug*.

Spectators rush to the scene of Orville's crash at Fort Myer, September 1908.

hundred on behalf of the society—audiences whose fathers had shouted down the Aerial Transit Company.

When Brearey proposed to mass-manufacture the Crystal Palace steam engine, Stringfellow refused to allow it. Yet he still received optimistic updates from Brearey on the progress of the latter's undulating wing craft, a fanciful machine Brearey had patented in 1879. In theory, it would fly through the same motion that a manta ray used to swim. "Silk or other suitable fabric is extended from the arms and along the spar of the tail, thus giving a large supporting surface, and vibrations are imparted to the area which propels the machine by a wave-like motion," went Brearey's description. Alas, another great concept was rendered useless by an uncooperatively thin atmosphere.

Stringfellow remained loyal to Henson's ideas, though he had had no contact with his old partner since Henson left for America. Himself, he would remain involved in aerial navigation almost to the last, working alongside his son, Frederick John Stringfellow, who built a steam-powered craft of his own design—but which bore an elliptical wing and a deep car, the unmistakable imprint of a Stringfellow-Henson lineage.

Then one day in 1883 the elder Stringfellow told his son, "I have hung it up, Fred. I shall touch it no more." That December, John Stringfellow died at the age of eighty-four.

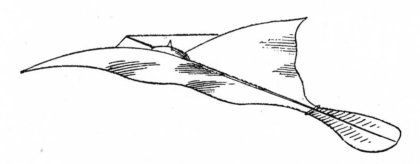

BREAREY, 1879: IT WORKED FOR MANTAS.

Five years later William Samuel Henson, age seventy-six, died in Newark, New Jersey. It went unreported in England.

Frederick John Stringfellow hoped to carry on with his father's work. To do so, Stringfellow the younger slowly began selling off the labors of Stringfellow the elder: the famed steam engines and models and documents left Chard piece by piece.

One of his customers was the U.S. government, in the personage of Samuel Pierpont Langley, secretary of the Smithsonian Institution.

Phillips Refines the Black Box

While Francis Wenham's 1870s tests with his black wind box were "crude and incomplete," a fellow Englishman, Horatio Phillips, nevertheless sought to refine and complete similar tests with a box of his own. His wind box was a trunk, through which he directed a jet of steam. Inside Phillips placed a series of shapes, and hoping to find out how fast the oncoming airstream should be to sustain each different form carrying the same weight, he let blast with the jet of steam. Along with achieving his goal—in 1884 he patented eight sections of various width and curvature—Phillips's experiments proved something more: In flying, a curved surface beats a flat surface any day.

Octave Chanute Wonders How to Get a Roof off the Ground

Octave Chanute was one of the most respected civil engineers in post–Civil War America. Almost single-handedly, it seems, he had built the nation's major railroads to the Mississippi and beyond.

Chanute born in France and came to the States with his parents at age six. He had entered the engineering profession in 1849 at seventeen, an unpaid apprentice laying rail lines along the Hudson River. In just four years he was earning a good salary as a division engineer in Albany. As the years went by he worked his way west, laying track almost all the way to Kansas, and then he built the railroads that brought the cattle from Texas to the Kansas City stockyards, and for good measure he built the stockyards there—the one in Chicago, too—and he built the first bridge to span the Missouri River, the Kansas City Bridge.

He was short, rotund, gray, and balding; his goatee gave him an elfin appearance. But so great was his reputation that they even named a frontier town after him: Chanute, Kansas.

At a dinner party in Kansas City one night, someone asked the esteemed builder what subject occupied him in his spare time.

"Wait until your children are not present, for they would laugh at me," said Octave Chanute. That subject was aerial navigation. What had initially gotten his attention, in Newtonian terms, was the behavior of solid bodies in a fluid. In the vernacular, it was flying buildings.

"I had been aware for years that there were a number of observed wind phenomena," he wrote, "such as the lifting of roofs, the blowing off of bridges, and the tipping over of locomotives, which the known velocity and pressure of the wind at the time was insufficient to account for." He realized that here lay undiscovered physical laws that would allow a man to fly as well.

Americans still gave as much credence to flying machines as General Grant had given to observation balloons during the Civil War. But when Chanute toured Europe in 1875, he discovered his fellow engineers there laboring seriously on the subject of human flight; he became acquainted with the work of Pénaud, Moy, du Temple and Le Bris; of Stringfellow and Henson, and Sir George Cayley. Upon returning to the States, he began a systematic study of the progress made in aerial navigation. And as a leader in the American Association for the Advancement of Science, he began forming aeronautical sessions during association meetings. At the first such session, in Buffalo in 1886, a near-riot broke out among scientists, in which a round of sarcastic bidding commenced yet failed to produce anyone in attendance with a flyable model.

In the audience quietly sat Chanute's counterpart in science, Samuel Pierpont Langley.

Chanute sponsored a second, less tumultuous meeting in Toronto in 1889; by the time he moved to Chicago in 1890, to settle down and set up a business preserving structural timbers, he had also set himself up as an unofficial clearinghouse of all aeronautical information.

Soon after, Mathias Nace Forney, an old friend (they'd worked together back in 1873 designing the system of elevated trains in New York City) who was now the editor of *The Railroad and Engineering Journal,* asked Chanute to write a short series for the magazine on the state of the art of flying machines—six or eight articles, how much could there be, anyway?—beginning with the October 1891 issue. They would call the series *Progress in Flying Machines.*

The fifty-nine-year-old Chanute agreed and started writing.

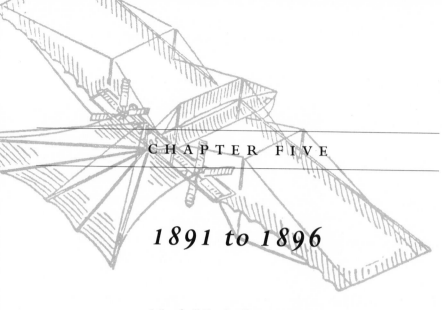

CHAPTER FIVE

1891 to 1896

Ader's "God of the Winds"

After his wing-flapping experiments failed, Clément Ader's local zoo had loaned him eagles and bats to observe, though he deemed these short-winged, fast-flying creatures insufficient for his purposes. So he got on a boat headed for the sand and the heat of Algeria, where he could watch the large indigenous vultures in their habitat and perhaps shoot a few to stuff and take home.

Too many hunters with the same intent had arrived before him, pushing the vulture population away from Constantine, Algeria. Ader merely disguised himself in Arab garb and headed to the interior, and there he found his large vultures, some with wingspans of ten feet.

He was impressed that vultures flapped their wings only to get off the ground. In soaring, he saw them adjust the angles of their wings to conditions of the wind. With this information, Ader decided to leave his first artificial bird packed away for good and headed back to rue Pajou, at Passy, in France, with a different form of flying machine in mind.

He christened it *Eole*, "God of the wind." This winged god more resembled a huge bat with feathers stuck perpendicularly in its nose.

A squat flying machine, *Eole* had little tail to speak of. Its control surfaces consisted of a simple rudder and a complex system for changing the wing angles. Its nose culminated in the four-bladed propeller, which was driven by a two-cylinder steam engine weighing 200 pounds yet generating 20 horsepower—much lighter than any steam engines that had come before. This apparatus sat between the pilot and the nose, completely blocking his view. A radiator protruded into the airstream above for efficient cooling—and poor aerodynamics. It rested on a tricycle undercarriage, with an additional wheel just off the ground in front to prevent the machine from nosing over while moving under its own power. From tip to tip *Eole* measured 54 feet and would fold up for easy storage. It weighed 653 pounds.

Some fifteen years and $120,000 in the making, *Eole* was ready for testing by October 1890. For his trials, the owners of the secluded Parc d'Armainvilliers placed their grounds at Ader's disposal.

"An Area was laid out in a straight line unturfed, beaten and leveled with a roller," he wrote in his autobiography years after, "so that one could see and record the traces of the wheels from the slightest lift to complete takeoff." During one trial from this leveled ground, *Eole,* its engine pocketing and wheezing, left the surface and hurled a distance of 164 feet, at an altitude of 18 inches.

Two gardeners and two foremen witnessed this leap. Though later that day the steam generator blew out, forcing a halt to further tests, one of the witnesses buried a handful of coal to mark the spot where the craft first left the ground.

"At that time," wrote Ader, "the *Eole* was considered, by the initiate and by the scientific press, as the first aerial apparatus piloted by a man to have flown at a small height over a short distance."

At that time, the French newspaper *L'Illustration* reported sightings of a "strange object resembling an enormous bird of bluish hue" that was reported to have "really flown several hundred yards, rising some 50 to 65 feet."

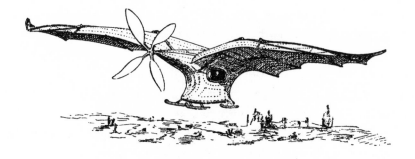

ADER, 1890: THE REAL WIND GOD
HAD WHEELS, NOT SKIDS.

Ader let speculation run wild. He himself would say nothing more at that time; nor would he take any foreign patents on the machine lest an enemy nation learn the secret, for the machine could have an important role in defending France. Just over one year later, he met with the minister of war and promised to construct a flying machine capable of carrying two men and 165 pounds of bombs.

What god would allow such a machine?

Langley's Travels

Samuel Pierpont Langley was two years younger than Octave Chanute; he, too, was born in the east, in Boston, and became a civil engineer and went west as a young man. But here their paths diverge. Langley returned to Boston and signed on as an assistant at the Harvard Observatory. He became an assistant professor in mathematics at the U.S. Naval Academy in Annapolis and ran the observatory there, then spent two decades at Pennsylvania's Allegheny Observatory as its director, writing papers and making a name for himself.* He dreamed of immortality, however, and knew he would achieve it if he became the one who conquered the air.

To do so, Professor Langley began to seek and receive grants to conduct tests on the aerodynamics of flat plates. He commissioned the construction of a small whirling arm, which escalated into a complex "whirling table," with two 30-foot arms and a ten-horse steam engine capable of spinning a flat plate at 70 miles per hour. Langley began hiring staff members to conduct the experiments and to build a series of rubber-powered models à la Pénaud, with light wooden frames and two propellers.

Meanwhile, Professor Langley accepted a position as an assistant secretary of the Smithsonian Institution. Within a year, the death of his superior had elevated him to the position of full secretary.

By the time the old Stringfellow triplane he had bought arrived from across the Atlantic, there was nothing new that Secretary Langley could learn from it. But that didn't really matter now.

Langley soon counted among his new friends in Washington the nation's most famous men—its richest, most powerful, most influential. With the thousands of dollars in grants that regularly rolled in to the Smithsonian Institution, Secretary Langley could steadily turn it into a national aeronautical research and development administration. And so Langley began assembling a team of the country's most talented engineers and machinists, with the goal of producing a powered model capable of sustained flight.

The Institution's staff and shops fairly buzzed with the construction of small paper-wing and tin-plate or shellacked paper-tube models, taken over now from Allegheny. The models soon numbered around a hundred, of all shapes and configurations: swept-back wings, superposed wings, single wings, tandem wings, one propeller, two propellers, one propeller pushing and one pulling, two pushing,

---

*It was as its director that he attended Chanute's 1886 Buffalo conference and sat in on the raucous aeronautical session.

two pulling—but none of the rubber-powered models flew to the
secretary's satisfaction. "[It] is not so much the power, but the skill to
guide it, which we lack," Langley said, and decreed that a new series
of models be built, larger models, with a steam engine sufficient to
sustain them in the air under control for perhaps a half minute.
Nothing like it had ever been achieved before in the history of the
world. This next generation of machines would need a name. Upon
the advice of an etymologist, Langley decreed they be christened
aerodromes, from the Greek *aerodromoi,* "air runners."

Work began in April 1891. The basic aerodrome configuration
had tandem wings, since "my most primitive observation with small
gliding models was the fact that greater stability was obtained with
two pairs of wings," Langley said. Their shape would be not flat but
cambered, curved to a ratio of one vertical inch to every twelve linear inches. Built from silk-covered aluminum frames, the forewing
measured 50 square feet, while the rear was 25 square feet. A four-
pound, single-horse steam engine drove twin 32-inch pusher propellers at 500 rpm.

In the end, one year later, the world's first aerodrome weighed almost 45 pounds and was too flimsy to bear its own weight. It had
been called, presciently, *Aerodrome No. 0.*

After rejecting it, the secretary commissioned three more aerodromes in quick succession: *No. 1* was much smaller but underpowered; *No. 2* was even smaller still, and still underpowered; *No. 3*
developed more power than any of them, but it just wasn't enough.
Thus far, the Langley bureaucracy had produced four machines unfit for trial. "While all of the machines were in the strictest sense
failures, in as much as none of them was ever equipped with supporting surfaces," wrote Langley in his official report, the aerodromes were of the finest material and exquisitely finished in every
detail.

Finally in March 1893, anxious staffers presented the secretary
with *Aerodrome No. 4,* which had 14 square feet of sustaining surface

between its two wings. By Langley's calculations, this one was powerful enough to fly and strong enough to survive a catapult launch.

Langley had decided a rolling start under its own power was a waste of time and fuel for an aerodrome. To get it into the air as quickly as possible, he directed that a catapult be developed simultaneously with the aerodrome by a separate team of mechanics and engineers. This complex system of springs, pulleys, levers, and launch cars was mounted atop a houseboat, which was towed downstream the Potomac by the Coast Guard to Quantico, Virginia, chosen by the site-selection team (with parameters handed them by Langley) for the stream's width, shallowness, and seclusion.

All the separate pieces had come together by November 1893, when *No. 4* was taken downriver and mounted upon the houseboat. Like a Stringfellow machine, the aerodrome seemed unable to function with any wind at all. After two months of delays, the secretary decided to scratch a catapult launch; *No. 4* would be held from the houseboat by a long arm and dropped. Langley was sure it would reach flying speed before it hit the water.

So with its steam engine running full tilt, the machine was released from the arm. And it plunged straight into the Potomac.

Phillips Knows How to Make a Venetian Blind

In 1891 Horatio Phillips returned again from his wind box and filed a patent for yet another wing section. In that patent he described how the section reacted in the airstream: "The particles of air struck by the convex upper surface . . . are deflected upward . . . thereby causing a partial vacuum over the greater portion of the upper surface. The particles of air under . . . follow the lower convex and concave surface . . . [and] are gradually put into motion in a downward direction, the motion being an accelerating one. . . . In this

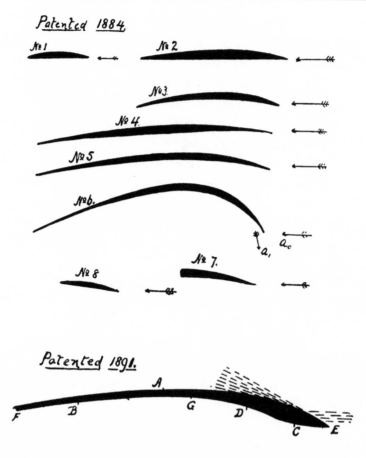

PHILLIPS, 1884 AND 1891: WHAT WAS
GOING ON ON TOP WAS AS IMPORTANT AS
WHAT WAS GOING ON ON THE BOTTOM.

way a greater pressure than the atmospheric pressure is produced on
the under surface of the blade." Simply put, low pressure is produced
on the blade's upper surface, while high pressure is produced on the
underside. Since high pressure always moves in the direction of low
pressure, the high pressure below pushes the blade upward to the
low pressure, and woosh—lift!

With this knowledge, Phillips two years later produced a flying machine resembling an open Venetian blind on wheels. Its wings were 50 slats, 22 feet long by 1.5 inches wide, mounted two inches apart. This apparatus measured 9.5 feet high and rested on a long wooden frame 25 feet long. A coal-fired engine turned a twin-bladed prop 400 revolutions per minute. The entire machine weighed 350 pounds, there having been "no attempt to provide exceptionally light machinery," reported Chanute from the pages of his column. On a circular track—shades of Moy—the Phillips machine proved it could sustain itself in the air for part of a lap, though "Mr. Phillips's experimental machine neglects any provisions for maintaining equilibrium in full flight, or for arising and alighting safely," Chanute wrote.

Otto Lilienthal Flies Every Sunday

Just about everything the wind box told Phillips, Otto Lilienthal had already worked out.

While Otto studied engineering, he and brother Gustav built and tried frail wings of wood and feathers, but they were interrupted by the Franco-Prussian War; after the war Otto worked as an engineer by day and experimented at night with a wing-beating machine, "which," wrote Gustav, "was launched from an inclined plane out of the window of our lodging on the fourth floor at 4 o'clock in the morning, so as to avoid being seen." Through this and more methodical experimentation, Lilienthal compiled more precise data than Cayley on the very forces that Sir George discovered were sufficient to sustain a common man in the air.

Not caring who knew what he knew about aerial navigation, Otto Lilienthal had published his findings in *The Flight of Birds as the*

Basis of the Art of Flying in 1889. And immediately he was chastised in the German scientific community.

"I am told that I should have come before the public with [these discoveries] immediately after my first discovery of the new laws of air resistance more than 20 years ago," he wrote in 1893. But the reason he hadn't was simple: "people in Germany still considered every man who occupied himself with this unprofitable art as little better than a lunatic. This was sufficient cause for our not attracting unnecessary attention to such studies."

The concepts he had kept from the world for so long? Lilienthal's analyses showed that "the construction of machines for practical operations in nowise depends upon the discovery of light and powerful motors" but rather, "in order to operate with the greatest possible economy, must be based, both in shape and proportion, upon the wings of the large, high-flying birds."

According to *The Flight of Birds,* that meant that the wing was to be a parabolic curve—"the greater curvature being to the front and flatter to the rear"—in its traverse section, so that it was concave underneath. The depth of that curve should be one-twelfth of its width (a 1-in-12 camber), though he advocated experimentation for wings larger than the one of 107 square feet he was presently building of cloth stretched over a willow frame.

So that anyone could try this at home, Lilienthal included handy air pressure tables, from which one could calculate the sustaining surface needed to support a given weight at a given speed.

After his book's publication, Lilienthal began practical tests by building his first *Flugapparat* in 1889 and a second in 1890; the first without a tail, and the second with. Both were failures.

Undeterred, he took what he'd learned and began his third flying apparatus, which he finished in 1891. Lilienthal whittled down its original 107 square feet of sustaining surface to 86 square feet. The final version had a long thin wing, with vertical and horizontal

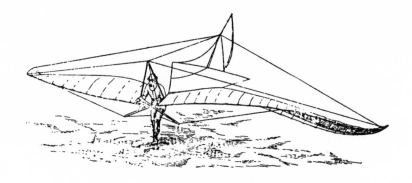

LILIENTHAL, 1891: THE ORIGINAL
SUNDAY AVIATOR.

rudders in back. Without himself aboard, the flying machine weighed 39.6 pounds.

Lilienthal's preliminary tests for this machine began in his garden. He would don the wings and run with them toward a springboard 26 feet away, which launched him forward into the air. Gliding a few feet, Lilienthal learned the basic handling characteristics of the machine, while he also practiced controlling it by shifting his weight. When he landed, he would run back and do it all over again. "After several hundred of these leaps I gradually increased the height of my board to 2.5 meters," he wrote, "and from that elevation I could safely and without danger cross the entire grass plot."

From there he moved his trials to the hills on the outskirts of Berlin, choosing one with a gentle, eroding slope facing the prevailing wind. Holding up the glider with a shoulder harness, Lilienthal ran down the hill toward the wind, until he was traveling fast enough for the wings to take hold—and they lifted him and carried him some 80 feet to the bottom of the hill. The flying apparatus actually flew—carrying an unheard-of 2.5 pounds per square foot.

But it flew imperfectly. Repeated flights—"almost every Sunday, and sometimes on week days"—showed that the machine grew surly and unstable when the wind reached speeds above 11 to 13 miles per hour, and "but for the circumstance that I was able to release myself quickly from my apparatus, I might have had a broken neck instead of the sprains in feet or arms which always healed in a few weeks."

Before Lilienthal would return to his hills, he needed to build a machine that would handle the ever-fluctuating temperament of the wind.

But the first round of tests supported Lilienthal's theories of the efficiency and worth of "concavo-convex" wing surfaces. And for the first time there was even convincing photographic evidence: Herr Lilienthal dangling in his glider, as he "sailed right over the head of the miller of Derwitz . . . and of his esteemed poodle dog."

Hiram Maxim's Fearsome First Kite O'War

All this evidence didn't convince the inventor Hiram Maxim of anything. Not one whit.

He wrote in the June 1892 issue of *The Cosmopolitan,* "It is neither necessary nor practical to imitate the bird too closely, because screw propellers have been found to be very efficient. . . . Without a doubt, the motor is the chief thing to be considered. Scientists have long said, Give us a motor and we will very soon give you a successful flying machine."

An expatriate American living in England, Maxim knew a thing or two about machinery. He had invented lighting systems and an electric telegraph, and he built a rifle that harnessed the recoil power of its cartridge: Firing it ejected the used shell and reloaded the weapon. By 1884, Maxim's machine gun could fire 600 rounds per minute. He patented this efficient killer and sold it to the British, which endeared him to the government there and also made him a rich man.

Suddenly Maxim was wealthy enough to take on the problem of aerial navigation his way: It was clearly an engineering problem, so he designed the machine first, then tried to work out the science through testing. And he did it in a big way, by designing a big machine: a biplane with 5,500 square feet of sustaining surface. The Maxim biplane could engulf nearly sixty-four delicate Lilienthal gliders and even dwarf Henson's conceptual aerial steam carriage of 1842. Size and subtlety of design didn't matter to Maxim—in his book it was all power.

He rented an expansive estate in Kent called Baldwyn's Park and there began assembling the pieces of his machine, while issuing statements to the press of his method and its makeup. The gravity and success of his automatic weapon, and his membership in Britain's Aeronautical Society—"Need I say that I am the most active member?" he confessed modestly—naturally added weight to his words, so the world listened when he spoke of building "the first kite of war."

To test the efficiency of propellers as well as the power needed to push a plane through air, he spoke of building "a very elaborate apparatus, provided with a great number of instruments," basically an updated whirling-arm device.

"Whether I succeed or not, the results of my experiments will be published, and as I am the only man who has ever tried the experiments in a thorough manner with delicate and accurate apparatus, the data which I shall be able to furnish will be of much greater value to experimenters than all that has ever been published before."

Lilienthal by Numbers

The years immediately after his first successful glides in the 86-square-foot glider, Otto Lilienthal and his mechanic, Hugo Eulitz, spent building and gliding in a variety of machines, each a variation on the same theme.

First they produced two successively larger man-carrying gliders, called *No. 4* and *No. 5,* and a standard shape grew and took form. In the *No. 5 Glider,* the wing became larger and had a dihedral angle, and the cruciform tail changed so that the horizontal surface was sandwiched between the wing and the vertical rudder. The wings of the *No. 6 Glider* of 1893 could be folded for easier transportation and storage, and its tailplane now could travel upward freely, since Lilienthal thought it might prevent upward gusts from pushing the tail up and the nose down. His *No. 7 Glider,* built that year, had an even larger wing, so the engineer and his mechanic could glide even on days when there was little wind. His *No. 8 Glider* was an average-size monoplane, which Lilienthal sold to one lucky customer.

On the *No. 9 Glider,* built in 1894, Lilienthal figured that even if he couldn't prevent his nosedives with the free-traveling tailplane of *No. 6,* at least he could come through a crash unscathed. This glider had a willow loop in front to absorb shock, which Lilienthal called the *Prellbügel.*

"During a gliding flight taken from a great height, the center of gravity lay too much to the back," Lilienthal wrote. "At the same time I was unable—owing to fatigue—to draw the upper part of my body again toward the front." So the glider zoomed up, then suddenly nosed over and slammed into the earth. Only the loop of willow with a funny name lay between Lilienthal and doom.

If he had a glider for light winds, he needed one for heavy winds, too; and so the reasoning behind *No. 10 Glider,* with its nine-square-meter, smaller-than-average wing. Lilienthal called it the *Sturm-flugelmodell.*

The next glider that Lilienthal and company built that year was, not surprisingly, called the *No. 11 Glider.* It was also named the *Normal-Segelapparat,* the "Standard" glider. Like its predecessors, it was a monoplane, though with a nice, average wing area, for Lilienthal, of 13 square meters. The horizontal tail now surrounded the vertical surface, though it was still free to hinge upward, as in the

No. 6 Glider. With this configuration Lilienthal thought he had licked the nosedive problem, so he dispensed with the *Prellbügel* as a standard feature. Lilienthal manufactured perhaps nine *No. 11s*, which were snatched up by buyers from Moscow to New York.

His gliding and writing had made the stocky German a celebrity at all points in between. And he used his status as the only flying human to fire off thinly veiled barbs at his main rival, the as-yet-earth-bound Hiram Maxim.

"I must confess," Lilienthal wrote, "that to us who abandoned *flat* wings fully two decades ago, it seemed almost inconceivable that experimenters should cling so tenaciously to the aeroplanes and to hopeless calculations on the resistance of plane surfaces, as practically all of them did during this whole period. Even to the present hour the majority of aviators expend much painful effort in attempting the hopeless task of trying to fly with flat wings."

Maxim's opinion on the issue was more concise. He called Lilienthal "a flying squirrel."

Maxim Takes Off Unexpectedly

For nearly two years now Maxim's shops at Baldwyn's Park, Bexley, Kent, England, buzzed with the sound of machinery machining and hammers hammering, of tubing being bent, of silk being stretched, of $45,000 being drained from Maxim's bank account.

As for the machine that took shape there, a village idiot viewing from a field might have mistaken it for a newfangled version of the locomotive, since it hissed steam and rolled with iron wheels upon some 1,800 feet of special eight-foot-gauge track.

A nearsighted deity might have blessed Maxim's 7,000-pound machine—175 times heavier than Lilienthal's—for it resembled a gossamer cathedral. The cross-shaped gargantuan wing spanned 104 feet and was ever-so-slightly concave, its outer panels rising in a stabilizing dihedral. Horizontal rudder panels on the nose and tail added to its fearsome symmetry; and Maxim threatened that others might be added if his original theory of control systems proved insufficient once testing was under way.

Its length was 145 feet, which, Maxim told the *New York Sun,* "is . . . so as to give a man time to think; its length makes it easier to steer and to change its angle in the air."

Like Langley's aerodromes, the machine was an engineering marvel to behold. It derived its power from twin 180-horsepower, two-cylinder steam engines, each generating one horsepower for every eight pounds it weighed—yet light enough for the aging inventor to heft alone—though part of its weight reduction had to do with its condenser: Steam would cool and condense by circulating within the hollow tubing frame of the machine itself.

Each engine drove a broad-bladed pusher propeller measuring nearly 18 feet in diameter. The engines were mounted on a sled, whose rising nose gave the whole machine an angle of incidence while on the ground; upon this sled too could be found the three-man crew.

As Maxim explained to the readers of *The Cosmopolitan,* unlike a boat, which has to be steered in one dimension, horizontally, a flying machine—like a torpedo—has to be steered in two dimensions: up or down, as well as left or right. Saying, "We should experiment with the more difficult one at first—namely the up and down or vertical direction," Maxim proposed the horizontal rudders, controlled in the air through a "Gyrostat," which consisted of a gyroscope that would keep the machine on some preordained angle of incidence. He did not see the necessity of a vertical rudder, not with two propellers on board: To turn the machine, "we should be able to partly close off the steam from the engine of one screw, and turn more steam on the other."

Before he began final assembly, Maxim tested the machine sans silk at various speeds on its track to measure the thrust of its propellers, the soundness of its engine, and the soundness of the whole design.

He wrote Chanute about what should have been: "I find a great number of steel stays are necessary in order to hold the machine in shape. . . . they appear to offer a considerable resistance to the passage of the machine through the air. If I were to build another machine I should aim more at getting less atmospheric resistance, because I can see now that everything else is assured except this single factor. If the machine does not go it will simply be because too much force is expended in driving the framework through the air."

Well, that wasn't its only problem.

Maxim had each of its wheels equipped with dynagraphs, instruments to measure their load. Then the machine's lifting surfaces were encased in silk, and he began the next series of tests, which ended when its steel bracings kept snapping. Back again with the repaired machine in early 1893, Maxim clocked it at 27 miles per hour with the propellers providing 700 pounds of thrust; the lift over the front wheels measured 2,500 pounds, while the lift over the rear wheels measured 2,800 pounds, "or quite all the weight resting on them," said Chanute. But on another test run in February, a gust blew the machine on its side, damaging its framework.

Again Maxim repaired the machine, and this time he had wooden guardrails built a few inches above the track, lest the flying machine should ever again try to become airborne. Maxim even took a reporter for a ride. "The action of the screws caused very little shaking through the whole machine," wrote journalist H.J.W. Dam. " . . . the commander yelled 'Let go!' A rope was pulled, then the machine shot forward like a railway locomotive, and with the big wheels whirling, the steam hissing, and the waste pipe puffing and gurgling, flew over the 1,800 feet of track. It was stopped by a couple of ropes stretched across the track working on capstans. . . . The ship was then pushed back over the track by men, it not being built, any more than a bird, to fly backward."

Tests continued off and on through July 1894. On the last day of the month, Maxim fired up the machine, and both shot down the track, accelerating from zero to 42 miles per hour in 600 feet. That was too much temptation for the kite to bear: It lurched upward, snapped through the guardrail, "and floated in the air," the surprised Maxim wrote. A piece of rail cracked one propeller, Maxim cut power, and the machine settled back to earth. Its unbridled flying days were over, for good this time.

Apparently, the foulest tonnage that the Maxim kite o'war ever threatened to rain down was the machine itself: All along, the biggest danger to humanity was that it might hurl uncontrollably among unsuspecting observers and crush them.

Progress in Flying Machines

By the time the year 1894 rolled around, Octave Chanute had completed the twenty-seventh installment of "Progress in Flying Machines" for Forney's *The Railroad and Engineering Journal,* a far cry from the six to eight installments originally proposed. He half-apologized for this: "investigation disclosed that far more experimenting of instructive value had been done than was at first supposed," he wrote in the introduction to a compilation of the series, published in book form that year. But in the foreword to that volume, he stated his intent: He wanted to prevent inventors from reinventing the wheel while they would invent the flying machine.

"It is intended to give sketches of many machines, and to attempt to criticize them"—though Chanute approached the subject with equanimity and was sparing with stern rebuke or ridicule: "We know comparatively so little of the principles which govern air resistances and reactions" that most every idea, every scheme, was thrown in for digestion; the volume was a dog's breakfast of up-to-the-minute aeronautical information.

He wrote extensively on the work of Mouillard, and Lilienthal; and Sir Lawrence Hargrave of Australia, who had just invented a highly successful box-shaped kite. Nothing was too obscure or outlandish for inclusion, from King Bladud to Besnier to Maxim. Indeed, as his statement about Moy's 1875 experiments reveal: "there was not sufficing knowledge to enable the public, or even scientific men, to distinguish the difference between a wild proposal, sure to fail to compass flight, and a promising experiment which was worth following up—a condition of affairs which has in a measure continued to this day."

There were mysterious holes in *Progress;* while eager to recognize Sir George Cayley's formula for calculating lift and drag, Chanute ignored Cayley's various flying machines, and gave only passing mention to *On Aerial Navigation;* perhaps he envied Cayley's title of Father of Aerial Navigation and wished to appropriate it for himself. Yet he gave an in-depth account of Le Bris, who first came to his attention through the pages of a romance novel.

He concluded with a note of optimism, and a set of reasons to develop the flying machine, other than the fact that it hadn't been done.

"[When] man succeeds in flying through the air the ultimate effect will be to diminish greatly the frequency of wars and to substitute some more rational methods of settling international misunderstandings. This may come to pass not only because of the additional horrors which will result in battle, but because no part of the field will be safe, no matter how distant from the actual scene of conflict . . . for a chance explosive dropped from a flying machine may destroy the chiefs . . . and must render nations and authorities still more unwilling to enter into contests than they are now, and perhaps in time make wars of extremely rare occurrence. . . .

"Let us hope that the advent of a successful flying machine, now only dimly foreseen and nevertheless thought to be possible, will bring nothing but good into the world; that it shall abridge distance, make all parts of the globe accessible, bring men into closer relation with each other, advance civilization, and hasten the promised era in which there shall be nothing but peace and goodwill among all men."

For all its flaws, *Progress* performed flawlessly: It catalogued the state of the art for experimenters, and perhaps gave some future giants the shoulders to stand upon. Secondarily it brought all the current experimenters in contact with Chanute. He seemed content with the role of their mentor, eager to distribute ideas and money, when necessary, among promising experimenters.

After finishing *Progress in Flying Machines,* Chanute had learned of a promising young engineer named Augustus Moore Herring. A native Georgian born at the tail end of the Civil War, Herring moved to New York to study mechanical engineering but dropped out of college before earning his degree. He worked as an engineer anyway and continued his college avocation: building Lilienthalesque gliders. After sending the galleys of *Progress* to the printer's in late 1894, Chanute hired the thirty-year-old Herring to build models based upon plans for a multiple-winged glider that Chanute himself had designed. With the younger man's help, Chanute was ready to move from theory to practice; he was finally ready to jump into the big game—and perhaps win it himself.

Lilienthal Meets Percy Pilcher

Otto Lilienthal sold a few Standard gliding machines and he continued to experiment, trying to solve his control problem. On his *No. 12 Glider* he tested out his newly patented full-span "flap" on the wing's leading edge. This device hinged downward; Lilienthal hoped it would lift the machine's nose and help it recover from its nose-dives. The wingtips of this model also had air brakes to help steer.

These new control surfaces didn't work as he had planned, so Lilienthal tried a different surface to increase his design's lift: His next three machines were biplane versions of his relatively ubiquitous *No. 11*, but the extra wing only seemed to hinder stability.

When he hit the slopes again in 1895 he had a little more company this time, besides the usual entourage of spectating Fräuleins and photographers and *Kinder*. His hillsides had become a mecca for the aeronautically minded; even Secretary Langley himself paid a visit to the workshop in Berlin—but he came away unimpressed by a Lilienthal machine under construction there. He found the willow frame "very crooked and irregular," and of the glider he wrote, "The aspect of the whole was heavy and clumsy."

He had to admit, though, that at least it flew, and it flew relatively well, for now Lilienthal was making up to 1,150-foot glides in his crooked and irregular, heavy and clumsy machines.

Others came calling as well, like Percy Pilcher, a Scottish lecturer in marine engineering at the University of Glasgow. Pilcher had built a tailless glider of his own design, which he called the *Bat*. He arrived at the foot of Lilienthal's hill seeking what only Lilienthal could offer: flying lessons in tested machines. Pilcher left not only with basic flying instruction and experience but also with Lilienthal's sound aeronautical advice to improve Pilcher's more colorfully named machine.

As for Lilienthal himself, his experimenting was about to enter a new phase. In the past he'd fitted a glider with a one-cylinder, two-horse carbonic gas engine that flapped surfaces on the wingtips, but he never flew it with the engine running; lately he had begun fitting a monoplane gilder with a larger two-cylinder engine, also powered by carbonic acid gas and also flapping six featherlike surfaces on either wingtip. As soon as he perfected this powered machine in the shop, flight testing would begin.

Langley's Aerodrome No. 5

While the Smithsonian crew in Washington strengthened and reengined and rewinged *Aerodrome No. 4,* they also completed construction on the next aerodrome, *No. 5.* The wings of the latter spanned nearly 14 feet and had spruce ribs covered with silk; they were set on the machine's body at a 20-degree dihedral angle for stability. By October 1894, both were ready for testing.

With its new engine running at full speed, *No. 4* was shot from the catapult—and headed straight to the shallow bottom of the Potomac.

Now the crew placed *No. 5* on the catapult and launched it. After release, the aerodrome arced upward at a 60-degree angle, then splashed into the river. Elapsed flight time: three seconds.

Acting upon recommendations from observers on the houseboat, Smithsonian staffers strengthened both aerodromes. By May 1895, they had completed improvements (so extensive that *No. 4* was renamed *No. 6*), and moved back to the houseboat. On May 5, with Secretary Langley's friend Alexander Graham Bell in attendance as official timekeeper and trusted observer, *No. 5* was launched three times. The longest flight lasted six seconds. Once again, both aerodromes were hauled back into the shop for extensive modification.

Word of Augustus Moore Herring's gliders reached Langley, and the secretary came to see his workmanship in New York. Langley immediately hired Herring away from Chanute and placed the young man in charge of rebuilding *Aerodromes No. 5* and *No. 6.*

Herring proceeded to redesign and replace both sets of wings on each aerodrome, making the fore and aft sets the same size. And then he changed the tail to a cruciform shape mounted on a spring so that it would flex in gusts and maintain the craft's equilibrium automatically, as Pénaud's writing recommended.

Herring did all this, but he couldn't do it fast enough to please Secretary Langley and was released. After more delays and staff shuffling, both aerodromes were once again ready for launch by May 6, 1896.

Aerodrome No. 6 was launched first. The catapult sheared off one of its wings, and it flopped into the drink. Quickly *No 5*. was mounted the catapult and prepared for launch. Bell was in place with a camera, while Secretary Langley stood on the river's edge. He ordered the launch at 3:05 P.M.

The aerodrome left the catapult, dipped a few feet, then began a slight climb into the gentle breeze. Bell snapped the camera's shutter and watched.

"[It] rose at first directly into the face of the wind," he reported, officially, "moving at all times with remarkable steadiness, and subsequently swinging around in large curves of perhaps a hundred yards in diameter, and continually ascending until its steam was exhausted. At a lapse of about a minute and a half, and at a height which I judged to be between eighty and one hundred feet in the air, the wheels ceased turning."

Having covered 3,000 feet at between 20 and 25 miles per hour, *Aerodrome No. 5* settled gently into the Potomac.

The crew fished it from the river, straightened a kinked wing, and let the machine's fabric dry. In a couple of hours they launched it again, and *No. 5* once again rose and flew under its own power. It was no aberration.

"Just what these flights meant to Mr. Langley can be readily understood. They meant success!" the secretary shouted in exuberant third-person. "For the first time in the history of the world a device produced by man had actually flown through the air, and had preserved its equilibrium without the aid of a guiding human intelligence."

Yes, sustained, powered, heavier-than-air flight wasn't just possible, it was reality. And Secretary Langley was the man who had at last bestowed it upon humanity.

Lilienthal Flight Described

The whole world now knew of Otto Lilienthal, the stocky, red-headed little German who had made more than two thousand flights and had spent nearly five hours in the air. It seemed that everyone wanted a piece of him these days.

Newspaper mogul William Randolph Hearst bought himself a standard Lilienthal *No. 11* in June 1896, thinking pictures of it swooping above the wastelands of Bayonne, New Jersey, might somehow endear his *New York Journal* to New York readers; he had not yet thought of going so far as starting a war to boost circulation.

Now the *Boston Evening Transcript* wanted its own Lilienthal angle, and it dispatched reporter Robert Wood to meet Lilienthal at a Berlin railroad station early Sunday morning, August 2. Together they rode a train north to the foothills of the Rhinower Mountains, where Lilienthal assembled a biplane glider for flight. "So perfectly was the machine fitted together," Wood wrote, "that it was impossible to find a single loose cord or brace, and the cloth was everywhere under such tension that the whole machine rang like a drum when rapped with the knuckles. As it lay on the grass in the bright sunshine, with its twenty-four square yards of snow white cloth spread before you, you felt as if the flying age was really commencing. Here was a flying machine, not constructed by a crank . . . but by an engineer of ability . . . a machine not made to look at, but to fly with."

Atop the hill, Lilienthal put on the biplane glider like a chicken suit and waited for a good stiff wind. When it arrived, he took three steps "and was instantly lifted from the ground, sailing off nearly horizontally from the summit," said Wood. "He went over my head at a terrific pace, at an elevation of about 50 feet, the wind playing wild tunes on the tense cordage of the machine. . . .

LILIENTHAL, 1896: HE BUILT HIS OWN
HILL, AND THE CURIOUS FLOCKED TO IT.

"The apparatus tipped sideways as if a sudden gust had got under the left wing. For a moment I could see the top of the aeroplane, and then, with a powerful throw of his legs he brought the machine once more on an even keel, and sailed away below me across the fields at the bottom, kicking at the tops of the haycocks as he passed over them."

This flying game was so easy, even a reporter could do it—if he started safely, just a few yards above the hill's bottom. Holding the machine up—"As you stand in the frame your elbows are at your side, the forearms are horizontal and your hands grasp one of the horizontal cross-braces. The weight of the machine rests in the angle of the elbow joints"—Wood ran a few steps, and found himself "sliding down the aerial incline a foot or two from the ground. The apparatus dipped from side to side a great deal. The feeling is most delightful . . . as if gravitation has been annihilated."

LILIENTHAL, 1896: HE TOOK TO THE
SKIES BY THROWING HIS WEIGHT AROUND.

The article began appearing fourteen days later under such head-lines as: "Lilienthal's Last Flights."

Just one week after Wood's visit, Lilienthal was back gliding off the slopes, this time in one of his monoplane gliders, when a vertical gust threw the machine's nose straight up. While Lilienthal struggled to throw his weight forward, the left wing dipped, and the glider plunged 50 feet to the ground.

His spine was broken in the fall. Lilienthal was taken to a Berlin hospital, where he died the next day. He was forty-eight years old.

A Wright Gets the Fever

When a small businessman in Ohio named Wilbur Wright read about Lilienthal's fatal crash in the newspaper that summer, he was caring for his youngest brother, Orville, delirious with typhoid fever.

Wright remembered the Pénaud helicopter their father gave them as children, and remembered how as adults they had followed Lilienthal's exploits and debated his approach and his success. This news would interest Orv, he thought, and so he put it aside for him later, after the fever broke.

CHAPTER SIX

1896 to 1901

Chanute and Herring with **Katydid** and the Machine that Would Be Herring's

When Augustus Moore Herring and Samuel Langley parted company late in 1895, Herring wrote Chanute and asked for his old job back.

Though he had continued construction of the multiple-wing glider from his base in Chicago, Chanute put Herring back on the payroll and began making plans to conduct flight tests the following summer on this and another glider that he had funded. William Avery, who had actually built the multiple-wing, would be there; so would Herring, who had not only a proven Lilienthal glider but also some experience with flying. For good measure Chanute asked along William Paul Butusov, a Russian immigrant who alleged—somewhat to Chanute's disbelief—that his Le Bris–inspired *Albatross* had stayed in the air for 45 minutes.

For the test site, Chanute needed a place with a steady wind and lots of nice, soft sand to crash into. He chose the dunes near Miller, Indiana, which lay on Lake Michigan's south shore. Just a few miles from the Windy City, Miller was still a tough place to reach, and so might discourage the presence of reporters.

The group arrived one Monday in late June 1896, carrying tents, gliders, ballast, ropes, food, and a doctor with the ironic name of Ricketts and, Chanute said, "a slack practice and a taste for aviation." Anyway, this was dangerous business, and they were far from the nearest hospital. They had several visitors right away, who saw Herring setting up his Lilienthal-inspired machine; one of them hurried into town and cabled the outside world. Reporters started arriving the next day.

A short *New York Times* editorial appeared soon after. Attempting to be witty and urbane, the editorial made note of the recent discovery of an "airship farm in the wilderness of Illinois (whether within or without the municipal boundaries of Chicago is not specified)," and identified Octave Chanute as its supervisor. "The situation of the 'farm' is kept secret. . . ." the editorial added, though "hitherto, the builders of airships have courted rather than shunned the bright sunshine of publicity. They have, in fact, done rather more talking than flying. It seems hardly credible, therefore, that men engaged in inventing flying machines should care to prosecute their labors in silence and seclusion." Ah, but they did. To form a control group of data to compare the other machines against, the younger "farmhands" immediately made several glides in Herring's Lilienthal machine.

The longest flight that day was 70 feet, with a glide ratio of 2 or 3 to 1—that is, the machine sank one foot for every two to three feet it flew. Lilienthal himself could usually eke out an 8-to-1 glide ratio. Chanute called the machine "cranky," but it was all they had to learn from.

The following day Herring assembled the multiple-wing. Weighing 36 pounds, it consisted of no fewer than twelve separate 6-foot-long wings braced together, designed to pivot on ball bearings during fluctuations in the wind's pressure and angle and thus preserve the craft's equilibrium. It resembled a giant insect, but it should have flown as well.

In their first experiment they tried to locate the multiple-wing's center of pressure, but with the wind gusting too hard they couldn't. But the next day they got the machine balanced and took it flying. Over the following few days, while Avery and Butusov tried flying the Lilienthal—and while continually breaking and repairing the multiple-wing—the men reconfigured Chanute's machine in as many ways as they could think of: with just eight wings, then four wings in front and eight in back, then eight in front and four in back, then five in front and one in back. In this configuration it flew the best so far; Herring glided the machine 69 feet, for a 3.5-to-1 glide ratio. The men took to calling it *Katydid*.

They broke camp and returned to Chicago for the Fourth of July but were back experimenting in late August. This time they began preparing to launch Butusov's just-finished *Albatross* from its trestle and in the interim began gliding with the second Chanute glider, a triplane that he had designed. It was a clean-looking machine, with its silk-covered wings made with spruce spars and arc-shaped ribs. They were held neatly apart with six pairs of vertical struts, then braced crosswise solidly with piano wires. It owed its triplane configuration to Stringfellow's success, though its wings were an equal 16 feet long. Herring soon declared the bottom wing superfluous and discarded it, leaving 135 square feet of sustaining surface. The pilot hung below the machine on simple square frames, one under each arm, swinging his legs like Lilienthal in order to try and control the craft. Herring's trademark, cruciform, coopted-from-Pénaud "regulating" tail followed, mounted on a swiveling universal joint.

Avery and Herring soon made glides 97, 253, and even 359 feet long. Herring flew that final glide, then went to Chanute and said the biplane glider was stable enough to attempt powered flight. Chanute disagreed: He wanted to refine automatic stability further before putting an engine on it.

The next day Herring told a reporter from the *Record* of their conflict, and the day after that Herring went to Chanute and said

Paul Butusov had lied about ever flying the *Albatross*. Herring said he considered it "highly dangerous, and sooner than to be a party to its testing, he preferred to withdraw," Chanute recorded in the expedition diary. "O.C. let him go. Went to camp and took reporter into his confidence, who thought Mr. Herring's action prompted by egotism and jealousy. . . . Avery . . . then gave various incidents and remarks going to show unfairness on Mr. Herring's part in the tests of all the machines except the one which he called his own."

Everyone else could stay and watch the Butusov *Albatross* break stanchions and wing ribs and spars and otherwise adhere to the sand dunes near its launch trestle. As for himself, Augustus Moore Herring was going to attempt powered flight with that machine that he now called his own.

Ader Returns with Avion III

Upon cashing the French War Ministry's check, Clément Ader worked in secret to develop his design to the Ministry's specifications. Emerging in October 1897, nearly six years later—and putting behind him a false start with a machine he named *Avion II*—Ader said he was ready to demonstrate flight in a third machine, *Avion III*. This craft had a wing six feet longer than his first, and to overcome the destabilizing torque that a single engine placed on *Eole*, it was powered by not one but two 20-horsepower steam engines.

First Ader tried rolling the craft under its own power around the 4,800-foot circular track at Camp Satory, near Versailles. Then two days later, the Ministry let it be known it would wait no longer. With two generals observing, Ader climbed inside his machine and started its engines. And though the wind was strong and gusting, he began his takeoff run on the track—with the wing blowing hard from *Avion III*'s left rear quarter. Suddenly the machine was airborne.

Ader steered hard to the left, trying to stay along the circle's perimeter, but he was blown sideways to the right. He cut the engines and landed hard, 1,500 feet from his starting point.

The generals hurried to Ader, saw he was unhurt, and hurried away; in their report to the Ministry later that month they wrote that they observed *Avion III* "swerve suddenly from the track, describe a half-turn, incline to the side and finally stop." And, they reported, so damaged was the machine that further tests would be delayed indefinitely. As a result of the official report, the Ministry of War cut off further funding.

Percy Pilcher's Disparate Flock

The cause of Otto Lilienthal's death was much in debate within and without aeronautical circles. Everyone wanted to know: Did the fault lie in man or his machine? *The Saturday Review* called the glider defective, so the man whom Lilienthal trained romped to his mentor's defense.

"[On] this occasion [Lilienthal was using a] device by which when he moved his head the horizontal rudder moved, so as to give him greater command over the tilting of the machine," Percy Pilcher wrote to the journal. "His accident is very probably due to his not having been quite well acquainted with this new system." So the problem may have not been in Lilienthal's design but with his skill. Still, Pilcher could only theorize like the rest; the mystery remained.

In 1896 he had left Lilienthal's hills and traveled back home to Glasgow and modified his *Bat* according to Lilienthal's advice; then he had built more machines, the *Beetle,* the *Gull,* and finally the *Hawk.* This last was best of all: capable of 750-foot glides, with a hinged tail unit advised by Lilienthal, cambered wings, and something no Lilienthal machine had—a wheeled undercarriage. While refining the *Hawk,* Pilcher planned that next stage—adding power.

One rainy dismal day in late September 1899, before a well-heeled group at Lord Braye's estate in Leichestershire, Pilcher took off running down the hillside in the wet and heavy *Hawk,* which climbed' sluggishly to 30 feet. Then a bamboo strut in the tail snapped, and the machine collapsed and plunged to the ground. Two days later, never having regained consciousness, Percy Pilcher died at the age of thirty-three.

Herring Alone Develops a Powered Biplane

Across the Atlantic and half the American continent less than a year before, Augustus Moore Herring stood on a Michigan beach beneath the frame of his powered biplane glider, and prepared to start its engine.

Right after his split with Chanute, Herring had built a triplane glider in which he reported making glides of nearly 1,000 feet—and which he could steer in flight by shifting his weight, like Lilienthal. Then in 1897 he took an engineering job at a boatyard in St. Joseph, Michigan, and he found a rich backer named Mattias Arnot, who funded construction of a virtual replica of the biplane glider. At camp on the Indiana dunes that autumn, Herring's new biplane flew more than 600 feet. A reporter who tried it wrote, "one takes four or five running steps down the plank and jumps off expecting to drop like a stone in the sand. To his surprise and pleasure he experiences about the same sensation felt by a man when taking his first ascension in an escalator. There is a queer feeling of being lifted from beneath. . . . The wind rushes in the face . . . like a hurricane and hums through the network of fine wire that forms part of the framework with a high shrill note."

Perhaps those heady sensations were what helped Arnot decide to finance the next step, Herring's powered machine, to the tune of $3,000. This was a biplane powered by a light, simple, three-horse engine, driven by compressed air—but capable of only 30 seconds of operation—and turning a rear pusher and a forward tractor propeller producing an estimated 30 pounds of thrust. It stood on skids, but the operator would launch it by taking a few steps until it was airborne, then hoist himself onto a seat mounted under the bottom wing and ride it out. The biplane was finished by 1898.

According to Herring, on October 11, with the wind blowing at 20 miles per hour, he filled the machine's compressed air tank and placed the 88-pound biplane on his shoulders. He faced the wind, and ran a few steps, and started the engine. Immediately the biplane lifted into the air—and sputtered along for 50 feet before the compressed air gave out and the engine was still.

As soon as he skidded to a stop, Herring cabled Octave Chanute, who arrived from Chicago the next day. It turned out utterly windless. Chanute went back home without seeing the machine fly.

Ten days later, the wind got up to 26 miles per hour, and Herring again attempted powered flight. And this time the machine plowed 73 feet through the air along the beach; Herring said he was aloft eight to ten seconds.

With winter now setting in, Herring told reporters he'd return to his workshop and be back in 1899, fresh and with a refined machine.

Early that spring, the shop and its contents were destroyed by fire.

Langley Delicately Approaches the Next Stage

Secretary Langley himself had already achieved powered flight; he even published a few papers and magazine articles saying so. "I have brought to a close the portion of the work which seemed to be specially mine—the demonstration of the practicability of mechanical flight—and for the next stage . . . it is probable that the world may look to others," he wrote in *McClure's Magazine*. But he also began to search for further funds to reach the next stage—powered, sustained *manned* flight—while he had his team of engineers and mechanics still assembled. All he needed was a little money to continue. Just $50,000 would do it, he estimated.

The secretary knew that if anyone knew someone with that kind of cash who was interested in aeronautics, it would be Octave Chanute. But here he drew a lukewarm response and decided his last best hope lay in the treasury of the U.S. government. He got lucky. In 1898, with a little help from an explosion inside the battleship *Maine* and the newspapers of William Randolph Hearst, war broke out between the United States and Spain.

Secretary Langley let it be known around Washington circles that an enlarged, manned version of his successful *Aerodrome No. 5* would make an excellent weapon against the enemy. Eventually word—and photos of the machine in flight—got to President McKinley, who decided to assemble a committee to investigate the machine's wartime potential.

Representatives of the Army and Navy met with Secretary Langley at the Smithsonian, and the secretary showed them the models and pictures, and he told them that to build a man-carrying aerodrome, he could quickly and easily enlarge the present successful design, all for only $50,000.

The committee agreed that it would be a useful device and passed its findings along to the Army's Board of Ordnance and Fortification for final approval, which the board gave: the project would get half the money now, and the other half when that was gone and the secretary could show reasonable progress.

With staff intact and cash in hand, Secretary Langley could now build his man-carrying *Great Aerodrome*.

Wilbur Wright Twists Cardboard

It was important to a young man like Wilbur Wright that he make a name for himself, leave his mark on the world. He had a lot of time after his accident to think that the world might indeed pass him by.

Born in 1867, Wilbur had spent most of his life in Dayton, Ohio. He had planned to head off to college after high school, but while playing a variation of hockey called shinny one winter in his home-town of Dayton, Ohio, another player slammed him in the mouth with a shinny stick. It broke out all his upper front teeth, and in the long slow recovery his family believed he had developed a heart condition. Confined to his house with his mother, who had taken ill with consumption, Wright did little but look after her and read anything within reach. Though he was an excellent student—especially in mathematics—he never officially finished high school.

Neither did his brother Orville, younger by four years. And in truth, both regretted never going to college; higher education would have made their lives' work easier, Orville thought. Orville loved to tinker. He built impressive kites as a child—prodigiously light and strong. Later on he started a printing business, which Wilbur soon joined, even helping Orville build the printing press out of the top of an old buggy. When Orville got caught up in the nationwide craze for safety bicycles (so called because the two wheels were the same size and much safer than the old-style high-wheeled bicycle), Wilbur followed.

The brothers went into the business building and selling their own line of high-quality safety bicycles. The business grew mod-estly, and the boys' succession of redbrick bicycle shops was al-ways just a few minutes' walk from the family's small white house on Hawthorne Street. They didn't date and never married; they remained at home after their mother's death, along with their younger sister Katharine. Their father, Bishop Milton Wright of the conservative United Brethren Church, lived there as well, but he was traveling most of the time.

Since the boys were always together and had almost the same build—both stayed within the range of 140 pounds—it took a little practice to tell them apart at first. At five foot ten Wilbur was slightly taller and had sharp features and gray-blue eyes and was almost totally bald. Orville, about two inches shorter, had a tuft of hair on top and always wore a mustache. Folks thought he resembled Poe. Though he had a wicked sense of humor, in public, at least, he let Wilbur do all the talking.

After the Wright Cycle Company got going, Wilbur began feeling unsettled and thought about college before it was too late. "I do not think I am specially fitted for success in any commercial pursuit," he wrote the bishop in 1894, when he had turned twenty-seven. "I might make a living but I doubt whether I would ever do much more than this. Intellectual effort is a pleasure to me and I think I would be better fitted for reasonable success in some of the professions than in business."

He found his calling with the gliding flights of Otto Lilienthal. Debating with Orville the German's approach and mysterious death became Wilbur's chief passion. After absorbing everything on flight in the Dayton Public Library, he wrote to the Smithsonian asking the Institution's recommendations for research materials. ("I am an enthusiast, but not a crank in the sense that I have some pet theories as to the proper construction of a flying machine.") During slack times at the business he began to collect every word on the Smithsonian's list, from *Progress in Flying Machines* by Octave Chanute to the published papers of the late Lilienthal and the famous Secretary Langley of the Smithsonian. He devoured this material, and so did his brother. "[We] were much impressed with the great number of people who had given thought to it," said Orville, "among these some of the greatest minds the world has produced. But we found that the experiments of one after another had failed." They quickly recognized the two prevalent camps: The power-first approach of Langley and Maxim, versus the powerless gliders of Lilienthal and now Chanute. "Our sympathies were with the latter school," Orville said, "partly from impatience at the wasteful extravagance of mounting delicate and costly machinery which no one knew how to manage, and partly, no doubt, from the extraordinary charm and enthusiasm with which the apostles of soaring flight set forth the beauties of sailing through the air on fixed wings, deriving the motive power from the wind itself."

While debating with his brother the cause of each experimenter's failure, Wilbur became more and more excited by the idea of gliding like the late Lilienthal. The fault, Wilbur thought, lay in the chosen method of maintaining the machine's equilibrium: by the operator shifting his weight. There had to be a better way.

He noticed, when watching buzzards, that "they regained their lateral balance, when partly overturned by a gust of wind, by a torsion of the tips of the wings." That is, the buzzard would flex the trailing edge of one wing upward, creating drag, while flexing the trailing edge of the other wing downward, creating lift. Rolling along a line from its head through its tail, the bird regained its level.

Wilbur began thinking about building a biplane kite along the same pattern of the Chanute-Herring machine, while trying to find the right mechanism for twisting its wings without corrupting its structural integrity. He and Orv thought of using a system of shafts and gears running at the center of the machine, "which, being in mesh, would cause one wing to turn upward in front when the other wing was turned downward." But building the device strong enough to perform such a twist would make the gliding machine too heavy.

Then one July night in 1899, Wilbur was in the bicycle shop selling a new inner tube to a customer. While they chatted, Wilbur handed over the tube and held on to the empty pasteboard box, absentmindedly tearing off the ends of the box and flexing and twisting the hollow remains.

When he realized just what he was doing, he shut down the shop and rushed home with the box to show Orville.

Over the next two days they built a kite with two superposed planes five feet long and 13 inches wide. Like the Herring glider, it was cross-braced laterally; but like the empty inner-tube box it was without fore-and-aft trussing to allow the ends, the wingtips, to flex. To control this kite they would use four cords: One led from the top wing's left forward edge to the bottom of a stick in the operator's left hand, and another led from the bottom wing's left tip to the top of the same stick; the same arrangement went from the right wingtips to the operator's right hand. Hinged joints on the upright struts allowed the top plane to shift forward or backward. Pulling the tops of both sticks backward shifted the higher wing forward, and that shifted the average center of pressure forward of the center of gravity, causing the kite to turn upward in front. Moving each stick in the opposite direction, however, would make the wings twist.

While Orville left on a family camping trip, Wilbur stayed in Dayton and tried the kite with a number of schoolboys present. "It responded promptly to the warping of the surfaces, always lifting the wing that had the larger angle," Orville said. "Several times, according to Wilbur's account to me, when he shifted the upper surface backward . . . the nose of the machine turned downward as was intended; but in diving downward it created a slack in the flying cords, so that he was not able to control it further. The model made such a rapid dive to the ground that the small boys present fell on their faces to avoid being hit."

Wilbur was so thrilled with the kite, he made a special trip out to the campsite and took Orville aside and spoke with him about it at length. Right then and there they started planning to build a larger kite, capable of carrying one of them.

Using Lilienthal's tables from *The Flight of Birds as the Basis of the Art of Flying,* they calculated that in a 16-mile-per-hour wind, they could lift one of their 140-pound bodies with a machine having 150 square feet of sustaining surface cambered 1-in-23. Now all they needed was to find that kind of strong wind, preferably steady as well.

Wilbur wrote to the United States Weather Bureau, asking for a chart of wind velocities for—where else—the Windy City, Chicago, in the autumn months, when the bicycle business was slack. And in May 1900 he wrote to the widely renowned Octave Chanute, introducing himself as an afflicted true believer in human flight ready to die for the cause, telling of his kite flying, and asking whether the older engineer knew of a good locale for their experiments. The sixty-eight-year-old Chanute replied promptly, offered to correspond further, and suggested Wilbur try experimenting, among other places, along the Atlantic Coast. By September 1900, Wilbur was on his way to the tiny fishing village of Kitty Hawk, North Carolina.

Langley $25,000 Later

Even before he had his government funding, Secretary Langley proceeded with developing his *Great Aerodrome.* After trying to find a major automobile manufacturer who could build him a 12-horsepower, 600-rpm, 60-pound gasoline engine, he settled on a minor manufacturer: Stephen Balzer, the man who unleashed the first automobile on an unsuspecting New York City—and who has been cursed for it ever since by untold, unknowing millions. Balzer promised to deliver a five-cylinder engine for a mere $1,500.

Then Langley hired another assistant to succeed the assistant who had succeeded Augustus Moore Herring. He was Charles Manly, a young engineer lately graduated from Cornell.

And he commissioned another launch mechanism, and while he was at it, the secretary bought a larger barge from which to base the new 15-ton catapult, and he contracted out more than $3,000 worth of modifications for the new barge, including an onboard shop.

By September 1899, Langley had gone through the first half of his government subsidy, even though work had barely started on the *Great Aerodrome.*

But that was okay: he gave the Board of Ordnance and Fortification a tour of his shops and of the new barge, and he showed them some more pictures and some finished parts for the full-scale *Great Aerodrome,* plus some models of what the final version would look like. The board quickly agreed to hand over the next $25,000.

Less than a year later, the completed frame of the secretary's newest flying machine awaited only the engine. While the power plant continued to be delayed, Secretary Langley kept his staff busy building a meticulously detailed quarter-scale aerodrome. It would be ready for testing in the summer of 1901.

The First Wright Glider

Before leaving Dayton on that five-day-long train-steamer-train trip to Elizabeth City, before what turned out to be a harrowing, storm-tossed two-day journey across Albemarle Sound in Israel Perry's leaky schooner, Wilbur Wright wrote to his father, away as always on church business.

"I am intending . . . a trip to the coast of North Carolina . . . for the purpose of making some experiments with a flying machine," Wilbur wrote. "It is my belief that flight is possible, and, while I am taking up the investigation for pleasure rather than profit, I think that there is a slight possibility of achieving fame and fortune from it. It is almost the only great problem which has not been pursued by a multitude of investigators, and therefore carried to a point where further progress is very difficult. I am certain I can reach a point much in advance of any previous workers in the field even if complete success is not attained just at present. At any rate, I shall have an outing of several weeks and see a part of the world I have never before visited."

Before Kitty Hawk, he'd only gone as far as the 1893 World's Fair in Chicago. Now he and his sister's best trunk (and enough clean collars to last the duration of the trip) were half a continent away, on a thin strip of sand that held a lifesaving station, the weather station that supplied the U.S. Weather Bureau with the steady wind-speed statistics that gained Wilbur's attention, a few sand dunes known as the Kill Devil Hills, and a few scattered houses as well. He'd pitched a tent near the home of Bill Tate, who had taken him in as a boarder, and there in the shade of an oak tree, Wilbur began assembling his glider.

It was a double-decker like their kite of the previous year. Initially, through judicious trammeling of its lateral trussing, its wings were bent upward to give them that stabilizing effect of dihedral. The way they planned it the wings would be 18 feet long, with spruce spars. Spruce that length was unavailable in Dayton, and the best stock he could manage to find along the way was 16-foot pine in Norfolk. So the wings he constructed in Kitty Hawk had wingtip bows to flesh out the length to 17 feet. Its ribs were five-foot-long strips of ash steamed and bent, with the peak of its 1-in-23 camber near the leading edge. They did it that way not out of homage to Horatio Phillips's wind tunnel experiments, but because they thought it would give the glider better fore-and-aft equilibrium. Still, they discovered that this also accidentally improved the wing's lift. The machine also had a horizontal rudder in front, which they hoped would more quickly change its fore-and-aft balance, help support the machine's weight, add some inherent stability, and act as a shock absorber in case they crashed, which they wholly expected to do. Many times.

By the time Orville joined Wilbur in late September, the modified glider weighed 50 pounds and had 165 square feet of sustaining surface—covered with extra-quality French sateen fabric. There was an 18-inch-wide gap on its lower wing to accommodate the operator, who, to reduce "drift" or drag, flew the machine while lying flat on the bottom wing but who would, they thought, hop up, pop through the hole, and start running when the machine got close enough to the ground to land.

All together, the glider had cost $15.

Meanwhile, their presence had created quite a stir in the sleepy settlement. Everyone for miles around already knew them on sight, and without introduction addressed them as "Mr. Wright," and secretly thought they were rich because they always wore suits—with fresh collars. Bill Tate had taken to following them around like a little boy—"He gets interested in anything we have," Orville wrote Katharine—and soon he was assisting them in their experiments. "Tate can't afford to shirk his work to fool around with us," Orville added, "so he attempts to do a day's work in two or three hours so that he can spend the balance with us and the machine."

First they tested it as a kite, using chains for ballast and fishing scales to measure its drag. "The greatest difficulty is in keeping it down," Orville wrote to Katharine. "It naturally wants to go higher & higher."

After flying it as a kite a few times—and after Wilbur put in a few hours comparing the flying characteristics of the local eagles and hawks with the buzzards back home—they decided to straighten its wing and found that it was easier to control. "The dihedral angle is of advantage only in still air," Wilbur wrote in his notebook. "It greatly increases the disturbing effect of side gusts."

They found it difficult to simultaneously control its fore-and-aft balance and its lateral stability, and "we almost gave up the idea of attempting to glide," Wilbur said, but before they broke camp and returned to Dayton, the three men carried it three miles to the largest sand dune of the Kill Devil Hills, *the* Kill Devil Hill, which had a rise of 1 in 6.

Wilbur lay down on the machine while Tate and Orville each held on to a wingtip and started running downhill for all they were worth. The machine began to rise, and the assistants held it down to gain speed, until they could no longer keep up with it. It shot away from them, flying just above the slope for distances of between three or four hundred feet.

"[I] then brought the machine slowly to the ground," Wilbur wrote Octave Chanute, "so slowly in fact that the marks of the machine could be seen for twenty or thirty feet back from the point where it finally stopped. . . . The wind was blowing about twelve miles. We found no difficulty in maintaining fore-and-aft balance. The ease with which it was accomplished was a matter of great astonishment to us. It was so different from what the writings of other experimenters led us to expect. This may have been partly due to the steadiness of the wind, partly to the fixed position of the operator, and partly to a fortunate combination of circumstances of which we were not aware. . . . We never found it necessary to shift the body."

But their experiment left them puzzled. The drag measurements on their machine were greater than those indicated by Lilienthal's tables. The Wrights would try to figure out why in Dayton the following year.

But for now, October was coming to an end. They said good-bye to their new friends at Kitty Hawk and packed up their gear and waited for their boat across Albemarle Sound. First, though, they took their gliding machine to the top of a dune and gave it a final shove, and after watching it glide to a rest in the bright, hot sand a few feet down the slope, they turned and walked away.

Mrs. Tate came down after they were gone and stripped the extra-quality French sateen fabric from the wings to sew into dresses for her little girls. It seemed a shame to use such nice fabric on a kite and then let it go to waste.

Trouble at Kitty Hawk

The Wrights returned to Kitty Hawk the following year, bringing with them a larger new glider, the lumber for building a shed, and an anemometer they borrowed from Chanute, even though, as Wilbur wrote him, "In general we are little disposed to use anything not our own but as in the present case we are already planning to spend about all we feel that we ought to on our this year's experiments."

Now that Chanute found they would accept one gift, he wanted to offer them more. He wanted to send a couple of young men along, but no need to worry: he would pay for everything. Then he wanted to show up, too. And there was more: To help the Wrights measure the angle of their glides, "I think you will need a clinometer, and if I find one downtown I will send it to you by express."

Wilbur was anxious about all this largess, especially the extra help; he made it clear that they were glad to have the two men come along, just as long as it was for Chanute's benefit, not theirs. Chanute replied that in fact it was for his benefit. As for the first man he'd be sending, Edward Huffaker, late a Langley assistant in his aerodrome trials, well, Huffaker would be bringing a gliding machine he'd built from cloth and paper tubing, which Chanute had paid for, and which Chanute had said earlier "I fear . . . will not stand long enough to test the efficiency of the ideas in its design."

As for the second, George Spratt, he was just a Pennsylvania farmer with a little medical training who was also interested in aeronautics, and Chanute said "I will be compensated by the pleasure given to him, even if I do not utilize him hereafter."

And as for Chanute himself, though he didn't say it, it would be just like the old days at Miller, Indiana: lots of sand, and wind, and gliders, and tools, and men living primitively together talking constantly about flying machines.

By the time the Chanute men had arrived circuitously at Kitty Hawk in July 1901—at the peak of summer this year, at the peak of mosquito season as well—the Wrights had finished building a long, low shed with a tarpaper roof just a thousand feet from the big Kill Devil Hill. Of course they wouldn't think of using the building for themselves; they'd live cramped inside in the tent next door. The shed was for their new glider.

They had stuck with the same general design as the last glider, with warping biplane wings and a controllable horizontal rudder again in front, only bigger this time. In fact, the entire machine was larger than any previous gliding machine in history. The new wings were 22 feet by 7, compared with 17 feet by 5 in the old machine, and they had a total lifting surface of 290 feet against 165. At 98 pounds the new machine weighed almost twice as much, too. Size aside, there was only one other major difference: Instead of using their earlier 1-in-23 camber, the brothers gave the new wing a ratio of 1 in 12, which Lilienthal preferred.

They took it gliding, and in less than an hour they could fly it over distances of more than 300 feet. But they also found its lift was just one-third of what the Lilienthal tables indicated it should be. And they expected the new machine to fly with a glide ratio of 1 in 12, though the machine would only do 1 in 6. They had designed the machine to fly at 18 miles per hour, which would let it hover above one spot in an 18-mile-per-hour wind, and let the operator rack up a few more minutes in the air. But they were able to fly only a fifth of the time they had hoped. And worse: The machine was not as docile as the first glider.

Wilbur first thought the rudder size was a problem and reduced it to ten square feet—to no good effect. Then the brothers spent a week streamlining the machine's leading edges and changing the camber to 1 in 18, which worked better: It would glide a little farther and was a little easier to control. Wilbur flew the changed machine 335 feet in 25-mile-per-hour winds and actually got it to turn gently to the left a couple of times.

Still, they were disappointed. They were assaulted by mosquitoes and the heat, by a "disagreeable Mr. Huffaker," who didn't place much emphasis on personal hygiene, and by the fact that they could actually rely little on knowledge that was thought gospel among the chosen. In mid-August they decided to break camp.

Orville expected he'd never see Kitty Hawk again. As for Wilbur, he was very quiet on the train back home. But once he leaned over to Orville and said, "Not within fifty years will man fly."

Further Success at Quantico

That June, the Smithsonian staff had the old houseboat towed downstream to Quantico again and mounted the new quarter-scale aerodrome on its launch platform.

Late in the afternoon of June 19, with its 1.5-horsepower gasoline engine spinning its two propellers, the aerodrome was shot from the platform four times, successfully flying 100, 150, 300, 350 feet, each time remaining aloft until its engine ran out of fuel.

It was yet another victory for the secretary: Not only had he demonstrated the soundness of his basic design, he had become the first to achieve sustained flight with gasoline power.

The next time one of his aerodromes took off, it would be with a man on board.

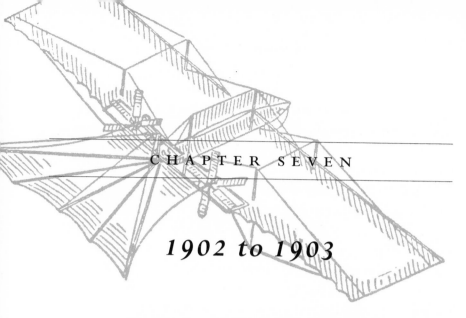

CHAPTER SEVEN

1902 to 1903

The Return of the Wright Brothers

Though Octave Chanute tried to put things in a positive light, he knew Wilbur was discouraged. If the brothers quit now, the best aeronautic work to date would be abandoned, maybe even lost, setting the cause back years. Chanute was getting old—and he wanted to see some results in his lifetime. Looking for a way to boost Wilbur's interest, Chanute told him that members of the prestigious Western Society of Engineers were interested in having him speak on his gliding experiments at an upcoming meeting. And, he wrote days later, the society would like to declare it Ladies' Night, if Wilbur approved.

"Will was about to refuse," Katharine wrote Bishop Wright, "but I nagged him into it."

"I must caution you," Wilbur replied to Chanute, ". . . I make no pretense of being a public speaker. . . . I will already be as badly scared as it is possible for a man to be, so that the presence of ladies will make little difference to me."

The invitation had its intended effect, however, and soon Katharine complained about hearing nothing but flying machines all day from her brothers. In mid-September 1901, she packed Wilbur onto the Chicago train looking like a swell. Since Orv was the more fastidious one—known for spending the day dressed to the nines, working on bicycles in the shop, then coming home spotless—Katharine had Wilbur decked out in Orville's shirt, collars, cuffs, links, and overcoat.

That gala evening, after his introduction to the society by the avuncular Chanute, Wilbur confidently expounded on the problems with building a successful flying machine. As he saw it, they came down to three: building wings, manufacturing power, and achieving control. For the most part, as Hiram Maxim's machine proved, the first two had been solved, but the third was still wanting. "When this one feature has been worked out the age of flying machines will have arrived," he said, "for all other difficulties are of minor importance."

What a subtle quagmire was that third problem. "The balancing of a gliding or flying machine is very simple in theory," he said. "It merely consists in causing the center of pressure to coincide with the center of gravity. But in actual practice there seems to be an almost boundless incompatibility of temper which prevents their remaining peaceably together for a single instance."

To make the two meet, his most successful predecessors had tried weight shifting, which was neither quick nor effective enough. Wilbur explained how he and his brother Orville used the forward horizontal rudder and wingwarping to achieve precise control over their gliders. "The control of the machine proved even better than we dared to expect," he said, but added that in their two years' worth of gliding at Kitty Hawk, the brothers had simply been unable to duplicate the results Lilienthal published in his tables of lift. The reason, this amateur explained before the roomful of professional engineers, was that the experts were wrong. Lilienthal's tables were in error. And now he and his brother would begin a series of experiments designed to get to the truth and "accurately determine the amount and direction of the pressure produced on curved surfaces when acted upon by winds."

Nevertheless, they had measured the drag on their latest machine, and it came to 40 pounds—2.5 horsepower. In level flight, drag equals power. "It must not be supposed, however, that a motor developing this power would be sufficient to drive a manbearing machine," Wilbur said. "The extra weight of the motor would require either a larger machine, higher speed, or a greater angle of incidence, in order to support it, and therefore more power. It is probable, however, that an engine of 6 horsepower weighing 200 pounds, would answer the purpose." A gasoline-powered engine that size would be within the bounds of current technology. Man might be capable of powered, controlled, sustained, and manned flight in much less than the fifty years he had just privately predicted.

Though it was ladies' night and he was no public speaker, that September evening in Chicago Wilbur Wright held the crowd in his palm. Engineers in attendance later approached Chanute about getting copies of the speech; eventually it was published in nearly every major scientific journal in the United States, from the society's own journal to *Scientific American* to even the Smithsonian's *Annual Report,* and a few other journals around the world.

Though too modest to ever admit it, Wilbur enjoyed the attention—he thought that he might make a good living lecturing on the Chautauqua—and his enthusiasm for aeronautics was fired like never before.

As he had indicated, he and Orville had decided to abandon Lilienthal's tables and work up some of their own. Orv had begun the process while Wilbur prepared the speech: Under no circumstances would he let his brother show up before a meeting of professional engineers and declare everyone wrong when their own work could be in error. He took an old starch box about eighteen inches long and cut a hole in it for a glass window, then inside he placed a surface cambered 1 in 12 like Lilienthal's, balanced it against a flat plate of equal area, and with a fan blew a stream of air into the box. Through the window he could see the angle at which both surfaces balanced; and after just one day he could tell for sure that something was off with the Lilienthal tables.

When Wilbur returned home, he fabricated another device to check Orville's results: He took another surface cambered Lilienthal-style, and a flat plate, and mounted both on a bicycle rim lying flat, which he in turn mounted on the front of one of their own gent's safety bicycles. If Lilienthal's tables of lift were true, the cambered surface at 5 degrees would balance the flat surface at 90 degrees. After tearing around the streets of Dayton with the contraption, the brothers found that, instead of 5 degrees, the curved surface balanced at a much greater angle: 18 degrees.

They backtracked through the lift formula and traced the discrepancy to what was known as the Smeaton coefficient for air pressure, a minute standard figure adopted by English engineer and steam fountain maven John Smeaton back in 1752, which the Wrights had accepted as gospel. The brothers realized the coefficient was too high and corrected it with a lower value. Now their findings began to make sense—on paper. But to double-check, they decided to test the aerodynamics of a wide range of cambered surfaces.

The bicycle-rim device would be too imprecise to measure the lift of surfaces at angles smaller than 5 degrees—angles that would be much more utilitarian for gliding experiments—so in the room above the bicycle shop, the brothers neatly built a second wind tunnel from pine lumber. It was six feet long and sixteen inches square, with a ducted fan on one end powered by a one-horse illuminating gas-powered motor that they had just built to drive some new equipment for the bicycle shop. They installed a glass window on top, through which to view one of two complex and fragile systems of balances that Orville built from a few pennies' worth of old hacksaw blades and bicycle spokes. Suggested by George Spratt at Kitty Hawk one night the previous summer, the first balance was for measuring the lift, and the second for measuring the lift-to-drag ratio, of small cambered surfaces—more than one hundred different tiny cambered sections in all, which Orville cut and hammered patiently from sheets of steel.

They played with the tunnel like kids with a new toy. They discovered that the balances were sensitive to variations in the airflow inside the building, even when one of them so much as moved—so nobody moved anything. They tested monoplane, biplane, triplane, and even the Langley tandem-wing configuration, and decided to stick with their biplane wings. They proved that a shallow parabolic curve shape provided the best lift; and that for their desires—a biplane glider able to hover above one spot in the winds of Kitty Hawk with one of them aboard—the best camber would be 1 in 20. They ran a series of tests to find the wings' most efficient aspect ratio—that is, the ratio of length to width first recognized by Francis Wenham; on a new glider the wing should be narrower: six to one, or six times as long as its width. They even discerned the precise distance by which to separate the two wings.

In early December the Wrights were finished playing with their toy.

"As soon as the results are put in tables," Katharine wrote to their father, "they will begin work for next season's bicycles." And after June, after the busy part of the bicycle season ended, they began work on the next glider. Its components took shape quickly, as always, among the spare spaces of the bicycle shop, and they were packed and shipped off to Kitty Hawk in a crate, with the brothers themselves not far behind. Arriving in late August, they repaired their old building and erected another (this time for themselves instead of the machine), and then they set about assembling the glider.

At a glance it bore a resemblance to their previous machines, having two cloth-covered, spruce-frame wings with 305 square feet of sustaining surface, and a horizontal rudder up front as always. But the new aspect ratio made the wings longer and narrower and gave them a birdlike grace. The brothers had also added a two-surfaced vertical rudder behind the wings, to counterbalance a tendency that emerged in the 1901 machine: When warped, the wing with the greatest angle would produce lift, of course, but the lift was offset by the drag it produced, and so the glider would turn in the air on that raised wing. Now the oncoming air, they hoped, would catch the new tail on the side that was turning and stop the machine from spinning.

They made changes in the controls as well. While before the brothers had worked the wingwarping mechanism with their feet, now they connected it to a hip cradle, which the operator would lie upon and shift sideways. It took only a few pounds' pressure to warp the wings.

At first they launched the glider as a kite weighted with ballast onboard.

"The machine flew beautifully," Orv wrote, "and at times, when the proper angle of incidence was attained, seemed to soar, although the angle of the hill was only a little over 6 ½ degrees."

The next day Wilbur climbed aboard, and Orville wrote, "Will made a number of glides in which he remained practically stationary in the air."

Now, for the first time, Orville started flying. After a few glides, he could travel 160 feet; during one glide he concentrated so much on keeping its wings level that he kept raising the machine's nose higher and higher—till it was 45 degrees above the horizon.

"By this time I found suddenly that I was making a descent backwards . . . ," he wrote in his diary. "The result was a heap of flying machine, cloth, and sticks in a heap, with me in the center without a bruise or a scratch." This, of course, was the same maneuver that had broken the tail on Stringfellow's 1848 model and killed Lilienthal in 1896. "In spite of this sad catastrophe we are tonight in a hilarious mood as a result of the encouraging performance of the machine both in control and in angles of flight."

As the brothers repaired the machine, they were nagged by one small problem: That vertical rudder corrected the glider's tendency to turn on the high wing all right, but now the machine would sometimes slide toward that low wing and dig its tip into the sand, spinning out. They called this maneuver "well-digging," and they couldn't stop it once it started.

Still, they were just learning to fly the machine. At the end of September their older brother Lorin arrived from Dayton, followed a day later by George Spratt, and suddenly the camp began to get crowded. Friday night they stayed up late talking, and frankly Orville drank a little too much coffee. Lying in the dark shed unable to sleep, he mulled over the well-digging phenomenon. Before drifting off, he knew he had a solution.

Orville, however, had long suspected that Wilbur thought new concepts were his domain as older brother, and when he didn't brush Orv's ideas off, he seemed to subconsciously adopt them as his own. So during breakfast the next morning Orville caught Lorin's eye to silently warn him: *Watch Wilbur's reaction.* Then Orville launched into his theory of well-digging.

When one wing dipped down suddenly, he said, the machine started to slide sideways and its speed began to build. As the glider slid, the wind struck the vertical rudder on the low side instead of the high side, causing the downward spiral. His solution was simple: Make the vertical rudder movable—under the operator's control. Then when he felt that the machine was going into a slide, he could turn the vertical surface toward the high wing and restore the machine's balance.

Wilbur sat silent as seconds ticked by. Then he broke his personal tradition and agreed with Orville's assessment of the problem, and he agreed with his solution as well.

But, Wilbur then suggested, instead of giving the operator yet a third control system to handle, and since the connection between wingwarping and the sliding seemed obvious, why not connect the rudder to the hip cradle and work the two systems in conjunction? The day turned out windless, so the brothers immediately built a new single-vaned rudder, installed it, and hooked it up to the hip cradle with control wires.

The next day being the Sabbath, the brothers did no flying, but they did greet another old friend, returning camp veteran Octave Chanute.

Immediately after the last season and before his Chicago speech, before the extensive wind-tunnel experiments, Wilbur had written in frustration to Chanute: "I cannot think of any experiment that would be of greater value . . . than an actual measurement . . . of some other machine than our 1901 model," and he asked whether any machine Herring had built for Arnot was still in flying condition. Well, now Chanute was in from Chicago as promised to test a pair of gliding machines he had financed and wanted to donate to the Wrights—and he had brought with him Augustus Moore Herring.

After Herring lost his flying machine and shop in the fire, he had sought further funding from his backer Mattias Arnot. But Arnot died from peritonitis in 1901, and that sent Herring to England for an interview with Hiram Maxim, who was then contemplating a return to aeronautics.

"Tell me confidentially what you think of his ability and experience," Maxim had asked Chanute, who replied that Herring "possessed considerable ability, [but] he cannot be easily managed."

Refused Maxim's job, Herring soon found himself back at Chanute's door asking for work, asking to be allowed to rebuild the 1896 gliding machine "to beat Mr. Wright."

Chanute hired Herring—for a third time—to refurbish the machine Herring had once claimed as his own design, and to test it along with an oscillating-wing machine that a C. H. Lamson had built for Chanute. When Chanute received his invitation that year to the Wrights' camp, he told them he wanted to donate the gliders to their cause and asked if he could bring Herring along, too. The Wrights now strenuously protested Chanute's glider gift offer when he mentioned it, insisting they would only fly their own machine. And Wilbur also said they felt reluctant to have Herring around.

"[Several] things I had heard about Mr. Herring's relations with Mr. Langley and yourself seemed to me to indicate that he might be of a somewhat jealous disposition," Wilbur wrote Chanute, "and possibly inclined to claim for himself rather more credit than those with whom he might be working would be willing to allow."

Sometimes their old mentor seemed to barely comprehend the philosophy and function of the machine's control surfaces. He remained convinced that automatic stability was the key to successful human flight and that propulsion should mimic that of birds. Still, they knew he was only trying to help, and so here he was now with his gliders and Herring, who set about assembling the rebuilt biplane machine. Flying against wind gusting between some 23 and 29 feet per second, Herring managed glides of just 15 feet from a dune with a 15-degree slope, while Wilbur in the new Wright glider flew as far as 280 feet at an angle of less than seven degrees.

Herring abandoned his old biplane for the automatically stabilizing Lamson machine and with it managed a 50-foot glide. Then as he watched the Wrights fly, he abandoned the Lamson machine, too.

Soon after—by mid-October—most of the campers had straggled away: Lorin to Dayton; Chanute to Washington, D.C., with Herring tagging along; and Spratt back to Pennsylvania. Orville and Wilbur were alone again with their glider.

But alone together they managed the best, and flew more in the final ten days than in the preceding weeks: All together they made a thousand glides, with the longest, 623 feet, lasting 26 seconds. "Day before yesterday we had a wind of . . . 30 miles per hour, and glided in it without any trouble," Orville wrote Katharine. "That was the highest wind a gliding machine was ever in, so we now hold all the records! The largest machine, the longest time in the air, the smallest angle of descent, and the highest wind!!!" In fact, they had achieved controlled, sustained, manned flight. As that wind grew colder, the brothers stuffed the Chanute machines in the loft of their living shed, closed the doors on their flying machine's shed, and boarded a boat for Elizabeth City, all the while knowing they faced that next step.

Langley's Great Aerodrome *Described*

Octave Chanute and Augustus Herring parted company in Washington, the former to drop by the Smithsonian castle for a brief visit with Secretary Langley, and the latter to seek an appointment with the same. With his diminishing stature Herring could only write a note to the secretary mentioning that he had recently come upon some fresh new ideas concerning wings and things, which he might be interested in discussing. After the disastrous showing of the rebuilt biplane, however, Chanute told Langley that Herring was a bungler, and so the secretary would have nothing more to do with Augustus Moore Herring.

Secretary Langley was very interested in the Wright brothers, though. Very interested indeed. He wrote them to ask if he could attend their trials at Kitty Hawk, and they replied that they were through for the season; he asked them to visit Washington at his expense, and they said they were too busy. He even asked Chanute to put in a good word for him, but it had no good effect.

Meanwhile, Langley's *Great Aerodrome* was slowly coming together under the supervision of the secretary's young, virilely named latest chief assistant, Charles Manly, the engineering school graduate in his early twenties given to straw boaters and walrus mustaches. What a great machine it was, too, with its two broad tandem wings measuring 48 by 11 feet and comprising 1,040 square feet of sustaining surface; it seemed to owe more to the failed and complex kite o'war of Maxim than to the relatively successful unpowered and artless gliders of his rival, that little German weight-shifter Lilienthal. The secretary had briefly considered using superposed planes for the sheer superiority in strength that trussing offered, but *his* tests showed them wholly inferior in lifting power; so he stuck with the configuration he knew best: very lightweight tandem wings held stable with Stringfellow and Henson's guy-and-post trussing, kept short and broad lest they collapse under the weight of their extremities.

The water-cooled, five-cylinder, 200-pound, 52-horsepower radial engine was so incredibly complex and impossible that subcontractor Balzer and Company went bankrupt trying to give it birth. Yet here it was, three years late, in all its gasoline-powered glory. Manly had romped to the Smithsonian's rescue and moved the unfinished pieces from Balzer's New York shop to Washington, where he completed the job at a total cost of more than $5,000. The engine drove two slim fans, each seven feet tall, made from cloth stretched between crossed wooden poles.

Having supervised its completion, who better to fly in it than Manly thought Langley? He agreed to the task. As operator, Manly would stand inside a tiny cloth-covered car slung beneath the great machine, attending the two control wheels: one to steer the aerodrome up or down, the second to steer it left or right, but neither of which the secretary expected to be important since the machine was designed for automatic stability. Once it shot from the catapult at a speed of 60 miles per hour, the *Great Aerodrome* would fly around for a bit with Manly, then settle into the water, Manly-first. While the operator/occupant fended for himself, the *Aerodrome* would float low on the surface like a leaf until Smithsonian workers reached it in small craft, for installed at strategic points on the machine were the finest floats the Smithsonian could buy. But then craftsmanship was really the paramount concern.

Including the new catapult and houseboat, the secretary had sunk $73,000 into the *Great Aerodrome,* diverting the last $23,000 to the project from various Smithsonian grant programs.

It was all in the name of science.

By November 1902, the whole machine had finally come together. And now—years behind schedule—testing could finally commence.

The Wrights Build a Whopper Flying Machine

In December, two months after returning home from Kitty Hawk, Wilbur wrote their friend George Spratt about the brothers' future.

"We are thinking of building a machine next year with 500 sq.ft. surface . . . [that] . . . will give us opportunity to work out problems connected with the management of large machines both in the air and on the ground. . . . If all goes well the next step will be to apply a motor."

Recently the brothers had neatly sketched the machine on a scrap of brown wrapping paper. Like all their machines, it evolved from the previous machine: It was a biplane with horizontal rudder fore and vertical rudder aft. It would have two wings forty feet by six, solidly held six feet apart by nine sets of spruce uprights with rounded corners (the most efficient shape for them, according to the wind tunnel). Its ribs had a one-in-twenty curvature, "probably not as easy in control as the shape used last year, but of better lifting capacity," Orville said. To make them light yet strong enough to hold the additional weight of an engine, and then flexible enough for warping, the ribs would be of two spruce strips spaced apart with small blocks, instead of a single solid strip as before. As always, it was covered with unvarnished Pride of the West muslin—127 yards' worth.

As always, the new machine would come to rest on the sand with skids, which doubled as a frontal framework upon which to hang the horizontal rudder. To take off on the skids under its own power, though, would be impossible: The sand would create too much drag for the machine to overcome. Their solution was quick and full of the Wright's cunning simplicity: With its propellers turning, the machine would run down a rail (consisting of about four dollars' worth of framing lumber) while riding atop a yoke that had altered bicycle hubs for rollers. When it reached the proper speed through the air, the machine would rise and the roller yoke would drop harmlessly aside.

Wilbur, of course, had publicly estimated that a six-horsepower, 200-pound motor could carry a manned machine into the air. Carefully now they calculated the drag that the estimated 625-pound machine would produce, allowing 200 pounds for the engine; then they wrote to between eight and twelve engine manufacturers, requesting information on vibration-free gasoline engines of eight to nine horsepower—weighing less than 180 pounds.

While waiting for a positive response, the brothers moved on to the next business: airscrews. From the start they knew they wanted two counterrotating propellers, to eliminate the powerful torque with which a single revolving propeller would sway their frail, unstable design. And also, because two propellers could push twice as much air. They also knew they would want the propellers mounted behind the machine, to avoid producing turbulent airflow over the wings. And that was all they really knew about propellers.

To design the most efficient airscrews for their particular machine, Wilbur headed to the Dayton Public Library and checked out the volumes there on marine screws. He found that all existing data was empirical, derived by trial and error since the days of Archimedes. The brothers didn't want to spend the money or the eons trying that approach, so instead they set about developing their own formula for airscrews. They argued and they calculated, and then it dawned on them that a propeller was simply a rotating wing. But they soon realized that a propeller never steps into the same airstream twice.

"[It] is hard to find even a point from which to start; for nothing about a propeller, or the medium in which it acts, stands still for a moment," Orville wrote. "The thrust depends upon the speed and the angle at which the blade strikes the air; the angle at which the blade strikes the air depends upon the speed and the angle at which the propeller is turning, the speed the machine is traveling forward, and the speed at which the air is slipping backward; the slip of the air backward depends upon the thrust exerted by the propeller, and the amount of air acted upon. When any of these changes, it changes all the rest, as they are all interdependent upon one another."

Complex as the issue was, they carved out a formula that gave them two eight-and-one-half-foot propellers, each 66 percent efficient and producing 45 pounds of thrust. Each was literally carved from three pieces of spruce laminated together, roughed out by hatchet, smoothed by a drawknife, covered with canvas, painted aluminum, and driven with a system of sprockets and chains. The brothers, after all, had a lot of experience with sprockets and chains.

The operator would lie on the machine's bottom wing as before, but to the left of the engine, which would be mounted just to the right of center so that at rest, the wings would be fairly well balanced laterally. They would cross the longest propeller drive chain, the one behind the operator's side, into the shape of a figure eight: It would make that propeller turn in the direction opposite of its mate. Provided both were revolving, each would cancel the other's torque.

Meanwhile, the engine remained hypothetical. No manufacturer who wrote back built such a motor; without a mass market for lightweight motors, no manufacturer had had a reason to develop one.

The brothers decided to build one from scratch. They had, after all, built the little single-horse engine that ran the bicycle shop's power tools. When they asked their assistant, Charlie Taylor, if he had any experience with gasoline engines, he said he had once tried to repair an automobile's motor. At least their engine experience exceeded their airscrew experience.

They had hired Taylor a couple of years back to help out at the bicycle shop while they let aeronautics consume more of their time. He turned out to be a crack machinist and began fabricating many of their gliding machines' metal fittings. Guided by rough sketches drawn on more paper scraps by either of the brothers, Taylor hewed a four-cylinder inline engine from solid metal in six weeks. The block was aluminum, and the pistons were cast iron. Its crankshaft he lathed down to size on the bicycle shop's tools. "It weighed 19 pounds finished and she balanced up perfectly, too," Charlie said.

For simplicity's sake the motor had no carburetor. From a half-gallon container suspended on an upright, gasoline dripped through a tube that led into a shallow chamber inside the manifold. There the fuel turned to vapor, then headed straight to the cylinders for combustion. The engine had no spark plugs for that, however. The electric system started with a portable battery attached to a magneto and ended with a spark coming from contact points opening and closing inside the combustion chamber.

During its first trials in February, the engine seized and cracked its block, which forced the brothers to have another forged at a local foundry. But this time they dared to try and mix the aluminum with eight percent copper, then heat temper the alloy—the first known instance of anyone risking such a hardening technique. Rebuilt by June, the shoebox-shaped black motor ran just fine: For the first 15 seconds it turned 1,200 rpm, a figure which, Orville calculated, translated into 16 horsepower; after that it dropped to 12 horses and stayed there. That was four more than the Wrights had asked for. And weighing in at 170 pounds—14 pounds per horse—it was 30 pounds under their estimate.

Poetically simple. And though she didn't work really well, she would work well enough.

Langley Flies the Quarter-Scale
Great Aerodrome

For months now reporters had been camped out at Widewater, Virginia. It was a little south of the secretary's old test waters at Quantico, but those press boys weren't fooled a bit by the shift downstream. They waited while the big new houseboat was set in position by the Smithsonian tugboats. And then they waited some more. Months passed, and Manly wouldn't tell them a thing.

But if they wanted to see something big and wanted to wait long enough, Manly was going to give it to them. At 9:30 in the morning of August 8, 1903, he shot a small aerodrome from the new catapult, and it flew sputtering for nearly 1,000 feet before settling into the Potomac. The Smithsonian men reached the aerodrome and had it draped in a cloth and out of the water before the press could splash there in their rowboats.

All they could get out of Manly now: The test was a success.

Wrights Glide More

By late September 1903, the Wrights had completed all the components of what they called their whopper flying machine and had the whole works crated and shipped to Kitty Hawk. The machine and the brothers' camp goods barely missed destruction, passing through Elizabeth City just days before a fire destroyed the freight depot there.

Arriving by launch at Kitty Hawk, the brothers first set about erecting a new larger building to house the new larger machine; as a small joke between themselves they called it the "hand car," corrupting the French for carriage shed, *hangar.* At Chanute's urging, they were studying European languages in their spare time.

Last year's glider was still in good condition, so they carried it up Big Kill Devil Hill to practice gliding. In one flight, Wilbur managed to hover in the air 30 seconds, while covering just 50 feet across the ground. Though Orville had less gliding experience and weighed five pounds more, he could do nearly as well.

The brothers also passed the time by playing a stock market game. "Flying machine market has been unsteady the past two days," Orville wrote Charlie Taylor. "Opened yesterday at about 208 (100% means even chance of success), but by noon had dropped to 110. These fluctuations would have produced a panic, I think, in Wall Street, but in this quiet place it only puts us to thinking and figuring a little."

Secretary Langley Leaves It to Mr. Manly's Discretion

Secretary Langley called the August test of the new gasoline-powered quarter-scale Langley aerodrome an official success. It "was the first time in history, so far as I know, that a successful flight of a mechanically sustained flying machine was made in public"—however unintentional—the secretary wrote later. Analyzing records of the flight, the Smithsonian team found that the aerodrome balanced perfectly; that its wings and guidance systems and equilibrium-preserving Pénaud-style tail functioned without flaw.

There was just one problem—okay, two problems. First, a workman overfilled the gas tank, which disrupted the machine's balance enough to cause the aerodrome to fly on a somewhat erratic path. In fact, the motor actually drowned out, so the mistake cut the flight short. But the secretary was satisfied, since he figured a long flight would have supplied no more pertinent data.

Now for that second problem. While resting over a river three miles wide with thick fog squatting on it most of the time, moisture saturated everything; rust formed and ate away at the flying machine's metal fittings and corroded its precise, delicate ignition system.

Still, the model flew, proving that the configuration was in itself sound. Secretary Langley left it to Mr. Manly's discretion to commence with tests of the full-size *Great Aerodrome.*

Of course, weather has its way with all things whether small or great, and now the humidity soaked the *Great Aerodrome*'s sensitive wings, softening its ribs so badly that they had to be replaced. Meanwhile storms destroyed some of the expedition's auxiliary equipment and damaged the houseboat (but even a gentle wind would set the top-heavy, flat-bottomed launch platform rocking hard enough to force Manly to cancel test flights).

With the great machine rewinged, Smithsonian mechanics finally started the engine for the first time, and the propellers promptly cracked under the strain. The mechanics just sent back to Washington for replacements.

By September 3 the time had arrived. Tugs and launches were in assigned position, photographers both official and unofficial were poised behind their lenses to record the moment for posterity. Smithsonian mechanics hauled out the battery to bestow the spark of life on the engine, and—nothing. No spark. The battery had been ruined by the damp, along with several dozen held in reserve.

Not until more than a month later, on October 7, 1903, would all the tugs and photographers be back into position downstream. Manly climbed down inside the *Great Aerodrome,* and this time its engine roared to life without so much as a tremor. The moment of truth had arrived: The butterfly had unrolled its wings and was ready to fly.

From the houseboat a skyrocket fired to signal the photographers.

Manly placed the goggles over his eyes and checked the altitude barometer sewn into the left leg of his white pants. After taking a deep breath, he finally gave the word—

Launch!

A second skyrocket went up! Photographers crouched behind their cameras! Tugs tooted their horns!

The *Great Aerodrome* shot down the 85-foot catapult launch rail! As it reached the end, it arced ever so gracefully into the Potomac.

Reporters paddled to Manly's rescue first and found him perched on a wing, muddy water dripping from his mustache. All he would say was that the machine was improperly balanced.

The Trouble with Propeller Shafts

While high winds and storms swept the Outer Banks and kept the brothers groundbound, a description and photos of the *Great Aerodrome* along with a newspaper clipping arrived from Octave Chanute: "Prof. Langley accused of using government time and money on visionary flying machine tests; congressional investigation likely," read the headline. Still, Wilbur couldn't help but notice that the Langley machine weighed about the same as theirs, yet carried four times the power.

Competition or not, the two had begun assembling the new flying machine, and even they were impressed. "It is the prettiest we have ever made," Orville wrote the bishop. George Spratt arrived in camp to help as the machine neared completion; in early November it was ready for testing. But now the engine vibrated so badly that it bent the propeller shafts. Deciding that Kitty Hawk was getting too cold for him, Spratt left camp while he still could and took the shafts with him to ship back to Charlie Taylor in Dayton. On his way out he passed Chanute, stopping by briefly; then he, too, left, but he sent back a pair of gloves for each of the brothers.

"It will be a week before we are ready for trial," Orv wrote his sister. "Stock in Flying Machine sells one day at 175 and the next at about 17. Last night it got down to around 3. . . ."

While they waited for Charlie to repair the new propeller shafts, they tried out the new launch system, setting the 1902 glider on the roller yoke and running it along the new rail; five times out of six they succeeded in lofting the old glider. By November 20, the rebuilt shafts arrived from Dayton, and the brothers reinstalled them. Again they shook hard—hard enough to loosen the nut that attached the shaft to its drive sprocket. They applied some Arnstein's bicycle cement, "which will fix anything from a stop watch to a thrashing machine," said Orville, though it was used mainly for sealing bicycle tires to rims. "We stuck those sprockets so tight I doubt they will ever come loose again." On Wednesday, November 25, they tested the engine and it ran perfectly.

But rain began to fall at noon and kept up the rest of the day. A cold, hard wind blew in from the north for two days straight. On November 28 the brothers pulled the machine from the hangar and started the engine—and cracked a propeller shaft. Tired of fooling around, Orville packed the shafts up and headed back to Dayton, leaving Wilbur alone at camp.

With the year coming to a close, with winter setting in, with time running out, Wilbur scrapped the idea of carefully testing the new machine as a glider. From the first, they would risk flying it under its own power.

Manly Takes Another Dive

While Charles Manly said the *Great Aerodrome* failed because of balance, a sharp-eyed observer from the Board of Ordnance thought he saw the machine's front guy-post snag on the launch mechanism. Either way, the machine needed rewinging yet again, and while the Smithsonian men were doing so in Washington, an October storm at Widewater swept away most of the project's fleet of small craft. The houseboat survived, though, and got towed back to Washington as November came to an end.

The project's funds had finally run out. Secretary Langley needed some positive results, and fast.

The earliest opportunity, December 8, turned out bitter cold, but Manly thought the wind calm enough to try another launch. He quickly had the houseboat towed a few miles down the now-icy Potomac and anchored at Arsenal Point. The wind began to pick up, gusting to 18 miles per hour, but Manly decided to make the attempt anyway and stripped down to his long underwear. Whether the *Great Aerodrome* succeeded or failed, in the end he would still be swimming.

As gray sky began to darken, he took his position in the machine and started the engine. It sputtered to life; with the propellers spinning, Manly hurriedly gave the signal.

Woosh! it shot down the rail—then it rose straight up in the air. With its rear wings twisting and folding in agony, the *Great Aerodrome* slid tailfirst into the Potomac.

Rescuers hurried to reach Manly, who was trapped beneath the machine. They managed to pull him from the icy river, shivering and swearing violently. Smithsonian boat crews attached a line to the *Great Aerodrome,* and in minutes they had pulled the machine apart.

Still, the secretary tried to cast a positive image on the whole incident.

"While the injury which had thus been caused seemed almost irreparable to one not acquainted with the work," Langley acclaimed, "yet it was found upon close examination that only a small amount of labor would be necessary in order to repair the frame, the engine itself being entirely uninjured."

But only an act of Congress could redeem the secretary's reputation now.

Mr. Daniels Takes an Amazing
First Photograph

Three days later Orville arrived back at Kitty Hawk carrying two new solid-tool-steel propeller shafts and a newspaper clipping describing the Langley aerodrome's latest plunge, and reporting the total cost of the project at $73,000. Including the latest trip home for shafts, Orville figured he and Wilbur had spent almost $1,000 so far on their machine.

By the next day, Saturday, December 12, the brothers had the new shafts installed and spinning beautifully. The wind, though, was too light to start the machine from the level sandy plain of their camp, and it was too late in the day to drag it halfway up Big Kill Devil Hill for a run down the incline, so they decided to test how well it would run along the launch rail. On the last run the machine snagged its tail on the rail, snapping a support. They put the damaged machine away in its hangar over the Sabbath, though when Mr. Etheridge of the lifesaving station stopped by to visit with his wife and children, the brothers laid aside their reading to show the machine and explain how it worked.

The damage being minimal, they had the support spliced by early afternoon on Monday, December 14. It was clear, cold, and calm—almost too calm. Still, the winter wouldn't wait much longer: They agreed to make an attempt starting down the side of Big Kill Devil Hill. One of them hung a sheet onto the ocean side of their shed; everyone within five miles knew what it meant and had an open invitation from the brothers to come witness the event.

Someone at the lifesaving station a mile away spotted the sheet and told the other men there. They gathered together and put on their coats and set out trudging across the cold sand to help, with a couple of small boys and at least one dog tagging along.

After they arrived, the stationmen and the brothers set the machine on its launch rail, then shoved and pulled the contraption backward toward the big hill. Like ancients moving a strange stone burden to the summit of some grand temple, they slid the machine to the end of its launch rail and then relayed the rail's separate pieces over and over again behind the machine. They kept this up for forty minutes, until they had pushed it a quarter-mile up the hill. Then fastening the machine to the rail with a rope, the brothers grabbed the propellers and pulled down. The whole thing shook as its engine caught and roared, and the propellers blew angry tornadoes of sand.

Two little boys scrambled for home.

While they let the engine warm, one of the Wrights dug into his pocket for a coin and flipped it while the other called. Wilbur got to take the first whack. He lay down on the machine's lower wing and took the forward rudder's control bar in his left hand and pushed it back and forth; then he shifted in the hip cradle. All the control surfaces functioned normally. Everything was ready.

Wilbur tried to slip off the restraining rope, but the machine's thrust held it so taut, he didn't have the strength to budge it. While Orville and another man shoved the machine back and held it for a moment, Wilbur slipped the rope away.

Then Orville signaled for the other man to let go of the left wing. But before he himself was ready, the flying machine sped off down the track. Orville tried to run and keep up with it and balance it on the right—it was a little heavy on that side—but after only a few feet it left him behind in a sandstorm.

Wilbur pulled back on the rudder bar, and 35 feet down the rail the machine leaped into the air. When it passed above the rail's end already at least six feet in the air, Orville clicked his stopwatch. The machine kept nosing too high upward, then settled down into the sand tailfirst. Its left wing struck, and the machine spun around spraying sand. Orville clicked the stopwatch again. In just 3.5 seconds Wilbur had flown more than one hundred feet—and had broken a skid, a strut, a brace, and a front rudder spar. He had pulled up too steeply too soon, before the machine had built up enough speed to stay in the air.

Laying rail before rail once again, they slid the injured machine back down to camp and put it back into its hangar. The brothers spent the next day splicing struts and spars and skids, though Wilbur took the time out to walk to the Kitty Hawk weather station send a telegram to his father.

Misjudgment at start reduced flight one hundred twelve power and control ample rudder only injured success assured keep quiet

Bishop Wright had spent that previous day typing copies of a brief description of the machine and a biographical sketch of his boys to hand out to the press.

Repairs were completed by noon on December 16, and once again they got the machine out and set it up on the rail, this time on the level plain near camp. But the wind died away, and after waiting several hours, they slid the machine back into its shed.

Early that morning, December 17, 1903, a cold, strong wind blew in from the north. They rose early and as always put on their business suits complete with collars and ties and caps, and they checked the wind speed: gusting 20 to 27 miles per hour. They hoped that it would die down, but it wouldn't; they waited and talked about how risky it was to try flying an unfamiliar machine in such strong winds, and they thought about missing Christmas at home, and then they discussed how the risk of flying in strong winds would probably be offset by being able to crash at a slower speed over the ground.

At ten that morning they put out the sheet for the men at the lifesaving station.

While they set up the rail just west of their camp sheds in the biting cold, John Daniels, Will Dough, and Adam Etheridge arrived from the station, accompanied by lumberman W. C. Brinkley of nearby Manteo, and Johnny Moore, a teenager from Nags Head who scavenged a living with his fortune-telling mother on the Outer Banks.

With the men's help, the brothers placed the machine in position on the rail; then Orville set up his Korona camera on its tripod, focusing its lens on the end of the rail. He asked Mr. Daniels if he had ever taken a photograph. Mr. Daniels said he had not.

It was easy, Orville explained: Mr. Daniels should hold the rubber bulb and squeeze it once he saw the machine reach the end of the rail. The camera would do the rest.

The brothers primed the engine and pulled the propellers through, and their machine shuddered and rumbled to life. They shook hands.

Now it was Orville's whack. He lay down on the flying machine's lower wing and tried the controls. At 10:35 A.M. he released the restraining rope, and the machine started rolling slowly down the rail into the fierce headwind. Running alongside Wilbur kept up easily, holding the machine steady while it lifted slowly away from him into the gray sky. He stopped transfixed in time at the end of the rail, watching it sputter past, its heavy wings sagging in the air as it flew away from him.

At that moment, Mr. Daniels squeezed the camera's bulb.

The same moment, Orville was having a rough time keeping things balanced onboard the machine. That the forward rudder itself was out of balance didn't help things any, and the machine rose, then darted down, then rose, then darted, until it splashed into the sand 120 feet from where it had left the ground, cracking a skid.

"This flight lasted only 12 seconds," Orville was to write, "but it was nevertheless the first in the history of the world in which a machine carrying a man had raised itself by its own power into the air in full flight, had sailed forward without reduction of speed, and had finally landed at a point as high as that from which it started."

Everyone gathered around and carried the machine back to the rail, where the brothers spliced the cracked skid. Then they all went inside to warm up for a few minutes with a little small talk about the weather and the prodigious laying abilities of the camp chicken.

Now it was Wilbur's turn. They started the machine again, and he lay on the lower wing and released the restraint. The machine ran down the rail, lifted, and weaved 175 feet through the air before skidding to a halt in the sand. Again they hauled the machine back to the starting rail; Orville now took off trying to hold it steady while it oscillated, then a gust from the left tossed the machine on its right. He tried to compensate for it with the wingwarping cradle and did only too well—the left wing touched down and the machine came to a rest, 15 seconds and 200 feet after it started.

On Wilbur's second turn the machine lifted off and wobbled, but he got it steady and held it that way while the machine kept going, going, going, just flying off toward the beach, then once again the oscillation began, and the machine pitched down and slammed into the ground, smashing the front rudder. It had flown straight ahead for 59 seconds—nearly a minute—and 852 feet, almost a sixth of a mile. They removed the damaged rudder, figuring it could be fixed in a day or so, then everyone pitched in and carried the machine back to camp. As they stood there in the cold wind, a sudden gust lifted the flying machine, and everyone rushed to hold it down. But the machine picked up and turned over and Daniels was caught inside a mesh of wires and chains. They extracted him, badly bruised but not injured seriously.

He would later boast of taking the fifth flight that day.

They turned to the machine: Several ribs were smashed, a wing spar had snapped, the engine mounts were broken, the chain guides twisted.

It would never fly again. But that didn't matter.

After lunch the Wright brothers walked to the telegraph office at Kitty Hawk's weather station, and Orville handed the operator a message, which he tapped out right away.

success four flights thursday morning all against twenty-one mile wind started from Level with engine power alone average speed through air thirty-one miles longest 57 seconds inform Press home Christmas.

Two Stories Reach Circulation

The telegraph operator got the speed wrong, of course.

He relayed the message through Norfolk, Virginia, where it seemed to splinter in two. The first version headed on otherwise un-altered to Dayton; the second version found itself in the hands of a friend of the Norfolk operator, where it began picking up baggage. This friend worked for the Norfolk *Virginian-Pilot,* and with a few details of his own he fleshed out the message into a page-one story. This version grabbed more luggage on the Associated Press news-wire, and eventually it said that the flight in the two-propeller ma-chine—one propeller behind, and one underneath—lasted three miles, at an altitude of 60 feet over the Atlantic in the teeth of a gale, and upon landing, the swarthy "Wilber" Wright cried, "Eureka!"

As for the other, more accurate message, Lorin Wright carried it and the bishop's announcement over to the Dayton *Journal,* as planned.

"If it had been 57 minutes instead of 57 seconds, we might print it," the editor told him. "But we're glad to hear the Wrights will be home for Christmas."

Meanwhile, reporters familiar with the less prosaic account bom-barded the house at 7 Hawthorne Street, and the bishop did his best to correct the Norfolk version with what he knew about the capa-bilities of what he called the "Wright Flyer," and he promised to pass on requests for interviews to his sons, whom he expected to arrive back under the parental roof any day now.

"I suppose their sister Katharine or maybe the bishop came over and told me about it," Charlie Taylor remembered years later. "I know I thought it was pretty nice that they had done what they set out to do, and I was glad to hear that the motor ran all right. But I don't remember doing any jig steps. The boys were always so matter of fact about things; and they never made any effort to get me excited."

The brothers arrived home December 23, refusing to give out interviews, or descriptions of the machine, or any details of their methods.

They did, however, have a nice Christmas dinner with the family.

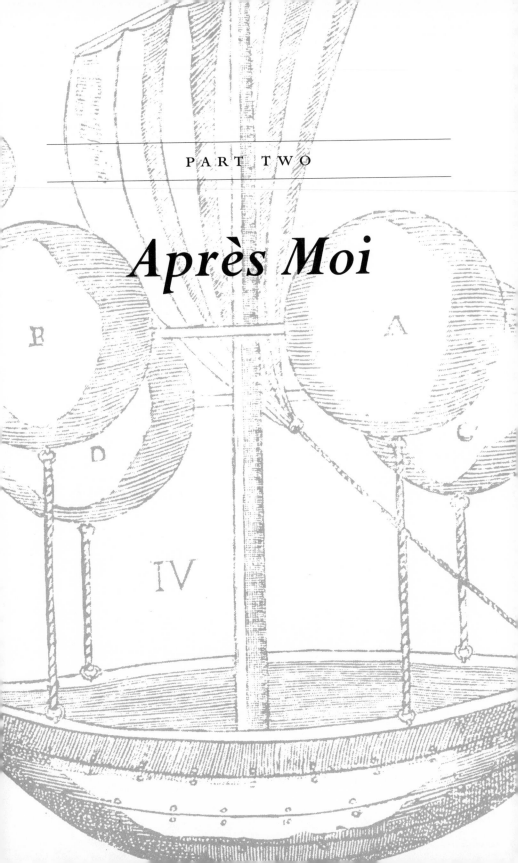

PART TWO

Après Moi

CHAPTER EIGHT

1904 to 1908

France Struggles with the Truth

On a cold day the preceding April, Octave Chanute had traveled to Paris to speak before members of the Aéro-Club de France. An account of the speech by Parisian attorney and Aéro-Club leader Ernest Archdeacon, printed in *La Locomotion* and in *L'Aéronaute,* introduced Chanute as "a veritable celebrity among 'aviators' " who had been "working with indefatigable earnestness on the most difficult problem of aerial navigation."

"Admitting that he was no longer very young," Archdeacon continued, Chanute "took pains to train young, intelligent, and daring pupils, capable of carrying on his researches. . . . Principal among them, certainly, is Mr. Wilbur Wright."

What Chanute told them in his native French shocked their very blood.

"Americans," he said, "have rather favored aviation. As elsewhere, many visionary projects have been advanced, but nevertheless the beginning of a practical solution seems to dawn on the horizon."

He briefly outlined the experiments of Secretary Langley and better described his own Indiana group, naturally, but concentrated on the methods and accomplishments of *les frères Wright:* The "time is evidently approaching when, the problems of equilibrium and control having been solved, it will be safe to apply a motor and a propeller," he assured the audience. "In point of fact, the Messrs. Wright are now gliding very nearly as well as the vulture."

The French weren't upset that Chanute seemed to be getting a little more than his due credit for the Wrights' work. This was a matter greater than personal honor.

"Will the homeland of the Montgolfiers suffer the shame of allowing this ultimate discovery of aerial science . . . to be realized abroad?" Archdeacon shouted from the journals. "Gentleman scholars, to your compasses! You . . . gentlemen of the government, your hands in your pocket . . . or else we are beaten!"

Archdeacon himself vowed 3,000 francs to the first to fly a powered machine more than 25 meters, and the Aéro-Club followed with a 1,500-franc prize for the first to cover more than 100 meters. But before the government could put its hand in its purse, a story originating more or less in Norfolk, Virginia had sailed across the Atlantic. Its message, if the outlandishness were true: the Wrights had left a coat of dust settling on the home of the Montgolfiers. To Archdeacon's shame, Frenchmen resorted to copying the Wrights' last and best glider from the information and drawings Chanute provided in his lecture.

Archdeacon himself had a glider built, and he paid a young engineer named Gabriel Voisin to fly it following the course that Chanute outlined: Master control over sand before trying to apply power. In this crude copy one year after Chanute's lecture, Voisin and one Ferdinand Ferber began trotting off the dunes of Berck-sur-Mer—with poorer results than Chanute said to expect. Another took the leap in his own *type de Wright* glider. But, declaring wing-warping structurally unsound and unaerodynamic, Robert Esnault-Pelterie modified his machine so that it had two moveable horizontal surfaces placed forward of the wings, controllable with a steering wheel. Initially, this machine, too, was a disappointment.

Archdeacon proclaimed loudly that since the French were ahead in other matters of aeronautical importance, especially lightweight engines, the Wrights must be lying about their achievements. *Bluffeurs!*

He wrote them to issue a direct challenge: Be seen flying in America, or come give us lessons in France!

Congress Answers Langley

Congress convened in January 1904 and focused its attention on the government's once and future support of Langley's *Aerodrome*.

Though the machine was in pieces, the project still had solid potential, or so maintained Representative James Hemenway, chairman of the House appropriations committee. If a fleet of aerodromes could "sail over the enemy's camp," Hemenway said, ". . . and ascertain all about him, and still be out of danger themselves, that would be an instrument of war more formidable than any that the world has ever yet seen."

But the impetus Congress had to initially approve Langley's funding, the Spanish-American War, was over long ago. While war threatened Europe—as it seemed to do constantly since the German victory in the Franco-Prussian War—there were no immediate challenges to America that would merit the long-term investment needed to develop such extraordinary weapons. Representative Gilbert Hitchcock of Nebraska spoke for just about everyone when he said, "[If] it is to cost us $73,000 to construct a mud duck that will not fly 50 feet, how much is it going to cost to construct a real flying machine?"*

That was also the sentiment of the Army Board of Ordnance and Fortification, which had inspected the dripping remains of Langley's

---

*During the same session, the House also voted to halt the War Department's practice of buying "French novels," which had been going on for years.

Great Aerodrome and concluded that a practical flying machine was years and thousands of dollars away. Though it would allow him to retain the machine and all its associated equipment, and challenged him to keep trying (tee-hee), the board declared it was through funding the secretary's experiment.

Wrights Add to Bee Culture

Just after the new year, Charlie Taylor was waiting around for the brothers to return to the bicycle shop, half expecting a small celebration. When they came in, the only thing they said was that the *Flyer's* engine had been damaged and they would now want three new ones built. Charlie got to work right away.

Orville redesigned some engine parts and prepared a statement for the Associated Press to correct the erroneous accounts of the Wrights' flights. They just wanted to get the facts straight; for now they were not going to make their secrets public. "We paid the freight, and had a right to do as we pleased," said Wilbur.

The brothers also answered a flood of congratulatory mail from the world's aeronautical aficionados—all except one letter, from Augustus Moore Herring. Herring wrote to say that he had separately solved the problem of powered flight, that he had in fact designed and developed the Chanute biplane glider. Now he had a little proposition for the two brothers: They would form a business partnership with him, each having a third interest. He added that someone interested in bringing an interference suit against the brothers had offered a pretty nice sum for the patent rights he possessed— and which the Wrights had violated with their machine.

"This time he surprised us," Wilbur wrote Chanute. "Before he left camp in 1902 we foresaw and predicted the object of his visit to Washington, we also felt certain that he was making a frenzied attempt to mount a motor on a copy of our 1902 glider and thus anticipate us, even before you told us of it last fall. But that he would have the effrontery to write us such a letter, after his other schemes of rascality had failed, was really a little more than we expected."

"While I could wish that you had applied for patents when first I urged you to do so," Chanute replied, "I think that your interests are quite safe."

The year before, as they were building the powered machine, the Wrights themselves had filed for patents covering the control surfaces used on the 1902 glider and especially the wingwarping mechanism. For now they would ignore Herring, sure of the quality of their work versus his, but they also retained a patent attorney to handle their affairs from now on.

Then the brothers turned to building the replacement flyer. It was much the same as the first one, which they had barely had a chance to fly and so could offer few hints for improvements; the new wings, though, had a 1-in-25 camber and were made with pine spars instead of spruce, still unavailable in Dayton; the new machine weighed a few pounds more, but by regearing the engine, they thought they could get it flying at up to 40 miles per hour, compared with 30 to 35 mph for the first machine. They would need the extra speed: Instead of the high, steady winds of Kitty Hawk, they would now try flying from a cow pasture outside of fairly windless Dayton. They knew that the first practical flying machine was anything but practical: Of what practical use was a flyer that almost had to be crated up and hauled halfway across the continent in order to live up to its name? Kitty Hawk was nice and secluded, but it was not a practical place to develop a practical flying machine that could be flown practically anywhere. Nor was it entirely practical to ignore the bicycle business for ever-lengthening periods. And the brothers were practical men.

Owned by Dayton banker Torrence Huffman, the hundred-acre field known as Huffman Prairie lay alongside the Springfield electric road—the interurban trolley—near a stop called Simms Station.

It was an old swamp filled with half-foot-high grassy hummocks ("it resembles a prairie-dog town," Wilbur said), but it was away from town, easy to reach, and Huffman would let the brothers use it for free just so long as they didn't hurt any of his cows. They built a hangar for the machine there and laid out a launch rail four times longer than the one at Kitty Hawk to give the machine extra time to build speed for takeoff.

Wilbur contacted the local papers and told the editors what he and Orville had planned for Huffman Prairie beginning May 23; on that first day they would gladly meet representatives of the press. He said they didn't want anyone to think they were being secretive, but they wanted to get the attention over with and get on with their work. They would allow no cameras, though—and forbade sensationalism of any sort.

Aside from two dozen family members and friends, about a dozen reporters showed up, along with rain and high winds, then utter calm. Not wanting to disappoint the crowd, the brothers tried to launch, but the machine plowed down the rail and plopped off the end without rising an inch. Without showing emotion, the brothers announced that they would try again the following day. Three reporters came back and got to see the machine fly a distance of between 25 and 60 feet—accounts vary—at an altitude of between six and twelve feet. Then, "It dropped," according to *The New York Times*. "This was due, the inventors said, to a derangement in the gasoline engine that furnished the power. In the fall, the propellers were broken, and the test could not be repeated." It was exactly what the reporters would have expected from a couple of crank bicycle mechanics who said that they could fly. After that, the newspapers left them alone.

Even without the jinxing eye of the public, the brothers continued having trouble with the new flyer. The brittle pine wing spars kept shattering from the force of landing, and finally they had to be replaced with the more flexible spruce. The machine was so unstable that if the pilot's attention slipped for an instant, the machine might climb into the air at such a high angle that it would no longer gain lift and drop tail-first to the ground—the same maneuver that had finished off the *Great Aerodrome,* killed Lilienthal, crippled Oliver the Flying Monk, broke Stringfellow's 1848 model, and had happened to Orville gliding and Wilbur when he attempted that first powered flight at Kitty Hawk. Wilbur gave it a name that to this day confuses nonfliers who have had their engine die on them while puttering about in an automobile: He called it "stalling."

But they couldn't even stall and crash if they couldn't launch first. In the first three months conditions were so calm that the brothers reached flying speed only forty times, and then they had used up so much of the pasture to take off that they had to set the new flyer down after only a few hundred feet before they plowed into the trees and telegraph wires along the edge of the field. "It is a pity we cannot trade a few of our calms to Prof. Langley for some of his windy days that used to trouble him so," wrote Wilbur.

By September, they had devised a solution that required no extensive modifications to the machine. It was a catapult that harnessed the force of a 1,600-pound weight plunging from a derrick. Now they were able to launch in the calmest wind after a run of only 50 feet. And now they were ready to attempt a complete circle in their machine.

On the first try they turned too wide and almost went outside the pasture—and that wouldn't do—so they shut off the engine, landed, and carted the machine back over bumpy ground to the rail for another launch. After more runs they started to get a feel for it: how much they needed to slide the hip cradle and lower the wing in the direction they wanted to turn; then while the machine was turning, how much they needed to slide the hip cradle the opposite direction to hold the angle they wanted and to turn the rudder at an angle that wouldn't drive the machine's nose into the ground. At times they would lose control of the machine and spin into the ground, but near the end of the month Wilbur managed to circle the field, and fly a record distance of 4,080 feet in the process. Though it was not exactly like he was born doing it: sometimes the brothers couldn't get the machine to stop turning.

On the very day the machine flew its first circle, a journalist arrived to investigate the Wrights' story. Following rumors, Amos Root had driven one of those newfangled automobiles nearly two hundred miles across poor roads to witness the brothers' experiments firsthand.

Now that he saw it with his own eyes, Root thought the flyer seemed magical—like something from *A Thousand and One Nights*. "The machine," he reported, "is held until ready to start by a sort of trap to be sprung when all is ready; then with a tremendous flapping and snapping of the four-cylinder engine, the huge machine springs aloft. When it first turned that circle, and came near the starting-point, I was right in front of it; and I said then, and I believe still, it is one of the grandest sights, if not the grandest sight of my life. Imagine a locomotive that has left its track, and is climbing up in the air right toward you—a locomotive without any wheels, we will say, but with white wings instead . . . with the tremendous flap of its propellers, and you will have something like what I saw. The younger brother bade me move to one side for fear that it might come down suddenly; but I tell you friends, the sensation that one feels in such a crisis is something hard to describe."

Root wrote the first eyewitness account of powered, controlled flight for *Gleanings in Bee Culture,* a journal catering to the apiculturist trade. He was no crank who thought studying bees might unlock the secret of powered flight; but still, he didn't need an excuse for what he wrote in *Gleanings.* Aside from being the sole reporter and the editor-in-chief, he was also the publisher.

"Up to the present we have been very fortunate in our relations with newspaper reporters, but intelligence of what we are doing is gradually spreading through the neighborhood," Wilbur wrote afterward to Chanute.

They made sixty more flights in the remaining months of 1904—one in which they circled the field four times and stayed aloft five minutes—yet the Wrights still managed to log just 45 minutes in the air the entire year. Even though they tried to adjust its fore-and-aft balance with steel bars for ballast, the new flyer still had a "tendency to undulation" like the 1903 machine. Winter had set in, so they dismantled the second flyer and crammed its pieces away into the crannies of the bicycle shop to be used for spare parts on the next machine.

"As we have decided to keep our experiments strictly secret for the present, we are becoming uneasy about continuing them much longer at our present location. In fact," Wilbur added to Chanute, "it is a question whether we are not ready to begin considering what we will do with our baby now that we have it."

You Can't Fool the Board of Ordnance and Fortification Twice

Yes, achieving powered, controlled flight about forty-eight years ahead of Wilbur's exasperated 1901 prediction had forced the brothers to recast their purpose. Of what use was this newborn baby?

Of what use? Well, for sport, surely; rich men were always interested in purchasing new devices that threatened their necks. But what of the Wrights' liability for the machine, for the safe performance of an inherently dangerous product? They could spend the rest of their days and modest fortune being sued in court by rich and powerful men.

What of the machine's practical business applications? A flyer might quickly deliver loads of cargo, though in the foreseeable future it couldn't carry much save for light loads of mail, and then the machine would preferably need predesignated safe areas to alight. Governments, however, might still be interested in using flyers to observe enemy emplacements in times of war. That was why Langley received *his* funding, after all. Selling the flying machine as a weapon, then, would be the most sensible goal of the bishop's sons.

Over the Christmas holiday they invited their local congressman for dinner, and at his suggestion they wrote a letter to him giving a vague description of their machine's performance ("It not only flies through the air at high speed," they wrote, "but it also lands without being wrecked"), and capabilities ("The numerous flights . . . have made it certain that flying has been brought to a point where it can be made of great practical use in . . . scouting and carrying messages in time of war"), and adding that they were ready to build and deliver such machines to the U.S. government—for a price, of course. They would also consider supplying the American government with "all the scientific and practical information we have accumulated in these years of experimenting, together with a license to use our patents; thus putting the government in a position to operate on its own account."

The congressman promised he would personally deliver the letter to Secretary of War William Howard Taft and then arrange for the brothers to meet Taft themselves, but he forwarded it by mail instead. Taft bounced the letter routinely to the Board of Ordnance and Fortification.

Having been inundated with such requests from every hayseed and charlatan who knew it was willing to give away fortunes to fund harebrained flying schemes, the board replied to the congressman with a somewhat personalized form rejection letter, saying, in short, "[the] Board has found it necessary to decline to make allotments for experimental development of devices for mechanical flight. . . . It appears from the letter of Messrs. Wilbur and Orville Wright that their machine has not yet been brought to the stage of practical operation, but as soon as it shall have been perfected, this Board would be pleased to receive further representations from them in regard to it."

These public servants of ours were by no means fools. After the greatest American scientist had failed, why would they believe that a flying machine could be patched together by a couple of backwater mechanics from a tiny city in Ohio?

At least the brothers had tried.

"We would be ashamed of ourselves if we had offered our machine to a foreign government without giving our own government a chance at it," Wilbur said, "but our consciences are clear." Which was good, because even before they had their reply back from the U.S. War Department, they had written to Great Britain's War Office with a similar offer. In less than a month the British asked the brothers' terms and said they would soon meet an official representative sent to observe their machine in action.

The Wrights still had to improve their basic design. In May 1905 they started building the third powered machine, and had it completed by late June. Like its predecessors, it had 40-foot wings. In fact, other than a larger forward horizontal rudder modified with semicircular vanes to improve the design's turning instability, an independently controlled rear vertical rudder that added a second-hand lever to master, a more powerful engine of 20 horsepower, a larger fuel tank to hold the extra fuel it would burn staying aloft for several minutes at a time, and several minor improvements in construction, it was just like the previous powered machines.

It flew no better than the previous machines, either. Days full of ten-second-long hops would end in spar-busting, rib-cracking crashes, and the third flyer would be put out of commission while they and Charlie Taylor sawed new spars and spliced ribs.

One Friday in mid-July the machine shot down the rail with Orville flying, and after a few seconds it began undulating out of control. Suddenly its nose stabbed into the ground, crushing it and throwing Orville through the top wing. He emerged bruised and shaken. Clearly, something had to be done before one of them got himself crippled permanently—or killed. As Wilbur dryly observed while correcting proofs of an article Chanute wrote describing their work, "I doubt whether the expression *'in perfect safety'* . . . is quite justifiable."

To help the machine's longitudinal stability they rebuilt the front rudder and increased its area from 50 to 84 square feet and stuck it way out in front almost twice its previous distance—a whole 12 feet. After further short flights, they also enlarged the rear rudder from 20 square feet to 34 and moved it three feet farther behind. Lengthening the machine made it more stable indeed, and after a few minor adjustments they were flying a circle once again, then two circles, then four—then so many that they lost count—around 16 circuits, or 11 miles, in 18 minutes. They even flew the first figure eight. But a problem from last year resurfaced: Sometimes while turning a short circle, the flyer would stall for no reason, then fall to the ground. They started thinking it must be caused by some invisible major flaw in their design—they might have to scrap the whole configuration and start from scratch.

One day Orville was circling a thorn tree in the center of the field when the flyer began to nose up out of control and head right into the tree. Orville instinctively shoved the machine's nose down to miss the tree and found that he had regained control. They realized then that the machine was stalling as it turned.

"The trouble was really due to the fact that in circles," Wilbur said, "the machine had to carry the load resulting from the centrifugal force, in addition to its own weight . . . a limit was reached beyond which the machine was no longer able to maintain sufficient speed to sustain itself in the air." The solution lay in more skilled piloting instead of major changes in the machine.

What a machine it was now that they had that skill! They chased birds with it—and killed one with a propeller! Their endurance record jumped daily—from five minutes to 18 minutes to 21! They could even fly it till it ran out of gas! They fit it with a larger three-gallon fuel tank, and 25-minute flights became common, then 30, then 34, then Wilbur stayed in the air 39 minutes! They were flying so many circles around Huffman Prairie, they were covering some 25 miles! They could climb up to 40, 60 feet high!

Word started getting around that a couple of locals had built a machine like those dirigible balloons that a little Brazilian named Alberto Santos-Dumont flew in Paris, only different, and lots of folks started coming out to watch at Huffman Prairie. If the brothers were flying, conductors on the electric road would stop the trolley and show passengers the miracle unfolding above a cow pasture. These same folks were soon streaming into the offices of Dayton's newspapers, jabbering on about the huge white mechanical bird circling trees in a pasture. Even the most hard-boiled, cynical editors took pause.

One day in late September, Wilbur looked up from tinkering on the machine and saw three reporters. Since the best place to find a fresh new story idea is in the competitor's pages, other reporters soon followed, and the sight of them became fairly commonplace. Then a young man showed up, said he wasn't exactly a reporter though he did some writing for various publications, and asked to see the machine up close. No photographs, the Wrights said, but they told the man to make himself at home. After he left, Charlie Taylor spoke to the brothers.

"That fellow's no writer," he said. "At least no ordinary writer. When he looked at the different parts of the machine he called them all by their right names." Later they recognized the same young man in a newspaper photograph: He was Charles Manly, Secretary Langley's chief engineer.

The brothers would have to stop flying the machine before a cunning description and a fortuitous photograph revealed the secret that was still theirs alone. Yet day after day went by, and still no appearance by the British military. They decided to give the U.S. government one more shot at the weapon of the century.

"We are prepared," Wilbur wrote Secretary of War Taft, "to furnish a machine on contract, to be accepted only after trial trips in which the conditions of the contract have been fulfilled; the machine to carry an operator and supplies of fuel, etc., sufficient for a flight of one hundred miles; the price of the machine to be regulated on a sliding scale based on the performance of the machine in the trial trips; the minimum performance to be a flight of at least twenty-five miles at a speed of not less than thirty miles an hour." He added, "We are also willing to take contracts to build machines carrying more than one man."

Of course, he also wrote Great Britain's War Office on the same day, upping their previous offer: They would now provide a machine that could fly 50 miles instead of just 10.

The response from the U.S. government came again from the Board of Ordnance and Fortification: "It is recommended the Messrs. Wright be informed that the Board does not care to formulate any requirements for the performance of a flying-machine or take any further action on the subject until a machine is produced which by actual operation is shown to be able to produce horizontal flight and carry an operator."

You have to hand it to the board: It was alert this time. No one—repeat, no one—was ever again going to use it and a flying machine to make the United States Army look like wasteful morons. The Wrights also found out from the British military attaché in Washington that nothing would start to happen until he showed up in Dayton to see the machine fly, so they wrote him that they weren't going to show their machine to any government unless there was a prior agreement on the terms of sale.

The Brothers Wright still had one business card up their pressed sleeves. They had been contacted by Captain Ferdinand Ferber, who was now attached to the aeronautical division of the French army, and who had written to them twice before describing his own glider experiments in France. Eager for them to talk to his government, Ferber had helped arrange a visit from a representative of a syndicate charged with purchasing a flying machine for France. In late December 1905 the Wrights agreed to supply that syndicate with a flyer for one million francs. That was $200,000 in U.S. currency—two thousand times what they'd gotten for a typical Wright bicycle.*

They could finally pack away the third machine. The next time they would fly, they would do so in France.

Gabriel Voisin and Kites, or Alberto Santos-Dumont and Ducks

Gabriel Voisin believed that the Wright glider replica he had flown—badly—from the dunes of Berck owed its origin to the work of Lawrence Hargrave, the Australian who had managed to lift himself in the air briefly with a train of his highly stable box kites in 1893 (and yet who clung tenaciously to the concepts of steam power and motive flapping). If the Wrights would reveal none of their secrets, then Voisin would follow the trail leading straight from Hargrave.

He built a large box kite with rudders front and rear, all mounted on floats, which on a July day in 1905 he shoved into the River Seine and tied behind a racing boat. "The big Panhard engine . . . was idling," Voisin wrote. "Gradually and cautiously [the helmsman] took up the slack of my towing cable. . . . I had the controls ready. I

---

*In 1904, the average worker earned around $10 per week (the average man, $11; the average woman, $6). Bishop Wright had never earned more than $900 a year.

waited for a time and then I applied the elevator." His glider leaped from the water and climbed smoothly to the tops of the poplars that lined the quay, then settled back into the Seine.

The crowd that gathered to watch held two important men, both active Aéro-Club members: Louis Blériot, who made his fortune manufacturing automobile headlights and who immediately hired Voisin to built a glider for him; and Alberto Santos-Dumont, the thirtyish diminutive Brazilian, invariably described as dapper for his style-setting floppy Panama hat and high collars, whose father had done very well with the family coffee plantation back home. Santos-Dumont himself was renowned in America for his sequentially numbered series of dirigible balloons that had little to control them but had the latest, lightest gasoline engines. He was revered by the French for his sputtering circumnavigation of the Eiffel Tower with *Dirigible No. 6* in 1901, and he was beloved by the sentimental for dividing the 100,000-franc Aéro-Club prize that he won for the feat between the poor of Paris and his mechanics.

Inspired by Voisin, Santos-Dumont had those same mechanics build a box-kite machine of cotton-covered bamboo and pine, to test and perhaps launch slung beneath his *Dirigible No. 14;* and so he painted on its side *14 bis.* Driven by an incredibly light 78-pound, 24-horsepower Antoinette motorboat engine turning a four-blade aluminum pusher propeller, its 33-foot box-kite wings arched upward in dihedral. Its box-kite horizontal rudder, which Santos-Dumont called the "elevator," stuck far out and down in front; the machine rolled on a pair of knock-kneed wheels set in a narrow track beneath the wing, and its long snout rested upon a skid set behind the elevator. The operator stood in front of the wings inside a tall wicker basket with a control wheel. It looked as if Santos-Dumont were preaching to the elevator.

He thought this machine resembled a bird of prey, and he called it such with manly swagger, but to the casual observer it looked like a fleeing duck, and thus most called it the *Canard*. History has re-membered it by what was painted on its side: *14 bis.*

Before he tried flying from a level surface as the Wrights had said they had done, Santos-Dumont needed to test the machine, of course. To check the elevator's function, he had *14 bis* suspended from a wire run and towed along by a reluctant donkey on the ground, the ass itself being pushed and pulled by human assistants. This arrangement failed to produce the requisite speed and served to frustrate all involved, including the donkey. The Brazilian tried dragging *14 bis* with *No. 14,* and the canard plowed so powerfully ahead of the dirigible that both flew dangerously amok. The me-chanics managed to wrestle all safely to the ground, and Santos-Du-mont confidently declared he would now test the bird of prey under its own power.

He had his mechanics install a new, more powerful engine—the 50-horsepower Antoinette, weighing less than 200 pounds. On a cavalry field near the outskirts of Paris that September, Santos-Dumont and *14 bis* jumped 23 feet into the air and stalled, crashing to the ground. Both undercarriage and propeller were flattened, but Santos-Dumont felt that *14 bis* was finally ready to fly in public.

After a month and a half, the ruptured duck was repaired, with its elevator reconfigured to be more responsive. A group of official ob-servers arrived at the parade grounds on October 23, 1906, repre-senting the Aéro-Club of France and the Fédération Aéronautique Internationale, a record-keeping organization established the prior year by representatives of eight nations, including France, Britain, Germany, and the United States.

Before this audience that morning, the powered Voisin machine contracted by Louis Blériot refused to do more than roll on the field. Standing at the helm of *14 bis* that afternoon, Santos-Dumont started his engine and began his run. The canard whizzed past the enthusiastic spectators picking up speed, then it lifted into the air and hurtled out of control for 50 meters before touching ground again.

The crowd went wild and carried Santos-Dumont off the field. Then the sage men of the FAI checked their stopwatches, measured skidmarks, and mumbled and nodded: Alberto Santos-Dumont had become the first man in history to successfully fly a powered, heavier-than-air machine.

The Wrights in Exile

While newspapers erupted with coverage of Santos-Dumont's first flights, back in the States the Wrights remained mysteriously quiet. Fueled by Archdeacon's rantings, speculation about the brothers began building: Had they or hadn't they? Could they or couldn't they? If they could, why wouldn't they do it in public?

Bemused by the criticism while they waited for the confirmation of their patents, the Wrights really weren't worried about the experiments of their rivals: They had clearly been the first to achieve powered, controlled flight, and they had the documentation and witnesses to prove it, too. With competitors like Santos-Dumont hurtling dangerously out of control in such tenuous machines, they might have nothing to worry about for a long time, perhaps until their patents ran out in 1923.

"Even you, Mr. Chanute, have little idea how difficult the flying problem really is," Wilbur wrote a few days before Santos-Dumont's first run. "When we see men laboring year after year on points we overcame in a few weeks, without ever getting far enough along to meet the worse points beyond, we know that their rivalry and competition are not to be feared for many years."

Wilbur also said, "The fact that the American public does not know the difference between a flying machine and an airship has been a great help to us in maintaining secrecy." Another help had been that Orville started giving a coat of aluminum paint to all the framework, uprights, and control cables so that they would wash out on any unauthorized photographs. It also helped that the always-respected small businessmen now moved with increasing ease and frequency among the region's elite circles—Wilbur seemed to thrive on it. When an unapproved report about their machine threatened to leave Dayton through an issue of one local newspaper, the Wrights managed to have all copies suppressed. What was good for the Wright brothers was good for Dayton. But one fact remained: Since the previous winter they had not actually flown their machine for fear that someone might discover its secrets.

Toward the end of 1906, Bishop Wright wrote in his diary, "There is much in the papers about the Wright brothers. They have fame, but not wealth yet. Both these things, aspired after by so many, are vain."

It looked as though business would start to move faster than it had, with the mysterious French syndicate promising to buy a flyer. But those negotiations dragged on for months with niggling over specifications, which the brothers attributed to the increasing success of the nation's indigenous experimenters and to the cooling of French tensions with Germany. British interest seemed to fire again, then, it too, cooled.

Finally, in late 1906, some good news arrived: The Wright control systems were protected in Germany, then in the United States. Every patent office around the globe officially followed suit: The brothers now held worldwide licensing rights to the flying machine, based upon patents granted them for their 1902 glider.

A company with strong ties to Russia (which had lost its recent war with Japan) offered the Wrights half a million dollars for exclusive foreign rights to their patents. Wilbur put that deal off to travel to New York for negotiations to sell the Germans fifty machines at

$50,000 apiece—$2.5 million—the Germans perhaps being more tense with the French than the French realized.

As the spring of 1907 arrived, even the U.S. Board of Ordnance and Fortification approached them, through a letter quietly saying it would now like to look at flying machines. A clipping about the Wrights from *Scientific American* magazine had made its way to aeronautically minded President Theodore Roosevelt, and he passed it along with a personal note to Secretary of War Taft, who passed it along with his personal endorsement to the Board of Ordnance.

"We have some flyers in course of construction," Orville wrote back, "and would be pleased to sell one or more of them to the War Department, if an agreement as to terms can be reached." They asked for $100,000 for providing one flying machine with two seats capable of flying 200 kilometers.

Wilbur now headed to Europe for negotiations. The brothers had signed with Hart Berg, a professional American business representative there (who thought Wilbur would make a "capital Exhibit A"— to be tucked away later during the nitty-gritty negotiating). Meanwhile, Orville set up a new two-man machine. He placed the seats side by side, "with the controlling levers so arranged that either man alone, or the two together, can manage the machine. In this way we think it will not be difficult to train others." He found it "a great improvement over the old system" of shifting on the hip cradle, though he had yet to test it in the air. In July it was crated up and on its way to Paris, along with Orville, Katharine, and Charlie Taylor.

In Europe the Wrights bought evening clothes, dined in fine restaurants, strolled in the Tuileries gardens, flew in a hot-air balloon, visited the Louvre, ascended the Arc de Triomphe, eluded reporters, met with important French officials, and met with important German officials; then they watched the French negotiations fall through and the German ones drag on inconclusively, and they left for home with their flying machine still packed up and waiting in French customs.

Fastest Man on Earth

The Wright brothers woke up one day to realize they were no longer alone: There were by now other serious fliers in America— a group springing from an unexpected corner of the Langley camp.

The secretary himself had died in 1906 of a broken heart, it was said, over the public vilification and his subsequent inability to gain redemption by successfully completing the aerodrome experiments; though his age, seventy-two, and a series of strokes added complications, too.

Yet his good friend, telephone inventor Alexander Graham Bell, now sixty-two, continued fanning the interest that began during his role as official observer for Secretary Langley a decade before. Portly and white-bearded, Bell had learned a thing or two over the years from his experiments in voice communications, from watching the Langley project, and from his own experiments with increasingly larger multicelled "tetrahedral" kites: He came to believe that combining money and bright young men of like mind could produce results. Now at his Nova Scotia retreat in the summer of 1907, he had assembled the requisite group of bright young men. Funded with $35,000 donated by wife Mable Bell, the group of twenty-year-olds solemnly voted to form an organization dedicated to produce America's first powered flight. They named it the Aerial Experiment Association.

Dr. Bell himself was president and took no salary. Two Canadians, Casey Baldwin and J. A. D. McCurdy, signed on as chief engineer and assistant engineer at annual salaries of a thousand dollars apiece; treasurer was Lieutenant Thomas Selfridge of the U.S. Army, attached to the group by the orders of President Theodore Roosevelt himself, and so he drew no AEA salary. Early on, Selfridge was nearly killed while riding Dr. Bell's latest tetrahedral kite, *Cygnet,* as it was being towed with a motorboat. He and *Cygnet* plunged into the icy water, ruining the kite and nearly drowning Selfridge.

There was one more post that needed filling at the AEA: director of experiments. For that spot Bell was willing to pay five thousand dollars for the Fastest Man on Earth.

That's what folks called Glenn Curtiss, a thin, serious-looking man in his thirties with a receding hairline, tight mouth, moustache, and a passion for tinkering with machinery—especially motors. A former bicycle racer, Curtiss started setting speed records on motor-cycles that he designed and built himself right down to the engines. During races in Florida in January 1907, the leather-clad daredevil rocketed 136 miles per hour on his huge V-8 powered, belt-driven motorcycle. No human had gone faster.

He started trying to making a name for himself with his light and powerful engines. In 1904 he sold one to dirigiblist Thomas Bald-win (no relation to the AEA's chief engineer); both had attended a late-summer aeronautical exhibition at the Dayton fairgrounds in 1906, where a chance meeting with the Wrights—the brothers had helped retrieve Baldwin's runaway dirigible—led the four to spend the following few days together talking flying machines. The brothers and Curtiss seemed to take to one another; they had much in common (except, well, Curtiss had married).

"I sometimes suggested to Curtiss that he was asking too many questions," Baldwin recalled later, "but he kept right on. The Wrights had a frankness of schoolboys in it all and had a rare confi-dence in us. I am sure Curtiss at that time never thought of taking up flying."

Curtiss wanted to sell them motors, but the brothers said they preferred their own, which were a little heavy but at least they knew what they were getting. Anyway they had parted friends, and now Curtiss had come to Bell's summer home to deliver the engine he'd built for the *Cygnet*. After Bell offered him the directorship, Curtiss ended up staying in Nova Scotia. Winter arrived, so he moved that the group reconvene at his home base and machine shop at Ham-mondsport, in upstate New York. The AEA members voted in favor of the measure, and in early 1908 they were busy jumping off a local hilltop in their own bamboo glider modeled on and updating the old 1896 Chanute (or was it Herring?) design, while building their first powered biplaned aerodrome.

Red Wing it was called, from its silk cloth covering of leftover kite material donated by Dr. Bell. The wings were 43 feet long, a narrow six feet at the widest, then each tip tapered to a point. Crisscrossed with wires, the bottom wing curved up and the top wing curved down, so that from certain angles *Red Wing* resembled Gulliver's football as captured by Lilliputians. The main objective was just to get the thing moving through the air in front of as many witnesses as possible, so the AEA's bright young men engineered it to be as light and streamlined as they knew how, with the lightest, strongest motor that Curtiss could supply: a 40-horsepower V-8 weighing just 185 pounds. The *Red Wing* project leader, Lieutenant Selfridge, placed a wicker seat on the bottom wing, mounted behind a forward eleva-tor held in place by a rectangular bamboo framework, silk-covered for streamlining. The operator worked a steering drum controlling the elevator. A lever controlled the square vertical rudder mounted with a fixed horizontal surface (for fore-and-aft stability) on more bamboo poles protruding behind the wings, the engine, and the sin-gle pusher propeller, Selfridge either not being aware or not too concerned about the torque. With its operator, *Red Wing* weighed just 570 pounds, 1.5 pounds per square foot of wing. By compari-son, the 1903 Wright machine had a wing loading of 1.25 pounds per square foot, but it weighed more than 600 pounds and only had a 12-horse motor.

Red Wing had to work.

The aerodrome rested upon two short skis, appropriate consider-ing it was to be tested on the flat frozen expanse of nearby Lake Keuka. There, on March 12, 1908, Casey Baldwin sat behind the controls on the machine, started the engine, and started sliding across the ice. After a 100-foot run *Red Wing* took to the air, climbed to between 10 and 20 feet, then slammed back down on the surface after hurtling 319 feet.

If you didn't believe the Wright brothers—and really, who could? they had grown so secretive—then this was the first powered flight on American soil to be held in public, out in the open for anyone to see. Of course if you did believe them—as Curtiss should have, since the brothers had showed him pictures of their machine in flight—then this was almost three times longer than their first flight and therefore superior to their three earliest flights.

Other short flights followed, but five days later a good crosswind turned *Red Wing* over in midair and demolished it. Baldwin dragged himself and the engine from the wreckage, and the AEA started work on its next machine, *White Wing,* which Baldwin supervised. Except for its choice of fabric covering—Dr. Bell ran out of red—in outward appearances *White Wing* was a ringer for *Red Wing.* It even had the same engine. But its wings were a bit shorter, the tail and vertical rudder a bit smaller, its elevator a bit larger, and the propeller had a slightly different pitch.

Its control system was a little more sophisticated, too: A wheel now steered the rudder right and left, as in a motorcar, while a lever attached to the steering post moved the bow elevator up and down. But more important, "In this machine it was deemed advisable to get some positive method of controlling lateral stability," Baldwin wrote (AEA legend says Bell did the advising), so its wingtips were "hinged about their fore edges." To operate them, the pilot wore a shoulder harness; when, say, the right wing went high and the pilot naturally leaned to the right, the harness's steering ropes would increase "the angle of incidence of the tips on the lower side and decrease the angle of incidence of the tips on the high side," and the machine would resume its upright and level flight.

Trials began in May 1908, and thus the machine was outfitted with a trio of wheels and hauled to a local racetrack. After three days Curtiss had succeeded in flying it 1,017 feet at 37 miles per hour "under perfect control at all times," he pointed out. On its fourth day of testing, on its fifth flight ever, McCurdy as pilot hit a strong quartering wind that made *White Wing* touch the ground with its right wing; it turned turtle and came to rest on its back, a complete loss after having flown a lifetime total of just 674 yards. The engine remained unharmed.

The next machine was Curtiss's baby. To say that it resembled *Red Wing* and *White Wing* would be repetitive, but it did—right down to its salvaged, indestructible engine; again though there were minor changes. Curtiss set the wingtips at a neutral angle when they were not being used, and he changed the mechanism's gearing a little. The entire machine was lengthened for stability, the undercarriage strengthened for landing, and the elevator enlarged further for better steering control. To make the wings impermeable to the air, the builders coated its surfaces with paraffin and turpentine, and they tinted the mixture with yellow ochre—the color of a june bug—because *White Wing* had washed out in photographs, and these folks wanted people snapping as many pictures as possible. They completed the third aerodrome in June; Curtiss began trials on the twenty-first. In three flights he covered between 456 and 1,266 feet, "This last flight . . . the longest ever made in public in America at that time," he wrote. In four days he was doing "record flight" after "record flight"—up to 3,240 feet.

Right away the AEA notified the newly formed Aero Club of America that Curtiss was going to try for the first *Scientific American* Trophy, which offered a $2,500 prize for the first public flight of one kilometer in which the flying machine left the ground *on wheels*—something the Wrights had refused to try. The *June Bug*—that's what Pa Bell called it—would attempt the distance patriotically on the Fourth of July, in Glenn Curtiss's hometown of Hammondsport, New York.

It stormed that day, but the sky cleared after five P.M. and spectators quickly packed the stands and grounds of the Stony Brook Farm racetrack. AEA members started the *June Bug*'s engine, and

Curtiss took off on his first try, landing just 100 yards short of the mark. He adjusted the tail and tried again. This time, said Curtiss, the *June Bug* sailed above "the fields, fences, ditches, etc., as far as possible without going above the telegraph wires and trees" and flew 1.25 miles before the watchful eyes of the official observer: Charles Manly. For Curtiss, he took home the first aeronautical cash prize offered in America, along with a year's possession of the trophy—an ornate and bulbous sterling phallus topped with an engraving of Langley's *Great Aerodrome*—and an immeasurable amount of public adulation.

Found among the congratulatory mail flooding in to Curtiss that month was a letter from Orville Wright. It seems that in giving the *June Bug* "movable surfaces at the tips of the wings . . . for maintaining lateral balance," Mr. Curtiss had violated one of the Wrights' broad patents that protected their wingwarping mechanism. Indeed, Orville wrote, "We believe it will be very difficult to develop a successful machine without the use of some of the features covered in this patent," so if Mr. Curtiss cared to continue exhibition flights the brothers would be glad to license him the rights to their mechanism.

Give Mr. Baldwin (Thomas, not Casey) their regards, Orville said in closing, and have a nice day.

CHAPTER NINE

1908 to 1909

Kitty Hawk Revisited

Hart Berg had underestimated his clients. In short order, Exhibit A had become chief counsel. Of course, the Wrights weren't highly regarded while they were in Europe—one high-level French minister called them frauds—but it didn't bother them. Wilbur especially enjoyed a German newspaper cartoon showing the indifferent *Gebrüder* Wright coldly working France and Russia.

"Orville is at one end bargaining with France while I am working Russia at the other end," he wrote Katharine. "France has a wheelbarrow full of money and is down on its knees begging us to accept it. . . . At the other end I am almost equally indifferent, though Russia is represented as pulling its last rouble out of its pocketbook." Their as-yet undemonstrated invention was depicted as a cat in a bag.

The good *Gebrüder* had been working the United States as well. In October 1907, after months of negotiations, the Board of Ordnance and Fortification convinced the brothers that it was now prepared to negotiate seriously about purchasing a "dirigible" heavier-than-air flying machine, though their price was too high.

"If we can obtain assurances that we shall receive fair treatment and that our patents will not be palpably disregarded by the government officials," Orville replied, "we on our part will make every reasonable concession in order to provide a basis of agreement which it will be possible for your Board to accept. We care much more for an assurance of fair treatment than for an extreme price on the first machine."

Clearly, though, the brothers were delighted.

"During the past eighteen months," Orville wrote with a flourish part patriot, part bicycle salesman, "all our offers to foreign governments have contained provisions giving us liberty to furnish machines to our own government absolutely without restriction. Nothing would give us greater pleasure than to furnish the *first* machine to it."

With a little help from the Wrights on the specifics—the government was unsure about exactly what capabilities it should seek in a flying machine—the War Department in December issued a request for bids, "really for the purpose of forestalling criticism and sounding public sentiment," as Wilbur wrote to Chanute.

The brothers took their time to respond, allowing others—frauds, publicity seekers, and maybe even serious but inevitably less successful contenders—to step forward first and have their claims discounted. Fifty or so did. Of those, two parties actually had lower bids than the Wrights and were willing to lay down a ten percent deposit: One A. J. Scott, who quickly backed out and was never heard from again, and Augustus Moore Herring, who wanted to underbid the brothers and then hire them to build the machine for him. They, of course, refused to cooperate with such a scheme. Still, Herring had long told anyone who'd listen that he knew the secrets of the Wright brothers. Now was his chance to prove it: He let his bid stand.

After two months the Wrights wrote that they could supply a machine to fit the government's specifications—*their* specifications—

within two hundred days and for $25,000, which was exactly the amount the War Department had appropriated for such a purpose (and one-quarter of what they'd originally asked). Other submissions notwithstanding, the Signal Corps notified the Wrights early in February 1908 that it had accepted their bid and would issue them a contract. Less than two months later, they received word that France had also accepted their terms.

They would have to demonstrate machines for both countries simultaneously.

Wilbur and Orville had done nothing since the autumn of 1905 but try to sell their invention. The bicycle shop proprietors had become sharp international businessmen, true, but their flying had dulled after more than two years' absence from the air. They now needed to hone their skills, though with more privacy than available at Simms Station, Huffman Prairie. The brothers were comfortable with habit: In early April Wilbur packed up his trunk and boarded the train to Kitty Hawk.

It was drizzling when he arrived at the foot of Big Kill Devil Hill. While the wind blasted sand in his face, Wilbur slowly trudged around their old camp buildings. He saw nothing but decay. The roof and north end of their living quarters were gone, and the new hangar had collapsed completely, torn apart by the winter storms and drifting sand, by the power of the incessant wind that had brought the Wrights there in the first place. Vandals had broken in a few months before and ripped up their canvas cots and the Pride of the West muslin on the 1902 glider. That flying machine was worthless to the brothers now, but they needed the camp.

Soon the place fairly hummed—for Kitty Hawk—with crewmen delivering lumber and carpenters rebuilding the buildings; one day Wilbur was startled by a familiar face from Dayton, a mechanic named Charles Furnas. He had helped out some at Simms Station and then followed Wilbur to Kitty Hawk to get in on the ground floor of aeronautics. Wilbur found him a place to sleep in town and put him to work; by late April, they had rebuilt the camp. Orville arrived in early May, and they began assembling the flying machine.

It was not one of a half-dozen or so new machines that were now under construction back in Dayton and nearly identical to the 1905 flyer. Rather, it was the 1905 machine itself, modified with two seats and an extra control lever to train a novice pilot. Though they had more experience in the air than anyone alive, the brothers now had to learn how to fly sitting up, which they did gladly. "I used to think the back of my neck would break if I endured one more turn around the field," Orville said. The new dual control system consisted of only three levers: an elevator lever on the left of the pilot's seat, a wingwarping-and-rudder lever between the seats (that a novice pilot would work with his right hand while the passenger-instructor in the right seat would work it with his left), and a second elevator lever on the passenger's right.

Alerted by local telegraph operators, a half-dozen reporters from established East Coast newspapers and magazines showed up, kept their distance, appeared in camp only incognito (much to the brothers' amusement, since they knew all the natives for miles around), and filed reports on the mysterious, secretive Wright brothers' flights. Though not in that order: The brothers had barely gotten the machine into the air when the papers published an account of a 30-mile flight—which was possible—but also 3,000 feet high and eight miles out to sea, which would have been foolhardy. In reality, their voyages consisted of low, short (for them) meanderings among the Kill Devil Hills, trying out the machine's new controls and that new right seat; the brothers took up the world's first passenger in a heavier-than-air machine, Charlie Furnas.

After only ten days of practice, though, Wilbur crashed the machine. He was circling the various hills in a stiff breeze when, flying with the wind, the machine suddenly plunged to the ground. Wilbur was thrown against the top wing and emerged slightly bruised and stiff, and the flyer itself was barely damaged. But there was no time to repair it; their business in France demanded that one of them return to the continent.

It was another first for the Wrights: For the first time, business took precedence over their aeronautical experiments.

They gathered up the pieces of the 1905 machine, the first true practical flyer, and stuffed them inside the camp sheds among the fragments and skeletons and ghosts of all the other machines that came before, and left it all there as food for vermin and fodder for vandals.

Blériot's Epiphany

Chubby Louis Blériot had big, sad eyes and a big black moustache and a bewildered countenance, suggesting rather more bumble than passion. He had already produced a failed wing-flapping machine before his partnership with Gabriel Voisin, which in turn produced three powered machines that refused to part with the earth.

In fact, soon after Santos-Dumont usurped the Voisin-Blériot team and took his short 1906 ride on *14 bis* to win the 1,500-franc Archdeacon prize, Voisin left Blériot and went into business with his brother Charles. Having learned what not to do while bankrolled by Blériot, over the next year the dark, sleepy-eyed Voisin *frères* built a simple biplane with much longer 33-foot wings, and a 34-foot length consisting of a substantial box-kite tail and square framework jutting behind the wings, and an adjustable biplane elevator and a streamlined cotton-covered nose ending at the control wheel, and a wicker seat for its steersman, the *pilote*. Its pusher propeller was driven by the increasingly ubiquitous 50-horsepower Antoinette boat engine designed by marine engineer Léon Levavasseur and named for the daughter of his principle backer. The sculptor Léon Delagrange bought the first Voisin machine, while French bicycle and automobile racer Henri Farman bought the second, modified the tail, and named it *Voisin-Farman I*. At its controls in October 1907 he took the 50,000-franc prize that Aéro-Club president Ernest Archdeacon put up for the first official flight of more than one kilometer—which the *Voisin-Farman I* did in under a minute. Then just after the beginning of 1908, Farman took off into the cold dawn from a field near Issy-les-Moulineaux and used the machine's rudder to skid and crab (it had no lateral control surfaces) through the air around a banner set in the field.

This, the Aéro-Club proclaimed, was the first official circle in a flying machine.

But back to Louis Blériot. He personally took over testing his machines from the departed Voisin and hired a whole new staff of mechanics and engineers, which continued to turn out Blériots by the numbers, all of them Roman, all of them failures. Partial success came to him by the sixth Blériot machine. The *Blériot VI* resembled a lesser Langley *Great Aerodrome* but corrected Langley's oversights by having wheels and a reliable 24-horsepower Antoinette engine mounted, innovatively, in the nose. Its tandem wings were covered with vellum—parchment paper invented by the brothers Montgolfier—and had a generous dihedral for lateral stability; there was a rear rudder and a set of elevators on the forward wing. *Blériot VI* managed a 100-foot hop in July 1907. Though he demolished the machine in a spectacular crash two months later, it was enough to give Blériot hope. Better results emerged from *Blériot VII*, which was ready for testing that October. The rear wing had shrunk to span a few feet; overall it was larger than the prior machine. Right after testing commenced Blériot crashed this machine, too, and so it was on to *Blériot VIII*.

After unveiling the machine in April, Blériot's engineers spent the second quarter of 1908 refining it. Smallish like recent predecessors, it, too, had an engine in the nose, a single wing that crossed its square-section body, which was shaped like a spindle—a *fuselage*, as the French called it. The fuselage (which showed its naked innards past the cockpit) led to the elevator and culminated in a small squat rudder the same height as the fuselage. The entire flying machine rested on two wheels in front, with a slightly smaller one under its tail section, or *empennage,* as the French called the feathers of an arrow.

Like the shape of the machine, its control system had evolved within the line of machines since the *Blériot VI,* and had perhaps been derived from the system developed by Robert Esnault-Pelterie. A single lever was mounted atop a universal joint on the floor in front of the pilot's seat. When the pilot moved the stick left or right, he activated the narrow, pivot-hinged wingtips; when he moved the same stick forward or back, it also activated the elevator. To manipulate the rudder right or left, the pilot would push on a bar with his right or left foot. It was so simple, yet the movements of the stick and the rudder bar felt completely natural for the action they produced. Pull the stick back to go up, push it down to go down, sure; but now leaning it to the left tipped the machine left, and leaning it to the right tipped the machine right—how easy! Diving and climbing turns were now just simple single-lever operations: over to the left and forward dove the machine left; back and right meant climbing it to the right. There was nothing to it. The machine behaved almost as if it were responding to the pilot's thoughts. And once he learned how the controls operated, he rarely seemed to have to think about them again. It was like riding a bicycle or driving an automobile. The merging of man and machine would seem complete—if only the Blériot engineers could suitably refine the control surfaces.

Still, compared with his most successful machines so far, this was an eagle among ostriches. In *Blériot VIII* that July, he managed to remain aloft for eight full minutes and flew his first complete skidding circles.

But then he witnessed something that changed the course of aeronautics in his country for good. And it forced him to turn his back on his most remarkable machine to date.

Wilbur Takes France

Wilbur Wright had quietly left Kitty Hawk in late May 1908 and took a train to New York, the whole time being trailed by reporters of the mostly big-city and sensationalist variety. There he booked steamship passage across the Atlantic to France, where he hoped Orville would join him in a few weeks to get more flying practice before the all-important U.S. Army demonstration scheduled for September at Fort Myer, Virginia. He read that Lieutenant Selfridge was flying an AEA machine with wing-twisting features, and he wrote Orville urging him to start work on an article promised to the *Century* magazine. "It is important to get the main features originated by us identified in the public mind with our machines before they are described in connection with some other machine. A statement of our original features ought to be published and not left covered up in the patent office," he said.

Wilbur arrived in Paris still dodging the press, now mostly French and hostile—and now, for the first time, he was feeling competition nip at his heels. "Farman and Delagrange are visiting the big cities of Europe and giving exhibitions with some success," he wrote Orville. "They will probably make fifty kilometers before I am ready for the demonstrations."

He claimed the 1907 flying machine from French customs and opened its crate and found a shambles inside: ribs busted, cloth ripped, the radiators badly mashed. "I am sure that with a scoop shovel I could have put things in within two or three minutes and made fully as good a job of it," he said. Passage of time, customs officials, and Orville's "misrepresenting the amount of work remaining to be done" were to blame, and it cost Wilbur precious time.

He got to work fixing the damage and putting the machine together in a donated corner of an automobile factory. Though he spoke no French and dressed in his oversize flattened peaked cap and business suit, he behaved as if he were one of the common autoworkers: He automatically kept the same hours as they, right down to their breaks. Before he knew it, the entire factory thought he was simply grand.

But the papers were scathingly critical, and all predicted failure. Publicly, Maurice Farman sarcastically offered Wilbur $10,000 to meet him in a flying contest. (Privately, he let it be known he wanted to buy a Wright machine as soon as the brothers had one to sell.) Wilbur burned his arm badly when a radiator hose parted company with the engine. "Soon, others can do the flying," wrote his father, "but you have a field for truth and science that no one else can fill. I think you and Orville ought to take especial care of your health, as well as your lives."

It was nearly the end of July 1908 before he finished assembling the flyer, and a week into August before he and the French assistants that he had hired—who spoke no English—could move the machine to the racetrack at Le Mans. There, on a Monday, the racetrack grandstands filled with locals, newspapermen, and several prominent Aéro-Club members eager to see the *bluffeur*'s bluff called, to see Wright publicly humiliated. Ernest Archdeacon could be heard predicting a tragically flawed flight, loudly pointing out the faults of the Wright design. Wilbur just went quietly about his business, and when the time was right, he mounted the machine and released the catapult weights. He shot from the launch rail and flew two tight circles around the field, low and perfect and lasting under two minutes, and he landed smoothly and precisely right in front of the grandstands.

The stands erupted! Blériot, Delagrange and Archdeacon and the nation's other veteran aviators rushed to the machine barely able to speak. They had never seen—*had never flown*—anything like this! The machine was under perfect control! "This," Blériot said, "is the beginning of a new phase in mechanical flight! Wright is a genius. He is master of us all."

Wilbur Wright had conquered the air!

All the biggest newspapers reversed their positions the next day, and so did Archdeacon: Monsieur Wright, they all cried out, was no bluffer. They wanted to take up a public subscription and build a monument in his honor. He was presented medals, which he would only accept if they would give one to his brother, too. People made long journeys to Le Mans and camped out until they could see the miracle, see "Veelbare Vreecht" fly. "All the children within a dozen miles of my camp know me and as I ride along the roads they take off their hats and smile and say, 'Bon jour, Monsier Wright,' " he said. His face was lovingly and cadaverously caricatured on post-cards, and his backward peaked green cap started a fashion trend. Women even offered him their hand in marriage. Overnight, Wilbur Wright had become a French sensation.

Orville Flies for the U.S. Army

Back in the United States, Orville was finishing preparations for his demonstration before the U.S. Army Signal Corps in Virginia. "Both he and Wilbur peril their lives," wrote the bishop, "perhaps Orville most by the unsuitableness of the grounds at Fort Myer." Unlike Wilbur, Orville's proving grounds were thrust upon him—by the Signal Corps, for the proximity to Washington, D.C. Inspecting the area, he found the parade field too small to take off from comfortably and the proving field over which he was to fly lacerated with deep ravines. But it would have to do.

Augustus Moore Herring announced that he was going to fly his machine straight from New York instead of shipping it like the Wrights. He also asked for, and received, a thirty-day extension on his delivery date. Then without showing up, he faded back into the woodwork once again, forfeiting his two-thousand-dollar deposit.

With Orville and Charlies Taylor and Furnas working steadily, the Signal Corps machine was fully assembled as September began. After a few days' worth of false starts, Orville took to the air and flew a circle and a half around the field in little over a minute, then set down hard right before a host of official observers. "When the plane first rose," said Teddy Roosevelt, Jr., there as an observer for his father the president, "the crowd's gasp of astonishment was not alone at the wonder of it, but because it was so unexpected. I'll never forget the impression the sound from the crowd made on me. It was the sound of complete surprise." As the machine came to a rest, reporters rushed it with tears in their eyes.

The days passed and Orville rapidly logged more time and more circles in the air and set record after aeronautical record, and other than an overheating engine and an eighteen-inch split in one propeller that they fixed with canvas and glue, the machine held up pretty well. While at first he flew alone, he wasted little time taking up various young Signal Corps officers. The agreement the brothers had with the Army required that they train someone to fly the machine; one of the handful of officers assigned to the corps' new Aeronautical Division was Lieutenant Thomas Selfridge of the AEA.

"I will be glad to have Selfridge out of the way," Orville wrote his brother. "I don't trust him an inch. . . . I understand he does a good deal of knocking behind my back." Now, though, after a few delays for high winds, it was Lieutenant Selfridge's turn to fly with Orville.

They catapulted into a light wind, and Orville climbed the machine to 125 feet, circling the field three times in three minutes. On the fourth circle, Orville felt an unusual tapping behind him. He decided to set down immediately.

The flyer thumped and shook violently, and Orville cut the motor. The machine started sinking into a gully full of trees directly ahead. Coming down fast, Orville tried swerving left, but he had somehow lost control over the rear rudder. He straightened the wings—then the machine lurched and plunged 50 feet straight down.

"Oh-oh," Selfridge said.

With all his strength and all his skill, Orville got the flyer righted—

just before it slammed into the ground.

Spectators rushed to the cloud of dust boiling from the field and dragged the men from the heap of canvas and fractured sticks. Orville's hip, leg, and ribs were broken, but he could talk. The Signal Corps flyer, the world's first military flying machine, was demolished.

Selfridge's skull was crushed. He died in the night, never having regained consciousness.

He Only Looks Like Buffalo Bill

In England, almost a month had gone by since Santos-Dumont won the Archdeacon prize—more than a decade had passed since old Hiram Maxim's huge kite had broken its bonds unintentionally—and still things didn't look too promising for anyone in Old Blighty to be getting into the air anytime soon.

So Alfred Harmsworth, Lord Northcliffe, aeronautically minded as were all progressive men, took it upon himself to get things done. In his newspaper, the *Daily Mail,* Northcliffe soberly offered £10,000 for the first flight from London to Manchester, a distance of 200 miles. Right away the *Star* sarcastically replied that its offer of ten million pounds for the first flying machine of any sort that could fly five miles from London and back was still good: "One offer is as safe as the other." Days later the satirical magazine *Punch,* "deeply impressed as always with the conviction that the progress of invention has been delayed by the lack of encouragement," offered £10,000 to "the first aeronaut who succeeds in flying to Mars and back within a week."

Undeterred, the *Daily Mail* sponsored a less-ambitious model exhibition at Alexandra Park outside London during the spring of 1907, in which unmanned models would be flown indoors and out for £250 in prizes. Winner of the £75 second-place prize with his two biplane models was a young, tall, thin, and good-looking Englishman named Alliot Verdon Roe, who preferred to go by A. V. Roe. Each of his small biplanes had a wingspan of under eight feet and, powered by trusty rubber bands, would fly approximately 100 feet. There was, by the way, no first prize awarded; none of the entrants reached the published criteria.

After claiming his prize money, Roe spent it building a full-scale version of one of the models, with which he hoped to take the £2,500 *Daily Mail* prize for the first to achieve a complete circuit around the Brooklands racetrack. The Roe I Biplane, as it was officially called, lay low to the ground and had a 30-foot wingspan, a forward rudder, and a six-horsepower motorcycle engine driving a crude pusher propeller. This setup had to move a total of 650 pounds, but it did so with no great success—in fact, with no success at all.

Then Roe borrowed a 24-horsepower Antoinette engine (£75 only went so far in those days) and installed it with a different propeller in the biplane, meanwhile adding horizontal "winglets" between the craft's wings. In June 1908 he managed a brief hop of a few feet. It wasn't much, but for years Great Britain latched on to it and called it the nation's first flight.

Four months after Roe's biplane hop, on October 16, 1908, an American expatriate and kite-flying fanatic named Samuel Franklin Cody—no relation to Buffalo Bill, though he wore a droopy mustache and goatee, dressed like a cowboy, and toured England with his own Wild West Show—wheeled a huge biplane that he had built for the British Army in Farnborough, England. After starting its 50-horsepower Antoinette—borrowed, naturally—and making a short takeoff run, the Cody *British Army Aeroplane No. 1* flew almost 1,400 feet, then settled to the ground, and England was greatly comforted. After all, Cody was nearly a Brit, he had sustained flight on British soil, and most of the machine belonged to the British army—not even the Wrights had completed the sale of a machine to the military. Now that was a true first, the first military aeroplane, and the honour was all England's.

But across the Channel the very same month, and two months after Wilbur Wright's first official public demonstration, Henri Farman took his Voisin on a kind of landmark flight so daring that not even the Wrights had attempted it before: He left the vicinity of one city, Châlons, and flew to another, Reims, where he landed. Though it was only 16 miles, the flight was the perfect venue for hardly maneuverable French machines, and soon city-to-city distance competitions were announced in newspapers across France.

Not to be outclassed, Lord Northcliffe in the London *Daily Mail* stood up and offered £500—$1,250 in American money—to the first who crossed the English Channel in an aeroplane.

Wilbur Takes France, Part II

Once rescuers pulled Orville from the wreckage of the Signal Corps aeroplane—with a broken leg, three broken ribs, and as they discovered more than a decade later, three hip fractures and one dislocation—his first concern was for Lieutenant Selfridge, as his authorized biography highlights with the subtlety of a blowtorch. While sister Katharine rushed to his bedside, he had the two

Charlies bring him the propellers from the machine. Orville found a crack in one of them, which had probably created a vibration that loosened a wire that held a prop shaft, which started the whole shaft wobbling—into the stay wire of the vertical rudder, which flopped sideways. Just as he regained control during that fatal flight, a gust from below pushed the tail up and drove the machine into the ground.

In France, Wilbur himself felt nearly devastated by the accident. "The death of poor Selfridge was a greater shock to me than Orville's injuries," he wrote home. ". . . I felt sure 'Bubbo' would pull through all right, but the other was irremediable. . . . I cannot help thinking over and over again 'If I had been there it would not have happened.' " He postponed further flights for a week. Through Katharine, the Wrights asked for and received an extension on their Signal Corps bid.

Orville discovered that some of the AEA crowd had gotten inside the building at Fort Myer where the wreckage was stored, and Alexander Graham Bell himself was found taking measurements. Orville almost went into a seizure over that, but that was all he could do (Octave Chanute looked into the incident and assured Orville it was innocuous), and otherwise he recovered mobility fairly quickly and started looking after their growing business in America.

Meanwhile Wilbur had been giving demonstrations before Europe's kings and princes and giving rides to businessmen, and even to a woman, Mrs. Hart Berg, wife of their European business associate. He hobbled her skirt with a rope, and for that season hobbled skirts became the fashion rage.

He was reluctant, however, to subject royalty to the rigors and dangers of flying, and their highnesses understood—really, they only wanted to meet this magnificent, famous inventor, the odd Wilbur Wright—and so it became a tradition to participate in the flight by helping pull the rope that hauled the machine's catapult weight to the top of the derrick. Said one blueblood while watching another pull that rope, "I'm sure it is the only useful thing he has ever done in his life."

Wilbur, though, had grown irritated with the crowds that continuously packed the field. "I sometimes get so angry . . . that I feel like quitting the whole thing and going home," he wrote, "but when I think of the sacrifices some of them have made in the hope of seeing a flight I cannot help but feel sorry for them when I do not go out." Still he privately complained about people constantly watching his every move and said he hoped to give up exhibitions and demonstrations as soon as possible.

The French company they set up quickly had flyer orders in excess of $100,000, and with the orders came students to teach, starting with Comte Charles de Lambert, who bought two machines. Wilbur otherwise kept himself busy setting endurance records and winning prizes like an Aéro-Club prize for a flight of 48 kilometers in 55:30. He took the altitude prizes as well, flying more than 200 feet high in the air, and he also received the Michelin trophy for staying aloft for 2:20:23 straight. No one but the other pilots said anything about the flyer not having tires, and Voisin grumbled that, with a catapult launch, the Wright flyer wasn't *truly* flying. Still, Wilbur made more than a hundred flights in France, taking away the eleven records Orville had set at Fort Myer. To do so, Wilbur remained in Le Mans that Christmas.

"For three months I have scarcely had a moment to myself," he said. ". . . How I long for Kitty Hawk!"

On the first of January 1909, he left for the southern resort city of Pau, France, where he met a recovering Orville with Katharine and resumed his training flights with students. The brothers received the Legion of Honor and met more heads of state; and while Orville set up their factory in Paris, Wilbur went to Italy and met even more

heads of state and flew with more students and took up more passengers, including a Bioscope cameraman whose moving pictures—
the first taken from a flying machine—Bishop Wright saw in a
Dayton theater. Then, in May 1909, a year after Wilbur arrived to
French ire, the Wrights all boarded a ship and waved good-bye to
the crowds in Europe, and they waved hello to the crowds in New
York, where the newspapermen took pictures of them, Wilbur more
gaunt than ever and the still-recovering Orville looking even more
dapper with his cane. The photographers and newspapermen followed them on the train home to Dayton, where eleven carriages
met them at the depot and a four-horse carriage pulled them to
their little white house at 7 Hawthorne, surrounded by thousands of
spectators. Thousands more washed past by that evening.

"It is with great pleasure that I received your friendly letter,"
Octave Chanute wrote Wilbur. ". . . I have, of course, rejoiced over
your triumphs in Europe and was particularly gratified with the
sensible and modest way in which you accepted your honors, both
abroad and since your return to this country. It encourages the hope
that you will still speak to me when you become millionaires."

Then at the end of the month, Wilbur wrote André Michelin
complaining about a change in the Michelin trophy cup: a depiction
of the wings of Ader's *Avion* had been incorporated into its design.
"[The] incorporation of the *Avion* in the design of the Michelin cup
would be endorsement of claims which conflict with the reports of
those who witnessed the trials," he wrote. "This would be most un-
fortunate. If any legend is to be perpetuated in the cup would it not
be better to reproduce the wings of Icare?"

There was no confusion over how *that* flight ended.

While they built another Signal Corps flyer, the City of Dayton
held "an elaborate carnival and advertisement of the city under the
guise of being an honor to us," said Wilbur, which culminated in
the presentation of a special congressional medal by newly elected

President William Howard Taft—who as secretary of war had taken little interest in the Wrights but who could now hardly afford to ignore the biggest civilian heroes America ever had.

They shipped the new 25-horse Signal Corps machine to Washington, D.C., and on a sweltering July day in 1909, the Senate adjourned to gather at Fort Myer and witness a command performance from that which they had allocated funds. Because the wind was too high, the brothers refused to fly or to explain why or to even jolly the distinguished visitors. They just sat off to the side talking between themselves and waiting patiently, Orville natty as usual, Wilbur oilstained and wearing a sphinxlike grin, both of them looking nearly identical to the untrained eye (except one of them had a mustache), both of them quietly inseparable. General Allen of the Signal Corps, like all generals a realist about appropriations, flitted around nervously, then tried to keep up the distinguished visitors' interest by letting them out on the field for a good look at the miraculous device. That only irritated the brothers, and they asked what business all those people had poking about their machine. Pretty soon several of the young staff officers were herding the congressmen back into their special tents. The brothers finally gave up that day, the formal announcement amounting to quietly telling Charlie Taylor to roll the machine back into its shed, which both miffed and mystified a body of old men quite used to having a little more unctuous genuflection from businessmen, no matter how great their celebrity.

Soon after, though, Orville flew before a joint session of Congress, in the process easily breaking a couple of Wilbur's records. Congress quickly got over its snubbing and wrote the brothers a check for $25,000, plus $5,000 for having exceeded the 40 miles per hour speed they'd promised by 2 mph, and the government finally took possession of its first aeroplane—more than four years after it was initially offered, and one year after the government could have figured out that the machine would live up to the conditions the brothers had promised. At the moment it was the soundest, best-tested, nimblest, fastest, and highest-flying machine of its kind in the world. Moreover, Congress was proud to say that Americans had built it and Americans had the know-how to build bigger and better ones—better than any nation in the world.

Blériot Accepts Tips

Meanwhile, Louis Blériot's fortunes had taken a turn for the better—and it happened, not coincidentally, right after he saw Wilbur Wright's agile flying machine at Le Mans the year before. The reason? Wilbur explained to Blériot how the machine's control surfaces worked and even allowed the Frenchman to flex the wings for himself.

As Ross Browne, an American friend and soon-to-be flying student of Blériot, would recall in his later years, "Right away Blériot said, 'Look, we're going to throw out all those aileron things and start warping.' " He virtually ignored two recently completed and wholly inadequate machines, *Blériot IX* and *Blériot X,* and started work on the *Blériot XI.* It was compact and simple, clean and artless. The single wing was 25 feet long, nearly elliptical, and virtually lacked dihedral, and instead of having those pivoting wingtip ailerons, its trailing edges warped à la Wright. As with *VIII,* the fuselage, 26 feet long, was as open as a garden trellis behind the cockpit and ended with an elevator and a rudder, all controlled by the Blériot stick-and-rudderbar system. Its undercarriage resembled a brass bedstead resting on two bicycle wheels. Powered by the brand-new three-cylinder, 25-horsepower air-cooled Anzani engine (that took lightness in trade for the liters of castor oil lubricant it sprayed while running), the machine could fly up to 45 miles per hour—unofficially—and remain in the air for one hour. With *Blériot XI,* completed in January and modified into the summer of 1909, Louis

Blériot had sunk his entire headlight fortune into developing a machine that could fly. Now he needed it to be a machine that could pay for itself—and all its middling older brethren.

Blériot quickly entered the distance contests that sprang up between cities all over France after Henri Farman's Châlons-to-Reims trip the year before. On July 13, 1909, he took the 14,000-franc Aéro-Club prize for the first straight-line flight longer than 40 kilometers, flying from Étampes to Orléans and stopping in between. The distance was 25 miles, and he flew it in 45 minutes. Now Blériot turned his eye toward the London *Daily Mail's* prize for the first heavier-than-air crossing of the English Channel, recently doubled to £1,000. Drawing a straight line at its narrowest point, from Calais to Dover, the distance was just 26 miles, only a little longer than the Étampes-to-Orléans flight.

Stopping along the way, however, would not be possible this time.

The Race to Cross the Channel by Air

It only seemed ironic later, of course, but an Englishman concocted the *Daily Mail's* Channel prize. The paper's owner, Lord Northcliffe, hoped as always to spur on the development of the important new science of aeronautics in his own country. When he originally published the offer, only the American Wrights were capable of such a distance, and Northcliffe had privately offered Wilbur an additional $7,500 to try.

"I am personally inclined to chuck the prize business and get home as soon as possible," Wilbur, in France, had written to Orville, at home recovering from his crash. Orville's feeling was that he didn't care for Wilbur trying the flight when he wasn't around. "You seem to have much more trouble with the engine than I do," he said. And so it was that Wilbur turned down the lord.

By early July 1909, however, the *Daily Mail* prize began to appear like an open invitation to invade England by air. Several potential contestants declared themselves poised to head toward the abandoned Channel tunnelworks at Calais, able and almost ready to attempt a crossing there. The world press, especially the *Daily Mail*, played it to the hilt. Who would be the first to try—and risk failure and death at sea? Who would triumph? With little else to the story, reporters wrote profiles of the possible contenders: Like the balloonist Charles Rolls, one-half of the Rolls-Royce motor manufacturing firm, who had purchased a Wright aeroplane; or Léon Delagrange, who had a Voisin biplane but was now learning the controls of the more reliable Wright machine; his instructor, Comte Charles de Lambert, himself instructed by Wilbur Wright, who also had a Wright machine that could do the trip. And there was Henri Farman, the first man to fly distances, now almost ready to make his way there with an aeroplane of his own design, configured astonishingly similar to his old Voisin.

Everyone's favorite, though, was a tanned and good-looking playboy with mischievous sparkling eyes: a self-described man-of-the-world, twenty-six-year-old Hubert Latham. Known for the cigarette dangling from his lips and his casually icy nerves, legend has him flying straight into a rainstorm during one flight, taking the time to light up while his machine tossed about in turbulence. The first to reach the departure point at Calais, Latham would be piloting his huge stylish monoplane, *Antoinette IV.* Both the machine and its famous and complex 50-horsepower, eight-cylinder, liquid-cooled in-line V motor were developed by Léon Levavasseur, whose interest in aeronautics did not stop with engines. Proving he was almost more artist than engineer, Levavasseur designed the monoplane with a 42-foot trapezoid-shaped wing and a 38-foot slim fuselage, and he perched its Pénaud-style arrow tail high on a tricycle, formed by two wheels below midwing, and a nose skid that swept down from the fuselage then turned upward once it cleared the propeller. Its forward fuselage resembled a fine mahogany crew shell, save for the engine cylinders protruding upward at angles and the long radiators mounted along its sides. Details were important: Its cockpit, behind the wing, came equipped with an ashtray.

"My impression," wrote *The New York Times*'s correspondent, "after witnessing Latham's repeated flights . . . is that, unless he has installed a new and more powerful and reliable motor before he essays the water trip, he will probably have to swim."

With a couple of false starts behind him, Latham took off from Calais on July 19 and pointed the Antoinette toward England. Six miles over the Channel, his engine quit, but he managed to set the Antoinette down just a few hundred yards from the French destroyer *Harpoon,* dispatched ahead of time just in case Latham might need plucking from the Channel. His rescuers found Latham perched upon his sinking monoplane, smoking a cigarette. "I did not even get wet," he said, as if to prove that the *Times* correspondent was only half right.

Three days later, while Latham, Levavasseur, and ten hired mechanics furiously assembled another machine, *Antoinette VII,* Louis Blériot arrived at Calais, looking like a walrus on crutches: He had seared his left foot when an exhaust pipe exploded during one distance flight earlier that month, and he had burned it again preparing the machine for his Channel attempt. Only the day before, he had had surgery on the foot, but Blériot found he could still work the rudder bar, and now after notifying officials of his intent to attempt the flight, he could rest it while he sat out a required forty-eight-hour waiting period.

Comte de Lambert arrived in town and registered, and slowly his forty-eight hours ticked by as well. Then just before their waiting periods ended, high winds blew in, to Blériot's and de Lambert's frustration—and to Latham's delight, for his mechanics weren't finished until July 24. Then everyone had to wait for the wind to abate.

It broke early the next morning, Sunday, July 25, and Blériot was roused at 2:30 A.M. He dressed against the cold of altitude with tweeds, the blue coveralls of a French mechanic over the tweeds, and then with a khaki jacket over that, and finally he strapped on a cork lifebelt just in case. If he couldn't walk on his own, well, then, swimming might be a problem, too.

He waddled outside and fired four blanks from his revolver to alert his mechanics, then had his wife Alice driven to the *Escopette,* his own personal destroyer assigned by the French government to steam across on his flight path. Blériot was taken to the *Blériot XI,* its vellum dirty and weatherbeaten from its young but rough life. A crowd had begun to gather.

"I won't need them until after I return from England," he said as he tossed his crutches aside and pulled himself into the cockpit. The crowd loved it.

After a short test flight, he sat and waited for sunrise, the earliest he could take off according to the rules. As a quarter of an hour crawled by, Blériot's entourage trained a telescope on the Latham-Levavasseur camp, but they saw no signs of life. Someone must have overslept.

At 4:35 the sun rose as scheduled, and right away Blériot took off under full power, loaded with fuel, into a slight southwest breeze. He climbed over some telegraph wires, crossed over the cliffs, pointed the machine's nose at Dover, and throttled back. "I begin my flight steady and sure toward the coast of England," he wrote. "I have no apprehensions, no sensation—*pas du tout*—not at all."

Back in Calais, Levavasseur woke to see Blériot's machine flying north. He rushed to wake Latham.

In a shot Latham was up, and while he and Levavasseur argued and the ten mechanics worked themselves into a frenzy getting *Antoinette VII* ready, the wind began to pick up. Now it would be too dangerous to start. Latham bit his lip, and tears welled in his eyes. He smoked. No one said it, but his only chance now rested on the hope that some disaster might befall Blériot.

After just a few minutes aloft, Blériot, his engine screaming along and spraying him with castor oil, overtook the *Escopette* while she plowed along harmlessly below at more than 25 miles per hour. He estimated that he was cruising at 42 miles per hour and at 260 feet above the Channel.

"The moment is supreme, yet I surprise myself by feeling no ex-ultation," he said, for he could tell the wind had grown stronger. "The motion of the waves beneath me is not pleasant," he added. "I drive on."

Ten minutes after passing the *Escopette,* Blériot turned his head to check his position against the destroyer, but the warship had fallen behind and disappeared into the mist. He was alone in a way that no one had ever been before, above seemingly endless water, behind the controls of a tiny flying machine of ash and bamboo covered with a roll of fancy stationery. He let the machine have its head, needing only to keep it level and balanced, and that he could do with a light touch on the controls. In ten minutes the unique solitude passed; just twenty minutes after leaving the French coast, he could begin to make out the White Cliffs of Dover.

They lay to the west, for the wind had blown him east, so with his bad foot he pressed on the rudder, and moved the control stick left and banked into the wind. Plowing west in fog, he continued along the coast until he spotted Dover Castle, and the break in the cliffs he was searching for: a green meadow scouted out by a French journal-ist eager to scoop the *Daily Mail.*

Blériot spotted his journalist waving the French tricolor and steered into the opening. Erratic winds there caught the machine and spun it around in the air like one of Sir George Cayley's de-scending sycamore seeds.

"At once I stop my motor, and instantly my machine falls straight upon the land from a height of seventy-five feet," he said, which broke the propeller and flattened the landing gear on impact. But for Blériot that was a good landing: "In two or three seconds I am safe upon your shore," he added.

The reporter helped extract the anxious Blériot from the damaged machine and told him that Latham was still on the ground in Calais. Word got out, and a crowd grew around *Blériot XI* and its sweaty, oily, but now relieved and elated pilot. The excitement spread to Calais and then the rest of the world. His machine was put on display, first inside a tent at Dover, then at a London department store. Tens of thousands filed past the monoplane in awe, as if paying respects to a foreign conqueror. Then the wonderment wore off, and reality settled in.

"A new point brought out," a *New York Times* reporter wrote, "is its striking appeal to the imagination of Englishmen that Great Britain's insular strength is no longer unchallenged; that the aeroplane is not a toy but a possible instrument of warfare, which must be taken into account by soldiers and statesmen, and that it was the one thing needed to wake up the English people to the importance of the science of aviation."

It was a cold, hard fact: Britain was now vulnerable by air, by foreign machines small like the Blériot and large like Count Ferdinand von Zeppelin's new rigid airships, and the nation's sovereignty could no longer be totally protected by its big navy and its bigger ditch. But with its greatest indigenous aerial feat being a recent 100-foot leap by A. V. Roe in a paper-covered triplane in Essex—and Cody's *Army Aeroplane No. 1* having broken the one-mile barrier—England did what little else it could and began looking into building a new kind of gun, an anti-aircraft gun, with which it hoped to protect its ships and shores by blasting tiny Blériot flying machines from its gray skies.

But for a while everyone was happy. The French were naturally elated at having such little machines while its neighbors did not. Louis Blériot was especially happy; he took orders for a hundred *Blériot XI's* in the following two days.

The only Frenchman who was miserable seemed to be Hubert Latham, who cabled his congratulations to Blériot upon his arrival, then just two days later he was again rescued from the Channel perched on his Antoinette's wing, puffing on a cigarette within sight of Dover.

The Wrights Consider Action on the Ground

The nation's reporters swarmed the Wrights when news of Blériot's flight hit Washington, D.C., during the second Signal Corps trials. The brothers told it honestly.

"Blériot's successful flight was splendid," Wilbur told *The New York Times*. "I know him well and he is just the kind of man to accomplish such an undertaking. He is apparently without fear and what he sets out to do he generally accomplishes. This recklessness makes him anything but a good aviator, however, for he lacks entirely the element of caution."

"I'm glad Blériot won the prize offered for the first aeroplanist to cross the Channel," Orville was quoted as saying "heartily" and added, "but I can't for the life of me understand how he ever managed to do it with the flier he has. His motor struck us both as being well nigh impossible, while he seemed to lack control over his machine. The great number of accidents in which they figured with his flier disclosed this lack of control, while his engine could never be depended on."

Even so, it was not that great a feat, they explained to the *Times* reporter: Because water reflects heat at a uniform rate, the air is smoother over the Channel. What the brothers were doing in the turbulent air over the hills and woods of Virginia was much more hazardous.

In reality, the brothers now had something more on their minds than prize flights: patent infringement. Orville, on his way to fly in Germany that August, sent a clipping to Wilbur that said Glenn Curtiss had announced he was going to represent the United States in the upcoming first international aviation meet at Reims, France.

"I think [the] best plan is to start suit against, Curtiss, Aeronautic Society, etc., at once," Orville said.

Curtiss Leaves the AEA

The members of the AEA had been shocked not only by Selfridge's death but also by seeing the vastly superior performance of the Wrights' machine in Virginia. They voted to continue experimenting for the time being, however, and after mounting the *June Bug* on floats and rechristening it *Loon,* McCurdy and company shoved the machine into Lake Keuka and tried to take off—but couldn't get the *Loon* to leave the water. Next, they built McCurdy's *Silver Dart,* an improved version of the basic AEA pattern but with a larger, 50-horse engine from Curtiss. In February 1909 it had become the first machine to fly in Canada; and it stayed in the air longer than any AEA machine yet: 19 miles.

Glenn Curtiss traveled to New York City to enter the *Silver Dart* in *Scientific American*'s second trophy competition, which would be awarded to the American machine that flew the longest distance that year, provided it was at least 25 kilometers, and done before its judge—Charles Manly, again. While in Manhattan, Curtiss met members of the Aeronautical Society of New York, who offered *him* $5,000 to build them a machine. He accepted and resigned from the AEA. With Curtiss now off on his own, the AEA had lost its best pilot and most skilled mechanic—the only one of them who could keep the *Silver Dart's* temperamental V-8 up and running long enough to capture the *Scientific American* Trophy. That May the Aerial Experiment Association quietly and officially voted itself out of existence, having fully met its original goal.

When Curtiss decided to go into business for himself, he took a partner: yes, Augustus Moore Herring, who couldn't build a flying machine for the U.S. Signal Corps but told Curtiss he could attract some $300,000 in backing, and who promised Curtiss that he held patents that predated and so voided those of the Wrights. Together they formed the Herring-Curtiss Company, based in Hammondsport, and there Curtiss built the Aeronautical Society's machine, officially the *Golden Flier,* popularly the *Gold Bug.* Differing slightly from the machines-by-committee of the AEA, the *Gold Bug* had two straight, rigid, and relatively short 28-foot yellow-colored wings with ailerons set midway between them for lateral control (and hopefully different enough from the Wrights' wingwarping patent to avoid infringement), bamboo outriggers to support the forward elevator and rear rudder, and a small, 25-horse water-cooled four-cylinder pusher motor. He tested the machine in the Bronx that June, and with the Aeronautical Society's permission, Curtiss flew the *Gold Bug* for the *Scientific American* Trophy on Long Island that July, circling for some 25 miles at an average speed of around 30 miles per hour. Since no one else beat that, Curtiss took home the $10,000 pot and the trophy for the second time.

Curtiss also had a second, similar machine under construction in Hammondsport for himself. It was a duplicate of the *Gold Bug,* except that it was to be powered by one of his big, 50-horse V-8 motors. When this machine was assembled, he figured it could outfly Blériot and Latham's Antoinettes and maybe even the Wrights now as well. With it, Curtiss announced, he would compete for the Gordon Bennett Trophy.

The Great Air Meet

Publisher James Gordon Bennett of the Paris *Herald* was perhaps best known for bringing to the world reporter Henry Stanley's immortal query, "Doctor Livingston, I presume?" (He was less known for getting ejected from his fiancée's house and New York society after urinating in the fireplace.) Bennett was also excited by emerging modes of transportation, and for several years he had offered a huge prize for some sort of speed competition: yacht races, balloon races, bicycle races, motorboat races, and automobile races. In 1909 the planners of the first international aviation meet knew whom to turn to for sponsorship for the first aeroplane race.

Officially the meet to be held at Reims was called *La Grande Semaine Aéronautique de la Champagne,* since it took place in Champagne country. Leading up to the competition for the Gordon Bennett Trophy was a week's worth of public flying by contestants from around the globe—contests designed to challenge the limits of the five-year-old flying machine. There was the *Grand Prix de Champagne et de la Ville de Reims,* a distance test; the *Grand Prix de la Vitesse,* for speed; the *Prix des Passagers,* for the one who could carry the most passengers; the *Prix de l'Altitude,* for altitude; and the *Prix de Tour de Piste,* a race around the meet's ten-kilometer (6.2-mile) course. The coup de grâce, the Gordon Bennett International Cup, was two trips around that course. Lest the competitions sound too prosaic, the London *Times* was happy to remind its readers: "So long as . . . it is difficult to strike a match and light a cigarette without shelter, the prudent man does not attempt flight, at least in a circuit."

In the weeks before showtime, workers assembled grandstands beside the racetrack near the plain of Betheny, north of Reims, built sheds for the flying machines, and set up red-and-white pylons to mark the aerial racecourse. They even laid tracks and constructed a special temporary train station nearby for the travel convenience of the spectators.

Nearly 200,000 people paid admission to the grounds that last week in August, while an estimated 100,000 watched from the surrounding hills. "All the hotels are full, and most of them have accommodated hundreds of people in furnished houses hired for the occasion, or in spare rooms placed at their disposal for a consideration by the tradespeople," said the London *Times*. While the Paris newspapers accused the good people from Reims of price gouging, the spectators and participants complained that the show's organizers seemed, well, disorganized. Perhaps that had something to do with the rain: It poured off and on throughout the week.

"[There] are such rivers of deep mud that enterprising individuals have placed planks across them and charge a penny per person for permission to cross," the *Times*'s special correspondent wrote.

Weather notwithstanding, everybody who was anybody in aviation brought their flying machines and paid the entrance fee (levied to prevent frauds, it would be refunded once their craft flew across the starting line). Everyone in aviation showed up, that is, except Wilbur and Orville Wright. The elder was home in the States; but the younger was right then demonstrating their flyer in Germany before crowds of thousands, and he implored the other to let him show up suddenly at Reims and sweep the meet. Wilbur said no—the meet organizers had refused to pay the brothers the licensing fee they demanded as patent holders of the flying machine.

Reims was billed as an international competition and indeed it nearly was: A total of thirty-five flying machines arrived from three different nations, including the United States, Great Britain, and France, but mostly France. (Though Germany had finally made it into the air through one Hans Grade and his triplane the preceding November, Orville was at the moment still the only one flying in that country with any of the necessary finesse.) Besides lone American Glenn Curtiss with his previously untested *Reims Racer*, pilots included Henri Farman, flying his new biplane which suspiciously resembled his old Voisin but which now sported the huge lateral control surfaces called *ailerons;* George Cockburn, a student and customer of Farman's and the meet's sole Englishman; Louis Blériot, who not a month before had flown across the Channel; his rival Hubert Latham, who had twice splashed down in the same and was hoping to rescue his and the Antoinette company's dampened reputation; and Louis Paulhan, who in a contest the previous year had won a new Voisin machine powered by an innovative new engine: the 50-horse, seven-cylinder Gnome rotary, which spun to cool itself and weighed but 3.3 pounds per horse.

Though the Wrights were absent, several of their machines made it on the field, including one flown by Frenchman Eugène Lefebvre, a pilot of less than two months but trained by Orville on his European tour.

When the weather broke late on the soggy opening day, the pilots quickly organized a slow parade of seven flying machines—the most ever in the air at the same time. Then Lefebvre stunned the crowd by performing "a series of daring evolutions before the grand stand, almost touching the banners on the roof," *The New York Times* reported.

"Well-known Americans, British aristocrats, titled Europeans, all went mad together . . . while a score of fresh-faced American girls . . . stood on chairs, dancing and screaming with the joy of a new experience.

" 'It's all Wright,' yelled Lord Northcliffe, unconscious of the joke."

Throughout the rest of the week, rain, records—and airplanes—fell almost daily. During the later speed trial Curtiss counted "as many as twelve machines strewn about the field, some wrecked and some disabled and being slowly hauled back to the hangars by hand or by horses."

Still, the weather worked in some fliers' favor. As Louis Paulhan flew in his Voisin for 2:43:24, beating Wilbur Wright's record by some 23 minutes, "an intense excitement prevailed among the public in the stands," while the sun breaking through the dark clouds "produced a succession of rainbows, which . . . enveloped the aeroplane and its pilot in tinted glory," said the London *Times*.

In his Antoinette, Hubert Latham spiraled upward to a height of 503 feet, claiming the altitude prize and reclaiming some of the dignity he had left dripping in the English Channel. Later he logged an impressive 95.6 miles to take the lead in the distance competition. But Henri Farman snatched that prize away and made the world's first flight of more than 100 miles, finally covering 111.847 miles around the circuit as darkness fell on Betheny Plain.

Meanwhile, Glenn Curtiss and Louis Blériot emerged as the leaders in speed. Having saved up the untried, irreplaceable *Reims Racer* for the later speed races, Curtiss flew at a blistering 43.385 mph, shattering the Wrights' official European speed record of 34.03 mph. Then the next day Blériot broke the new Curtiss record by flying 46.179 mph. Three days later, in the Gordon Bennett race, Curtiss flew 47 mph and beat Blériot by six seconds to claim the Cup for America.

Oh, and yes: With two whole passengers shoehorned inside the protective wings of his machine, Farman mushed around the official circuit and flew off with the *Prix des Passagers*.

After all the flying was done, six machines were put up for sale, bringing in from a hefty 30,000 francs for a licensed Wright machine to 10,000 francs for a small, speedy *Blériot XI*.

And then, "the meeting broke up amidst general satisfaction," reported the London *Times*. "It was felt that its success would do much for the future rapid development of aerial locomotion."

Curtiss Is Served

Having eclipsed the famous Louis Blériot on the Gordon Bennett, the spotlight now shone on Glenn Curtiss. He headed to Italy to further demonstrate the *Reims Racer,* and later he arrived back in America to a hero's welcome. Everywhere across the nation, aviation meets were popping up on the next year's calendar, and everyone wanted Glenn Curtiss at theirs.

But he had a nagging concern. On the opening day of the Reims meet, Hart Berg, the Wrights' business partner in Europe (and whose wife had made aviation history by flying with Wilbur earlier that year) walked up to Curtiss and announced casually that the Wrights intended to begin prosecuting him for patent violations. Curtiss was shocked.

"I should like to ask the Wrights if they really believe my machine is an infringement of their patents; it is quite absurd to say so," he told the *Times* reporter. It looked as though he would get the chance to ask them himself in court.

Now Curtiss would also begin to see exactly how much protection Herring's papers would afford him.

CHAPTER TEN

1909 to 1914

Backlash

The backlash began softly, almost imperceptibly, after the congressional bemedaling ceremony with President Taft, after the hometown parade and blowing factory whistles and living American flag made from red-white-and-blue-dressed schoolchildren singing "The Star Spangled Banner" and the massive fireworks display culminating in the flaming eight-foot-high profiles of the brothers, after Orville's own triumphant round of European hobnobbing with kings, queens, princes, counts, and countesses, and with high-ranking officers from every imaginable military branch of just name the powerful Old World state, after the formation of a Wright company in Germany and another one in the United States backed by the likes of Cornelius Vanderbilt and Robert Collier of the popular *Collier's Weekly* magazine (who would buy the first American Wright aeroplane sold to a private individual), and after the company brought a patent infringement suit against the Herring-Curtiss Company.

The backlash, in fact, began with the arrival of a letter from George Spratt written in late September 1909, delivered to the Wrights' Dayton residence at around the same time that Wilbur, for the Hudson-Fulton Celebration, had strapped a canoe on the bottom of his flyer and circled the Statue of Liberty about waist-high in front of hundreds of thousands of adulatory New Yorkers (and pocketed $15,000 for the feat). Spratt was depressed for not receiving due credit for his contribution to the Wrights' success: namely, for suggesting back in 1901 to the anonymous bicycle mechanics of modest means that to analyze the mediocre performance of their gliders, they should build the small balances and measure the lift and drag on surfaces of varying cambers—which they did. Spratt now told the famous and wealthy Wilbur that he wished to be justly compensated.

"I am surprised and a trifle hurt," Wilbur wrote back, "when you say that the advice and suggestions we gave you in return 'cannot be considered in any degree a fair compensation.' " After all, Wilbur had supplied Spratt with the precise and otherwise still-secret tables of lift that his balance idea had produced. And as long as Spratt's own aeronautical ambitions remained unfulfilled, Wilbur promised "any scientific information of practical knowledge which we have gathered in ten years of investigation and practical experience."

"Tell us your needs and we will help you," he now pleaded, and closed with reassurances of his everlasting friendship. But Spratt remained convinced that the value of his contribution—the very work that led to their immortality—was being concealed by the Wrights, and he continued to sulk and stew.

Ironically, the infringement suit the Wrights had brought against Herring-Curtiss in a New York court, while eloquently evoking the epic proportions of the age-old problem of human flight, nonetheless smacked of George Spratt's tone: The original work of the brothers—in this case the wingwarping technique of lateral control—had been stolen by Herring and Curtiss and used for their own profit.

In the case at bar this court is the first to be called on in the history of judicial proceedings, to pass upon the intellectual property of inventors who have mastered the intricate problems of human flight and invented the first machine, recorded in the annals of aeronautical history, having the capacity to rise from the ground, soar at the will of the operator and return obedient to his wishes— that, in a word, can fly as do the birds and has opened the era of human flight. No reported case exists involving a dynamic man-carrying flying machine, heavier-than-air, because no such machine was ever invented. This is, therefore, the first instance of such a machine and the first law-suit involving the subject-matter.

Curtiss had retained an attorney, and both contacted Octave Chanute in October, the former in person, the latter through post, each asking for a little historical information: They wanted to know whether the notion of warping a flying machine's planes preceded the Wright experiments.

"The bare idea of warping and twisting the wings is old, but there are several ways of accomplishing it," Chanute said, naming a few pre-Wrights who twisted their wings in one fashion or another, such as Le Bris, d'Esterno, and Mouillard. "It will be for the experts to determine what are equivalent devices," he said, adding, "I do not remember any balancing devices such as Mr. Curtiss used. I dare say, however, that they are quite old."

Injunction Junction

Over the following months, the Wrights, through their companies worldwide, filed patent-infringement suits against everyone, any-where, making money with heavier-than-air flying machines that were neither licensed nor built by them. This included the likes of Louis Paulhan, Charles Lamson, Louis Blériot, Blériot importer Ralph Saulnier, Santos-Dumont, Henri Farman, Robert Esnault-Pelterie, Clément-Bayard, and the Antoinette company. For each manufacturer, the Wright Company offered to grant licenses on an individual basis for up to twenty percent of each machine's value, levied retroactively; for promoters of aeroplane meets, it would grant licenses for twenty percent of the total amount of prize money and ten percent of the gross gate and grandstand receipts. Sometimes the company would grant licenses for a lump sum based on estimated receipts.

At first, the litigation approach looked positive. In January 1910 the Wrights received a preliminary injunction against the Herring-Curtiss Company. Less than two months later, they won a similar injunction against Paulhan, who had been competing with great financial success in America since the first Los Angeles Exhibition that January. When served, Paulhan had decided to unhook the lateral control surfaces of his Blériot and Farman machines, then capitulated and slipped away back to Europe. But Curtiss, who now had his entire business focused on selling aeroplanes through and for exhibition, decided to fight it out. Herring-Curtiss filed an appeal, and in June the appellate court temporarily lifted the injunction while the decision was under consideration. Curtiss was free to fly for the time being.

The Wrights themselves realized that if they gave in on one lawsuit—especially the first one—no aviator around the world would take them seriously. More important to them than the money, they wanted to receive full and proper recognition for their work. They alone had funded the research, had taken the risk, now they wished to receive nothing more or less than credit for inventing the first controllable flying machine capable of sustained flight.

The newspapers, in their coverage of the Signal Corps tests and in articles about the Wright patent battle with Herring-Curtiss, began to take a greater interest in the origin of flight, in the events that led to the Wrights' success. One feature, which appeared in the December 12, 1909, *New York World,* said, "Their persistent failure to acknowledge their monumental indebtedness to the man who gave them priceless assistance has been one of the most puzzling mysteries in their careers." It was referring to seventy-eight-year-old Octave Chanute. "I admire the Wrights," the article quoted him saying;

I feel friendly toward them for the marvels they have achieved; but you can easily gauge how I feel concerning their attitude at present by the remark I made to Wilbur Wright recently. I told him I was sorry to see they were suing other experimenters and abstaining from entering the contests and competitions in which other men are brilliantly winning laurels. I told him that in my opinion they are wasting valuable time over lawsuits which they ought to concentrate in their work. Personally, I do not think that the courts will hold that the principle underlying the warping tips can be patented. They may win on the application of their particular mechanism.

The fundamental principle underlying the warping of tips for the purposes of balance was understood even before the suggestion contained in d'Esterno's pamphlet fifty years ago. In modern times the warping tips were actually used in flight by Pierre Mouillard. . . . the idea is protected in a patent granted him by the United States Government in 1901.

The Wrights I am told, are making their strongest attack upon the point that they warp the tips in connection with the turning of their rudder. Even this is covered by a patent granted to an American in 1901.

There is no question that the fundamental principle underlying was well known before the Wrights incorporated it in their machine.

An Exchange Between Two Old Friends

Wilbur was aghast when he read this. Immediately after the first of the year, he fired off a cautious letter to Chanute.

[You] are represented as saying that our claim to have been the first to maintain lateral balance by adjusting the wing tips to different angles of incidence cannot be maintained, as this idea was well known in the art when we began our ex-

*periments. As this opinion is quite different from that which you expressed in
1901 when you became acquainted with our methods, I do not know whether it
is mere newspaper talk or whether it really represents your present views. So far
as we are aware the originality of this system of control with us was universally
conceded when our machine was first made known, and the questioning of it is a
matter of recent growth springing from a desire to escape the legal consequences
of awarding it to us. In our affidavits we said that when we invented this system
we were not aware that such an idea had ever suggested itself to any other person, and that we were the first to make a machine embodying it, and also that
we were the first to demonstrate its value to the world, and that the world owed
the invention to us and to no one else. The patent of Mouillard was cited as an
anticipation by the Germans and the English patent offices, and also by the de-
fendants' attorneys in the recent trial at Buffalo, and in each case it was decided
that it did not constitute an anticipation. I have also seen Le Bris and d'Esterno
mentioned as having anticipated us, but the accounts in your book regarding the
works and writings of these men do not contain any explanation of such a system of lateral control. Do the French documents from which you derived your
information contain it, and if so can you give information as to where such documents can be obtained? It is our view that morally the world owes its almost
universal use of our system of lateral control entirely to us. It is also our opinion
that legally it owes it to us. If however there is anything in print which might
invalidate our legal rights, it will be to our advantage to know it before spending
too much on lawyers, and any assistance you may be able to give us in this re-
spect will be much appreciated, even though it may show that legally our labors
of many years to provide a system of lateral control were of no benefit to the
world and a mere waste of time, and the world already possesses the system
without us.*

Chanute's reply was cool and direct:

*This [newspaper] interview, which was entirely unsought by me, is about as ac-
curate as such things usually are. Instead of discussing it I prefer to take up the
main principles at issue.*

I did tell you in 1901 that the mechanism by which your surfaces were warped was originally with yourselves. This I adhere to, but it does not follow that it covers the general principle of warping or twisting wings, the proposals for doing this being ancient. . . . The original sources of information are indicated in the footnotes [of Progress in Flying Machines]. *I did not explain the mechanism because I had not the data.*

When I gave you a copy of the Mouillard patent in 1901 I think I called your attention to his method of twisting the rear of the wings. If the courts will decide that the purpose and results were entirely different and that you were the first to conceive the twisting of the wings, so much the better for you, but my judgment is that you will be restricted to the particular method by which you do it. Therefore it was that I told you in New York that you were making a mistake by abstaining from prize-winning contests while public curiosity is yet so keen, and by bringing suits to prevent others from doing so. This is still my opinion and I am afraid, my friend, that your usually sound judgment has been warped by the desire for great wealth.

If, as I infer from your letter, my opinions form a grievance in your mind, I am sorry, but this brings me to say that I also have a little grievance against you.

In your speech at the Boston dinner, you began by saying that I "turned up" at your shop in Dayton in 1901 and that you invited me to your camp. This conveyed the impression that I thrust myself upon you at that time and it omitted to state that you were the first to write me, in 1900, asking for information which was gladly furnished, that many letters passed between us, and that both in 1900 and 1901 you had written me to invite me to visit you, before I "turned up" in 1901. This, coming subsequently to some somewhat disparaging remarks concerning the helpfulness I may have been to you, attributed to you by a number of French papers, which I, of course disregarded as newspaper talk, has grated upon me since that dinner, and I hope, that, in future, you will not give out the impression that I was the first to seek your acquaintance, or pay me left-handed compliments, such as saying that "sometimes an experienced person's advice was of great value to younger men."

Wilbur responded six days later:

Until confirmed by you the interview in the New York World...seemed incredible. We never had the slightest ground for suspecting that when you repeatedly spoke to us in 1901 of the originality of our methods, you referred only to our methods of driving tacks, fastening wires, etc., and not to the novelty of our general systems. Neither in 1901, nor in the five years following, did you in any way intimate to us that our general system of lateral control had long been part of the art, and strangely enough, neither your books, addresses or articles, nor the writings of Lilienthal, Langley, Maxim, Hargrave, etc., made any mention whatever of such a system. . . . If the idea was really old in the art, it is somewhat remarkable that a system so important that the individual ownership of it is considered to threaten strangulation of the art was not considered worth mentioning then, nor embodied in any machine built prior to ours.

The patent of Mouillard, to which you refer, does not even mention the control of the lateral balance, nor disclose a system by which it is possible to attain it. I have read . . . what your book says on . . . d'Esterno Le Bris, etc., but I do not find . . . any mention whatever of controlling balance by adjustments of wings to respectively different angles of incidence on the right and left sides. Have you ever found such mention? It is not disputed that every person who is using this system today owes it to us and to us alone. The French aviators freely admit it. No legal disclosure of the system prior to us has yet been produced. Unless something as yet unknown to anybody is brought to light to prove the invention technically known to everybody prior to 1900, our warped judgment will probably continue to be confirmed by the other judges as it was by Judge Hazel at Buffalo.

As to inordinate desire for wealth, you are the only person acquainted with us who has ever made such an accusation. We believed that the physical and financial risks which we took, and the value of the service to the world, justified sufficient compensation to enable us to live modestly with enough surplus income to permit the devotion of our future time to scientific experimenting instead of business. We spent several years of valuable time trying to work out plans which would have made us independent without hampering the invention by the commercial exploitation of the patents. These efforts would have succeeded but for jealousy and envy. It was only when we found that the sale of the patents offered the only way to obtain compensation for our labors of 1900–1906 that we finally permitted the chance of making the invention free to the world to pass from our hands. You apparently concede to us no right to compensate for the solution of a problem ages old except such as is granted to persons who had no part in producing the invention. That is to say, we may compete with mountebanks for a chance to earn money in the mountebank business, but are entitled to nothing whatever for past work as inventors. If holding a different view constitutes us almost criminal, as some seem to think, we are not ashamed. We honestly think that our work of 1900–1906 has been and will be of value to the world, and that the world owes us something as inventors, regardless of whether we personally make Roman holidays for accident-loving crowds.

You mention as a grievance . . . some disparaging remarks concerning your helpfulness to us . . . we also have a grievance extending back to as far as 1902, and on one occasion several years ago we complained to you that an impression was being spread broadcast by newspapers that we were mere pupils and dependents of yours. You indignantly denied that you were responsible for it. When I went to France I found everywhere and impression that we had taken up aeronautical studies at your special instigation . . . in short, that you furnished the science and money while we contributed a little mechanical skill, and that when success had been achieved you magnanimously stepped aside and permitted us to enjoy the rewards. I cannot remember that I ever spoke for publication regarding the matter. . . . However, I several times said privately that we had taken up the study of aeronautics long before we had any acquaintance with you; that our ideas of control were radically different from yours both before and throughout our acquaintance; that the systems of control which we carried to success were absolutely our own, and had been embodied in a machine and tested before you knew anything about them and before our first meeting with you; that in 1900 and 1901 we used the tables and formulas found in books, but finding the results did not agree with the calculations, we had extensive laboratory experiments and prepared tables of our own which we used exclusively in all our subsequent work; that the solution to the screw-propeller problem was ours; that we designed all our machines from first to last, originated and worked out the principles of control, constructed the machines, and made all the tests at our own costs; that you built several machines embodying your ideas in 1901 and 1902 which were tested at our camp by Mr. Herring, but that we had never made a flight on any of your machines, nor your men on any of ours, and that in the sense in which the expression was used in France we had never been pupils of yours, though we had been very close friends, had carried on very voluminous correspondence, and discussed our work very freely with you.

Wilbur ended the letter with a conciliatory gesture—"We have no wish to quarrel with a man toward whom we ought to preserve a feeling of gratitude"—but Chanute would have none of it. "I will answer him in a few days," he wrote Spratt, "but the prospects are that we are having a row. I am reluctant to engage in this, but I think I am entitled to some consideration for such aid as I may have furnished."

Chanute did not answer Wilbur in a few days, but rather in a few months—in May 1910—and then only after Wilbur had again written him, seeking reconciliation and stroking the old man's ego. In Chanute's letter Wilbur learned of his illness.

I am in bad health and threatened with nervous exhaustion. . . . Your letter of April 28th was gratifying, for I own that I felt very much hurt by your letter of January 29th, which I thought both unduly angry and unfair as well as unjust.

I have never given out the impression, either in writing or speech, that you had taken up aeronautics at my instance or were, as you put it, pupils of mine. I have always written and spoke of you as original investigators and worthy of the highest praise. . . .

The difference in opinion between us, i.e., whether the warping of the wings was in the nature of a discovery by yourselves, or had already been proposed and experimented by others, will have to be passed upon by others, but I have always said that you are entitled to immense credit for devising apparatus by which it has been reduced to successful practice.

I hope, upon my return from Europe, that we will be able to resume our former relations.

But that would not be the case. The close friendship—ten years—the voluminous correspondence—more than a thousand letters—had effectively ended. Six months after their final exchange, Octave Chanute died, nearly seventy-nine years old.

America's Channel

Even before the Herring-Curtiss lawsuit bogged down in appeals, Glenn Curtiss had carried on as if there were no restrictive patents on his machine's technology. His luck, however, seemed to collapse. With an untested, underpowered machine (Herring had surreptitiously promised the *Reims Racer* to a department store for display) he failed to get into the air at the same 1909 Hudson-Fulton Celebration in which Wilbur had girdled Liberty—he even met Wilbur and offered his hand, but Wright refused to shake, pleading grease on his own. Then during a company board meeting, the board members ordered Augustus Moore Herring to finally turn over his patents. Herring excused himself, detoured out the door, walked down the street and into hiding—this time for good. Herring-Curtiss quickly imploded under the weight of the Wright lawsuit, but Curtiss could afford to buy back the Hammondsport factory at the auction, and did, and started anew.

Meanwhile, though, Glenn Curtiss traveled to St. Louis, flew in an exhibition there, and then traveled on to the 1910 Los Angeles meet (where tens of thousands turned out just to see him fly) and won $6,500 in the speed and endurance contests. After making his way back across the States, he turned his attention to the *New York World's* $10,000 prize for the first to fly between Albany and New York City. It was touted as America's Channel Crossing, but even more dangerous.

"I fully realized that the flight was much greater than anything I had yet attempted," Curtiss said in his 1912 autobiography, "and even more difficult than Blériot's great flight across the English channel . . . news of which was still ringing throughout the world."

For starters, the flight from Albany to Manhattan would be nearly six times the distance from Calais to Dover, and instead of a nice broad Channel to splash-land in (should he have mechanical trouble), the two cities were linked by a fairly narrow river, the Hudson. "The Hudson flight meant one hundred and fifty-two miles over a broad, swift stream," Curtiss described it dramatically, "flowing between high hills or rugged mountains the entire distance and with seldom a place to land; it meant a fight against treacherous and varying wind currents rushing out unawares through clefts in the mountains."

Dramatics aside, Albany to Manhattan still presented none of the navigational problems inherent in flying out of sight from land: All Curtiss would have to do was just follow the river downstream; the first clump of skyscrapers off to the left would be Manhattan. He would have to stop about halfway for fuel and oil, so while he personally scouted the river for landmarks just before the flight, he kept his eye open for potential landing fields. One such field lay just above Poughkeepsie—on the grounds of the State Hospital for the Insane. Curtiss approached the hospital's superintendent for permission to use the ground.

"Why, certainly, Mr. Curtiss, come right in here," the superintendent replied. "Here's where all the flying machine inventors land." Curtiss decided he liked the looks of a field on the other side of the river instead, near a place called Camelot.

His aeroplane was christened *Hudson Flier* and looked similar to the machines he had built and flown since leaving the AEA—lots of bamboo framing and supports and planes protruding at odd angles in front and back—but with floatational cannisters bolted below the bottom wing, just in case. It was made ready for him at the Hammondsport factory and shipped to Albany. High winds kept it on the ground for four days, but in that time people came from miles around to look upon the machine. "One young [farmer] gazed at it so long and so intently that he finally fell over backwards insensible," Curtiss said. Early on May 31, 1910—a blue, calm Sunday—Curtiss, wearing goggles and sitting erect firmly gripping the high steering wheel with both hands, took off from Rensselaer Island, while an official press train steamed off in hot pursuit.

"The motor sounded like music and the machine handled perfectly," he said. " . . . I heard nothing but the steady, even roar of the motor in perfect rhythm, and the whirr of the propeller." In just over twenty minutes the train got up to 50 miles per hour and caught him. Curtiss matched its speed for a few miles, gaining on it when the railroad tracks meandered with the Hudson. Below he could see the train's great drive wheel working in apparent silence, while people onboard waved their hats. Likewise, he saw folks in the river towns, and on boats in the river itself, standing with their round faces turned skyward waiting for him to fly past, and they too would wave at him. He saw sudden blasts of white steam shooting from tugs and knew they were blowing their whistles for him.

The train turned inland, and pretty soon his little machine had flown far in front of it. Ahead he could now make out the Poughkeepsie bridge, roughly the halfway point. He aimed for the center of the bridge and flew over it at about 150 feet. He thought that just about the entire population of Poughkeepsie was down there—and that they looked like swarming ants. He found the pier that marked his landing field at Camelot and swung his machine wide and swooped in over a clump of trees and landed. A crowd of hyperventilating motorists soon piled around the *Hudson Flier*, and when Curtiss found his fuel had not arrived as scheduled, the motorists pooled their resources and donated a few gallons of gasoline (and some oil, too). Finally, the special train arrived, and the press corps and various dignitaries streamed out over the hill to offer him congratulations and not just for having lived through the flight: For flying that distance nonstop—87 miles—he was now the lead contender for the *Scientific American* Trophy, which would be presented at year's end for the longest nonstop flight.

His mechanic checked the machine over and pronounced it fit to continue, and once refueled, that was just what Curtiss did—this time letting the train leave first. It was the only time the locomotive got ahead of the *Hudson Flier* on this leg.

Curtiss headed down the Hudson at between 500 and 700 feet above the surface. He was rocked by turbulence briefly when the river narrowed at West Point, but all that cleared up as the river widened into the Tappan Zee.

"Soon I caught sight of some of the sky-scrapers that make the sky-line of New York City the most wonderful in the world," he crowed like a booster. "First I saw the tall frame of the Metropolitan Tower, and then the lofty Singer building." He also saw that he was about out of oil, and he landed on a grassy lawn at Inwood, in the verdant Bronx. Leaving his aeroplane unguarded, Curtiss walked to a working public telephone to inform the *New York World* that he had made it to New York City, as required by the prize. And once he got some oil, he said, he was going to continue on to Governor's Island, just to let the folks in the city have a chance to see him. Once again, a crowd had flocked around the machine, and once again a friendly New Yorker donated some oil. They helped turn his propeller over, and then Curtiss was in the air again.

"News of the approach of the aeroplane had spread throughout the city, and I could see crowds everywhere," he said. "New York can turn out a million people probably quicker than any other place on earth, and it certainly looked as though half of the population was along Riverside Drive or on top of the thousands of apartment houses that stretch for miles along the river." Over the roar of his motor, Curtiss could even hear the sirens and whistles of the ships and the cheers of the crowds. He flew the length of Manhattan, above its piers and below its tallest buildings, and before landing as promised on Governor's Island he swung west to circle the Statue of Liberty.

After the flight, Curtiss was herded to a luncheon sponsored by the *World* and then to a banquet at the Hotel Astor, where he was presented the *World's* prize. At year's end he was formally notified that the *Scientific American* Trophy was his—permanently.

But by the time he landed on Governor's Island, Glenn Curtiss had replaced the Wrights in the hearts and minds of Americans: He was now the country's—the world's—greatest aviator. The statistics, after all, were in his favor. The total air time was 2:51, and he had averaged 52 miles per hour, easily beating his own speed record of 47 mph (which he had set on the closed 20-kilometer course at Reims less than a year before). He was the first aviator to link two major U.S. cities. And he had also beaten the special train—although that was no real surprise to Manhattan commuters. But the feat was more than all that. Curtiss had flown America's officially designated successor to the English Channel flight, and for the time being, he had single-handedly allowed America to retain its worldwide leadership in world aeronautics.

Hair-raising Evolutions

The Wright Company had by now started selling its authentic, licensed aeroplanes in America, though prospective purchasers had to agree to not overfly crowded cities like New York. Nonetheless, from the moment it was founded, the company was a financial success. Could there possibly be a better name in aviation?

The brothers longed to get back to experimenting again, but the business of the business consumed their energies. They still found the time to continue perfecting the machine. As the power of their engines increased, they found the machine increased its tendency to undulate at higher speeds. To help stabilize his flyer, Wilbur took off one plane from its forward double elevator and fixed it behind the machine, just ahead of the vertical rudder. Finding his machine flew more stable that way, he made the rear plane a movable surface and chucked the forward elevator altogether. Lately, he had even taken off with wheels bolted under the machine's skids.

After collecting the $15,000 from his Governor's Island flight during that 1909 Hudson-Fulton Celebration, Wilbur reconsidered his harsh attitude toward exhibition flying: after all, the aeroplane-building business would take some time to get going; yet right now tens of thousands—maybe even hundreds of thousands—were willing to pay up to a dollar each just to behold the miracle of a flying machine in action. After all, cash receipts for the twelve-day Los Angeles air meet totaled $137,520. While this mountebank game was too low an occupation for the Wrights themselves, they could hire others to do it for them. And so Wilbur went about forming a flying team, like the loose group of fliers that had flown Curtiss machines at Los Angeles. The Wrights would charge the exhibition $5,000 for each aeroplane they supplied, plus $1,000 a day for each pilot, plus keep any prize money won by their pilot, who would for his trouble be paid twenty dollars per week, plus fifty dollars extra each day he flew. There would be rules of pilot conduct, of course: no gambling, no drinking, and especially no flying on Sundays. As team promoter the brothers hired a fellow Ohioan and dirigible exhibitionist from way back named Roy Knabenshue, who, before Fort Myer, before France, had approached them to ask if they would sell him a few machines for public exhibition. Now that they had reconsidered their position on exhibitions, Knabenshue agreed to handle the Wright team and booked them into aeronautical meets in the summer of 1910 at Indianapolis, Montreal, Atlantic City, and at the second international meet at Long Island in October, where the second Gordon Bennett race would be held.

Orville traveled south to scope out a site for a winter training school and ended up down in Montgomery, Alabama. There—from a hangar billboarded with the slogan, OUR PRICES LIKE "WILBUR" ARE "WRIGHT" BUT THEY ARE NOT "UP IN THE AIR"—Orville trained a trusted Daytonan, Brookie Brookins, who in turn instructed others handpicked for the team by the Wrights. Returning to the ever-expanding facilities at Simms Station in the early summer, Orville and Brookie continued instructing more pilots.

There wasn't much to training. Orville would tell a student some of what he knew, take him up, and let him get the feel of the machine. Should the engine quit, Orville often advised the student—perhaps facetiously—that he should consider plowing it into the nearest clump of trees. If he needed more instruction, the student could practice balancing on an old machine that Orville had rigged up inside one of the sheds at Simms Station. Usually after a total of around three hours' dual instruction, the fledgling was ready to fly solo.

One day late in May 1910, Wilbur and Orville took their eighty-two-year-old father out to Simms Station. Orville took Wilbur up, the first and only time they were up in the air together, and then Orville flew the bishop around for a few minutes, his first and only flight ever. Orv took him to 350 feet. "Higher, higher" was all he said.

There must have been something in the blood.

They shipped five machines to Indianapolis in June, and a few days later the Wright Aeronautical team followed, making its debut exhibition at the Indianapolis Motor Speedway. Brookins set a new altitude record of 6,234 feet, becoming the first man to fly an aeroplane above one mile—after which his motor died and he glided, sank actually, to an open field just off the racetrack. Pilot Frank Coffyn soloed, and besides a few lackluster laps around the Speedway, that was about as exciting as things got the first time out. And that was about as exciting as Wilbur wanted to keep it.

Their early shows got lukewarm reviews compared with those of the Curtiss team. So as the exhibition season progressed, the Wright pilots began taking more risks. Maybe they couldn't fly on Sundays like the Curtiss boys, but no one was going to say they were feather-weights.

Brookins, the leader, cracked up his machine during August's Asbury Park, New Jersey, exhibition. As he was trying to land, a group of about fifty newspaper photographers decided to try to capture the event and rushed onto the landing field. Brookins was low, coming down fast without power, and had no choice but to plow straight into them. Seven were injured, including one young boy who was trapped beneath the aeroplane, while Brookins received a broken nose, ankle, and several busted teeth. "And the machine was a complete wreck," he said.

The brothers rolled out a new machine to replace Brookins's machine. It was called a Model B, had a six-cylinder motor and two pusher propellers, two 39-foot wings, and a 28-foot length; it weighed 1,250 pounds and seated two, including the pilot. Both were left unguarded by the elevator, which was now mounted aft on open-to-the-air longerons behind the rudder. The skids had shrunk to vestiges and grew wheels and triangular blinkers, which helped stabilize the machine while it rolled over on its side in a banking turn. Not only was it less likely to break into uncontrolled undulations, the Model B was also faster and more maneuverable than the old-style machines that the team had been flying.

Wright team members Arch Hoxsey and Ralph Johnstone made the most of it. The pair, who nicknamed themselves the Star Dust Twins, had formed a rivalry of daring bordering on insanity. Now each took turns in the new machine, each wildly twisting, turning, dipping, sliding, curving, spiraling, and diving, each trying to out-fly the other. "Undaunted by the accident to young Brookins yester-day, they went through a series of hair-raising evolutions which made today's exhibition one of the greatest demonstrations of eccentric aeroplane riding ever seen in America," one paper reported. " . . . Pandemonium broke loose. Women cried their approval, while men yelled themselves hoarse."

One spectator not so positive: Wilbur Wright.

"I am very much in earnest when I say that I want no stunts and spectacular frills put on the flights there," he wrote to Hoxsey a few shows down the road. "Anything beyond plain flying will be chalked up as a fault and not a credit."

Still, it was evident to just about everyone: In exhibition flying, the Wright machines had maneuverability and sturdiness over their rivals, but they'd lost the edge on speed to the Blériots, the Voisins, the Farmans, and, especially insulting, their American rivals, the Curtisses. Orville wanted to change that fact and take the Gordon Bennett Trophy away from Curtiss at the same time during that second international aviation meet, at Belmont Park, Long Island.

He brought to the windy competition that October a new machine built for speed. It had a new, light, and powerful eight-cylinder engine, and small thin biplane wings 21 feet long with a total area of just 140 feet—less than a quarter of the Model B. Orville took the machine to Belmont and flew it unofficially at 70 miles per hour, and people started calling it the *Baby Grand*. But while trying it out on the blustery day he was to go for the cup, Brookins lost engine power, and the *Baby Grand* plunged into the ground and flipped over. Later that day, dashing Claude Grahame-White, a wealthy playboy Brit who couldn't care less about the Wrights' pesky patent-infringement business, took home the Gordon Bennett by flying 61 mph over the race's now-100-kilometer course in his unlicensed Blériot XI. In another highly watched race, in another unlicensed Blériot, Johnny Moisant was the fastest to fly from the Belmont racetrack, over Brooklyn, around the Statue of Liberty, and back, winning $10,000. At his victory party at the Astor Hotel that evening, Moisant promised a twenty-seven-year-old drama critic named Harriet Quimby that he'd teach her to fly Blériots.

The meet was not a total wash for the Wrights. Johnstone raised the world altitude record to 9,714 feet (compare that with the 508-foot record set a year earlier at Reims), and all together the Wright team took home $35,000 from Belmont, including $15,000 in prizes. The company, declaring a dividend of $80,000, voted the brothers $10,000.

The Wright team headed west, to a November exhibition in the mile-high city of Denver, Colorado, where the air was barely thick enough to support a flying machine. (In fact, the mile-altitude mark had only been surpassed by Brookins a few months before.) On the second day of the show, Johnstone pushed his machine to 800 feet above the ground, pulled off his power, and began his trademark spiral glide with its steep banks. But in the second turn, something went wrong: Johnstone seemed to lose control of the machine. Then from 500 feet it plunged straight into the ground. His broken body was found near the wreck. Spectators rushed to the crash and looted the site—they even tore the gloves from Johnstone's dead fingers.

From eyewitness reports, Wilbur figured that nothing was wrong with the machine; Johnstone had simply fallen out of the seat.

On the last day of the year, at the second Los Angeles meet, surviving Star Dust Twin Arch Hoxsey was climbing to beat the new altitude record of 11,474 feet—which he had just set a few days before. Before reaching his goal, Hoxsey suddenly started spiraling downward. "The cheering subsided to a silent prayer for the man in the frail thing of cloth and sticks," wrote one reporter. Just 500 feet above ground, the machine suddenly cartwheeled. The crowd swore they could hear spars snapping and cloth ripping, and then they saw the machine tumble to the ground.

When they pulled his body free from the tangle of wire and cloth, Hoxsey barely resembled a human being. This time Hoxsey's mechanics fought off looters with uprights pulled from the wreckage.

The team remained an entity for a few more months, though in reality the brothers were finished with the mountebank business.

Seat belts became standard features on Wright machines.

In November 1910 Orville left for Berlin again, to tour their holdings in Europe. He was met by Comte de Lambert with some bad news: the French company had just gone under and had turned its licensing rights over to another company, all of which the Wrights thought was part of some shadowy larger scheme. Even though French pilots were said to prefer Wright machines to the others, "our company is in such bad repute with the government that it could not do business," Orville wrote Wilbur. Things were not much better in Germany: "I had no more than got out of sight last year until every man in the shop was making improvements on the machine, and . . . in a short time they had so many on, that the machine couldn't carry them all." It got worse, too. While workmanship and materials the Germans used were first class, the Wrights were being paid no royalties for many of their own machines. "I have about made up my mind to let the European business go," he said. "I don't propose to be bothered with it all my life and I see no prospect of its ever amounting to anything unless we send a representative here to stay to watch our interests."

Amazing Firsts

From 1910 on into 1911, there seemed to be some new incredible aviation first happening everywhere. In Germany, Count Ferdinand von Zeppelin began flying passengers between cities with his fleet of six huge airships with rigid frames. In America, right after the Los Angeles meet, Louis Paulhan flew while his passenger, Lieutenant Paul Beck, tossed dummy bombs out of the Voisin. In Britain, Charles Rolls flew across the Channel in his Wright Model B, tossed a letter addressed to the Aéro-Club de France, and flew back with-

Wilbur flies a lucky passenger at Pau, 1909.

ABOVE
Louis Blériot flies his 1909 Channel-crossing monoplane, *Blériot XI*.

BELOW
September 1911: Cal Rodgers sets off from Brooklyn in the *Vin Fiz Flyer*.

ABOVE
A two-place Curtiss hydroaeroplane, circa 1911. Similar to the single-seat
1910 *Hudson Flier.*

BELOW
While hangers-on restrain her Blériot XI (these early machines had no brakes,
after all), Harriet Quimby gets some over-the-shoulder instruction on compass navigation before taking off from Dover on her 1912 Channel crossing.
Note flotation bag inside trellis fuselage.

ABOVE
The shape of things to come: A Déperdussin racer whizzes low and fast past an early airfield.

BELOW
Proof positive that Samuel Langley would have flown first had he had 1914's aerodynamic knowledge in 1903. The place: Lake Keuka; the pilot: Glenn Curtiss.

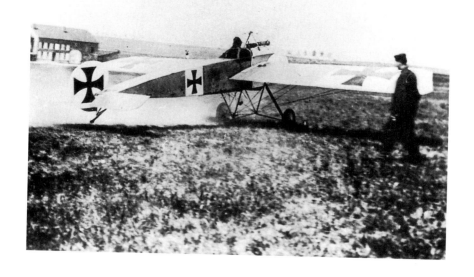

ABOVE
1915: With a machine gun mounted on its nose, a Fokker Eindecker goes hunting.

BELOW
A Sopwith Camel, introduced late in World War I.

America's ace-of-aces Eddie Rickenbacker, and the business end of his Spad
fighter.

The face of a modern combat pilot: Frank Luke, beside his 1918 Spad.

June 1919: Alcock and Brown's Vickers Vimy on the ground in Newfoundland, its nose pointed toward Ireland 1,890 miles away.

out stopping. Back in the United States, Glenn Curtiss managed to fly his machine while he tossed dummy bombs onto a target the shape of a battleship. Curtiss pilot Eugene Ely closed November 1910 by flying the *Hudson Flier* off the deck of the cruiser USS Birmingham and opened January 1911 by landing his machine—at about 40 mph—on a wooden platform mounted on the deck of the USS Pennsylvania. Ely hooked his machine on a series of sandbag-weighted ropes draped at intervals across the platform; they dragged him to a stop within a hundred feet. To make the machine more useful to the current needs of the Navy—naval commanders wanted a machine to hoist off and onto the deck of a battleship—Curtiss took what he'd learned from the *Loon* experiments and built a successful hydroaeroplane. It had a large pontoon with a stepped bottom, which broke the suction created when the float's hard surface sped over the water.

Each time there was some such grand new innovation, the conquering pilot—with the exception of the we-were-first Wright brothers—always spoke of his feat with grand, feverish zealotry: He and she weren't gladiators in latter-day Roman holidays but actually missionaries bringing the new and valuable science of aeronautics to the masses.

Wait a minute—she?

In France, Madame la Baronne de Laroche had received her pilot's certificate in March 1910, the thirty-sixth to be awarded by the Aéro-Club de France. After Glenn Curtiss formed his exhibition team, he wanted to add a woman pilot for the added draw of novelty and had begun instructing Blanche Scott. Scott soloed, in public, at an aeronautical meet in Fort Wayne, Indiana, but Curtiss cooled to the idea of Blanche flying. (She later asked Orville to finish her training, but he turned her down. Women were too nervous to fly, he said, though in truth he was probably too nervous to teach them.)

Alert American reporters had lately spotted a woman flying Blériots out at the new Moisant flying school on Long Island.

Johnny Moisant had made good on his promise to teach Harriet Quimby to fly, though he did so from the grave.

On a not-too-financially-successful tour with his own flying team, formed after the 1910 Belmont meet, Johnny died in a crash during a December show in New Orleans (and got the airfield there named after him; so began an enduring American tradition). His older brother, Alfred, realized the best way to get out of the exhibition business while staying in aviation was to start a flying school, which he did with a few Blériots and an instructor from France. Soon after, Quimby approached *him* about teaching her to fly, which she would write about in a series for *Leslie's Weekly*. Moisant recognized the potential for publicity and allowed Quimby lessons. Harriet then went to his sister, Matilde Moisant, and talked her into giving it a try, and Alfred had to say yes. But he made Matilde promise: No exhibitions.

They learned to fly like all Blériot students: alone, in the calm early-morning air. There were no two-seated, dual-control Blériot machines just yet, so the student's first series of lessons was in *Saint Geneviève,* an underpowered machine named for the French patron saint of fliers. Students would learn to roll *Saint Geneviève* across the field and steer in a straight line. (Trickier than it sounds because of the torque of its single engine's single propeller, *Saint Geneviève* always wanted to swerve to the right.) Once on the field's far side, the student would cut the power, mechanics would turn the aeroplane around, and the student would try rolling back to the starting point. After mastering that stage, students moved up to the *Grasshopper,* a Blériot with the throttle wired back to prevent the student from applying full power. In *Grasshopper* they could run down the field and hop six to eight feet into the air, cut power, be turned around, and run back again. Finally came the *Goat,* a real Blériot machine in which the student would take off, circle back, and land. Assuming they'd survived uninjured so far, the student could try for their Aero

Club of America license by landing within 165 feet of a designated point (a muslin marker on the ground), fly figure eights around a pair of pylons, and fly to an altitude of 164 feet. After 33 lessons of between two and five minutes each, Quimby passed the qualification requirements, becoming the first American female to do so. In the official letter recognizing the fact, the Aero Club stodgily offered her congratulations for a spot landing that was "the most accurate landing ever made in America on a monoplane under official supervision."

Too nervous, Orville?

A few days after Quimby, Matilde Moisant also received her official Aero Club of America pilot's certificate.

Matilde honored her brother's wish and flew no exhibitions; she lived to see old age. Harriet Quimby followed a different path. Hoping to become the female Blériot, in April 1912 she became the first woman to fly across the English Channel, but the event was overshadowed when the *Titanic* sank the day before. Less than three months later, at the Harvard-Boston air meet, Quimby was flying over Dorchester Bay in a sluggish Blériot machine modified to carry a passenger. The meet's organizer was in the passenger's seat and he shifted his weight; the Blériot dipped suddenly and threw both from its back like children off a fractious horse. They tumbled 1,000 feet and landed in five feet of water and mud. Both died on impact.

Vin Fiz

Louis Paulhan had skedaddled from the United States following the Wright-induced injunction, but he resurfaced in England, and after a closely watched race against Grahame-White, Paulhan won the £10,000 London *Daily Mail* prize for first flight between London and Manchester. The papers rounded up the usual suspects for comment, and they quoted Wilbur Wright as saying the first transatlantic flight would be the next big step in aeronautics.

He was wrong. A figure even more powerful than Wilbur had decided what the next big step would be.

Everywhere in America, exhibition pilots were making fortunes becoming the first to fly between two big cities: Philadelphia and New York, St. Louis and New York, Chicago and New York. Major newspapers in each put up the prizes to boost circulation. It was as if America, having in the last hundred years or so tamed a vast continent with great success, now had the chance to quickly relive the experience—only this time in front of witnesses, before the cameras, for the reporters, and from the air. In the autumn of 1910, after the bright storm of publicity died away from Curtiss's Albany-to–New York flight, William Randolph Hearst offered $50,000 to the first to fly America from coast to coast in under thirty days. Good for one year, the offer expired on October 10, 1911.

It was September 1911 before anyone got to work on the Hearst prize.

In San Francisco, a pilot named Robert Fowler took off in his Wright Model B, planning to head through the Donner Pass, 7,000 feet high, expecting to make 175 to 500 miles a day, and to streak across the country in twenty days. Two days out, a control wire broke on Fowler's machine, and he set it down in a clump of trees, for he was Wright-trained. Fowler was unhurt, but the machine was pretty well torn up, so he had to wait around for twelve days while it was being repaired. He hadn't even gotten out of California.

A few days later, on the other side of the country—Brooklyn, New York, to be exact—tall, sturdy, and solemn Cal Rodgers stood silently by his brand-spanking-new six-cylinder 32-foot span, single-seat, specially built Wright Model EX while a young woman poured grape soda on its skid and officially christened it the *Vin Fiz Flyer.*

The soda dripping from the skid was Vin Fiz, "The Ideal Grape Drink," owned by the Armour Company of Chicago. Armour is usually associated with meat-packing, but lest anyone mistake what product the company was promoting by sponsoring the flight (with five bucks per mile and a special three-car train stuffed with mechanics and spare parts), the Vin Fiz logo—a succulent bunch of purple grapes and VIN FIZ in green letters—appeared on the rudder, the blinkers, and very substantially on the bottom of the wing.

It was late in the afternoon before the thirty-two-year-old Rodgers climbed up in the pilot's seat, clenched a cigar between his teeth, and signaled for his props to be turned over. The engine came to life, and Cal took off and climbed over Sheepshead Bay. He rained Vin Fiz flyers onto Coney Island, buzzed Brooklyn and Manhattan, and banked toward New Jersey, where he picked up his iron compass, the railroad, following it to his first planned stop: Middletown, New York.

Eighty-four miles down; four thousand, two hundred thirty-one miles to go.

Landing inside a circle formed by five hundred automobiles in a field near Middletown, he was greeted by nearly ten thousand people, and there he spent the night. Up bright and early the next morning, Rodgers promptly hit a tree on takeoff and demolished the *Vin Fiz Flyer*. So Cal actually spent a couple of nights in Middletown. Luckily, his chief mechanic was Charlie Taylor, who had left the Wright Company to join Rodgers after a new Wright factory manager told him that the brothers kept him employed only out of nostalgia.* In two days Charlie managed to piece together a serviceable *Vin Fiz Flyer* from spare parts aboard the train. Once again Cal was off, "above the air currents going faster than the wind," and clocking 74 mph on the 95 miles to Hancock, New

---

*Orville was later shocked to hear this and offered to hire Charlie back after his services with Rodgers were no longer needed.

York, where a spark plug popped out of the engine and Cal broke a skid while landing in a potato field alongside the train tracks. The machine was fixed quickly enough, and the next morning he set out following the tracks for Elmira, New York—only to set down in Scranton, Pennsylvania. A delighted crowd gathered, told him he was lost, got him gas, and propped him, but mostly they descended on the *Vin Fiz Flyer* with pencils and covered the aeroplane with their signatures. "I nearly lost my temper when a man came up with a chisel to punch his autograph on an upright," said Cal, who doubled back and made Elmira before nightfall. Taking off the next morning, he slammed into a telegraph pole; when he got flying later that day, he blew out another spark plug and smashed a wingtip trying to land. Repaired again by the next day, he took off and was soon forced down with more ignition problems on the Allegany Indian Reservation. That afternoon, Rodgers slammed into a barbed-wire fence while trying to take off, again demolishing the *Vin Fiz Flyer*.

On the other side of the country, Robert Fowler had completed repairs to his machine and kept attempting to cross the Donner Pass like a puppy trying to jump a fence. He just couldn't get enough altitude. No fool, Fowler decided that if he couldn't leap over the Continental Divide, he would go around it, and he flew off down the coast to Los Angeles.

In the re-rebuilt *Vin Fiz Flyer*, Cal Rodgers took off and finally put New York State behind him, following the Erie Railroad into Ohio and landing just short of Akron's smokestacks 204 miles later. Bad weather held him down for a day, then he hopped another two hundred miles into Rivare, Indiana. The next day there was more foul weather, but Cal took off anyway and found himself overrun by a thunderstorm. He managed to let down through a hole in the clouds, landing in a shallow depression surrounded by trees, and sat out the storm under the wing of the *Vin Fiz Flyer*, puffing a cigar. He made Huntington, Indiana, by nightfall. Next day he tried taking off downwind—to mitigate the effects of gusts, he said—but the machine refused to rise. As Rodgers swerved to avoid a group of spectators, his wing dug into the ground, and the *Vin Fiz* was demolished yet again.

Two days later, Charlie Taylor again had the machine good as new, and Cal made Hammond, Indiana, where he was grounded two days by bad weather. On October 8, Rodgers finally arrived at the home of the Ideal Grape Drink—Chicago—three weeks and a thousand miles after setting off. (And to think only a year earlier it had taken Glenn Curtiss less than three hours to cover just under 200 miles.) Only one problem remained before Cal completed the journey: The contest expired in two days. Would he quit?

"I am bound for Los Angeles and the Pacific Ocean," Cal Rodgers said. "Prize or no prize, that's where I am bound and if canvas, steel, and wire together with a little brawn, tendon, and brain stick with me, I mean to get there. . . . I'm going to do this whether I get five thousand dollars or fifty cents or nothing. I am going to cross this continent simply to be the first to cross in an aeroplane."

With that Rodgers was off again, heading southwest from Chicago instead of due west because of the Rockies. He landed for the night just past Lockport, Illinois, then made Springfield, Missouri the next day; Marshall, Missouri, the next, and Overland Park, Kansas, the next. After two more days of bad weather, he got off and made Vinita, Oklahoma, sat out a day for bad weather, took off and stopped briefly for the crowds at the state fair in Muskogee, and made an evening of it at McAlester, Oklahoma. Cal flew a personal record of 265 miles the next day, ending up at Fort Worth. He flew the *Vin Fiz Flyer* over to Dallas and the Texas State Fair the next day. Then Waco, then Austin, then engine failure and a day waiting for its replacement, then San Antonio and a day of rest. He got to Spofford, Texas, the day after that but crashed taking off the next day, and the machine was destroyed yet again.

The mechanics had it rebuilt again by the next morning.

Off for Sanderson, Texas . . . Sierra Blanca . . . El Paso . . . Willcox, Arizona . . . and Tucson, where he stopped to chat with Fowler, who was heading as doggedly in the other direction but not making nearly as good time . . . then Maricopa . . . Phoenix . . . Stoval Siding . . . and finally into the Golden State, California. Over the Salton Sea his engine exploded, and he landed at Imperial and watched while a doctor plucked engine fragments from his arm for two hours. The old plug-popping engine was overhauled and installed by the next day, so Cal hopped up in the machine, took off, and got to Banning, California, before the spark plugs popped out again. By late the next afternoon, Cal Rodgers finally flew into Pasadena, where he was greeted by thousands, wrapped in an American flag, and paraded around the field. He had flown 82 hours over forty-nine days, averaging nearly 52 miles per hour. He predicted that soon it would be possible to make the trip in under thirty days—but he was no longer the one to do it.

"I prefer an automobile with a good driver to a biplane," he said.

Still, it really didn't seem over yet, not until he reached the ocean. A week after landing in Pasadena, Cal took off again, flying toward Long Beach. Halfway there he lost the engine and crashed into a plowed field. He was dragged unconscious from the wreckage. Though only his ankle was broken, the machine was destroyed for a fifth time. One month later, on December 10, he hobbled up to the waiting aeroplane, shoved his crutches under his seat, and took off. In only a few minutes Cal Rodgers landed the *Vin Fiz Flyer* before nearly fifty thousand screaming fans and symbolically washed the last of the sticky grape soda off his skid—though in truth only two uprights and the rudder remained from the original machine that had departed from Sheepshead Bay.

Less than five months later, Rodgers flew a Wright Model B into a flock of sea gulls and crashed into the surf just a few feet away from where the *Vin Fiz Flyer* had finished its cross-country trip. Trapped beneath the machine, Rodgers drowned while spectators fought over pieces of the wreckage.

Flying Too Near the Sun

While Cal Rodgers was winging his way toward Chicago, Orville Wright was on his way to Kitty Hawk for the first time in three years with a new experimental flying machine.

After the Wright Company was formed, Orville naturally became head of engineering and looked after how their machines were being manufactured, while Wilbur, as president, found himself immersed in the patent-infringement suits in the United States and abroad. It turned into an obsession for him: he gave up experimenting, and he even gave up aviating, except when he tried to fly a Curtiss machine out at Simms Station—which he found difficult. But then, he was flying it to gain grist for the litigation mill instead of furthering aeronautics.

While the Curtiss appeal continued to slither and crawl its way through the U.S. court system, Wilbur rushed to Europe, this time to testify in their major suit against twelve aviators in France. Their suit against Santos-Dumont was dismissed, since he had never tried to make a profit from his machines, but the Wrights won against the other eleven, who, instead of coughing up thousands of dollars in royalties, promptly decided to appeal the decision and buy some more time—perhaps until the Wrights' patent expired.

Wilbur then went to Germany, where the court ruled that his 1901 Chicago speech, plus the one Chanute gave in Paris in 1903— in which he said "to assure transverse equilibrium, the operator works two cords, which warp the right and left wings and at the same time adjust the vertical rudder"—constituted prior disclosure.* "The German Patent Office has taken the extreme position that these few words were sufficient to teach anyone how to build and operate a flying machine in 1903," Wilbur fumed in a letter to the editor of *Scientific American.* "It is rather amusing," he wrote to a friend, "after having been called fools and fakers for six or eight years, to find now that people knew exactly how to fly all the time."

Now it was the Wrights' turn to appeal, and that, too, would take years. Worse, the Wright companies in both countries had continued to decay, not only from mismanagement but also from bum motors. Wilbur returned home exhausted, at the same time that Orville was preparing that new Wright machine, a glider. With Wilbur determined to doggedly pursued domestic litigation, Orville left for the wonderful desolation of Kitty Hawk without him.

He did take along their older brother Lorin and his ten-year-old son Horace, and they all had a great time rebuilding camp and setting up the machine—which was configured much like the Model B, with the elevator in back.

They tweaked it for its best performance and flew it for astonishing lengths of time: seven minutes, five minutes, nine minutes and forty-five seconds, and covering just 40 yards! But the press had gotten wind of the trials, and as more reporters kept arriving, Orville decided to postpone testing the *other* reason why he had traveled all the way to Kitty Hawk. He had actually designed and built aerial navigation's Holy Grail: a device that created automatic stability, the advancement that would once and for all perfect the flying machine, silence the critics who said the Wright machines were too unstable, and stupefy the detractors who said that the brothers had begun to lose the edge on technology.

With the revolutionary device untried, they packed up and returned in November.

---

*Chanute's speech took place two weeks after the Wrights filed for their French patent, so that defense was overruled in France.

As winter turned to spring, Wilbur gave an exhaustive series of depositions in preparation for the Curtiss trials. "The amount of his intellectuality, in describing their invention was marvelous," wrote the bishop. "It must have greatly wearied him."

It *was* marvelous: Wilbur gave page after page of brilliant, equanimous testimony that chronicled their discovery of the flying machine, lucidly explaining complex principles of aerodynamics to jurists educated to pilot only a horse and buggy. Daedalus-like he once used a string to lead the court through the maze of the forces acting on a turning aeroplane: "If it hadn't been for Wright and that damn piece of string, we would have won," said the defense attorney.

And it *was* wearying: the stream of witnesses who stayed for dinner with the Wrights noticed that Wilbur grew ever thinner and paler. After an early May family picnic at Hawthorn Hill (a huge tract in Dayton that they had purchased to build a columned mansion Orville was designing), Wilbur went to bed with a fever. It was diagnosed as typhoid, the same disease that had almost killed Orville back in the beginning, in 1896. Wilbur recovered after a bit—these things seemed to last about a week—and wrote a letter insisting urgency to his patent lawyer, who wanted to delay the Curtiss proceedings. "Unnecessary delays by stipulation of counsel have already destroyed fully three fourths of the value of our patent," he said. "The opportunities of the last two years will never return again. At the present moment almost innumerable competitors are entering the field, and for the first time are producing machines which will really fly. These machines are being put on the market at one half less than the price which we have been selling our machines for."

Six days later, Wilbur's fever remained high. He called for his lawyer, Ezra Kuhns, who witnessed the signing of his will, along with the Wrights' secretary, Miss Mabel Beck. He slowly regained strength over the next week, though when he found out that Orv had left town briefly (to deliver their newest and latest, the Model C machine, to the government), Wilbur grew so agitated over his brother's absence that he had to be given a sedative intravenously. He slipped into unconsciousness, and Orville hurried back. Even older brother Reuchlin, living in Kansas and somewhat estranged from the family, was called for.

Wilbur seemed to get better over the next couple of days. Then slowly, he sank.

Thursday, May 30, 1912 *This morning at 3:15 Wilbur passed away, aged 45 years, 1 month and 14 days. A short life, full of consequences. An unfailing intellect, imperturbable temper, great self-reliance and as great modesty, seeing the right clearly, pursuing it steadily, he lived and died. Many called—many telegrams (probably over a thousand).*

—Bishop Wright's diary

It had come true, that sentence Wilbur had written to Octave Chanute in the very first letter between them only twelve years earlier—but already in another age. He had proved, as he said he intended to, that flight was possible to man. And not only had it cost him an increased amount of money, it had also cost him his life.

What a Show

When you took a good look around, it seemed as though aviation had stagnated in America.

Elsewhere, men had designed radical new machines, especially in France. Armand Déperdussin had built a sleek little bullet of a monoplane with a smooth one-piece "monocoque" fuselage of thin tulipwood, light and strong like an eggshell, and powered by the latest air-cooled Gnome rotary engine, which revolved on its crankshaft like a spoked wheel on an axle and thus cooled itself efficiently while kicking up a wicked torque. At the fourth Gordon Bennett Trophy in Chicago that year, the Déperdussin racer won with a top speed of 108 mph. There were other incredible innovations as well: the Antoinette Latham Monobloc, for example, was a big three-seater completely covered with aluminum sheeting (down to pants surrounding the wheels), and with all its bracing and control wires tucked away cleanly inside its thick wing. Though grossly under-powered and overweight, it held promise—had not company founder Hubert Latham gotten himself gored to death by a recalci-trant wounded buffalo while great-white-hunting in French Equatorial Africa. Weary himself of courting danger and always painfully finding it, Louis Blériot had retired at the end of 1909, though he kept his count going and was now up to the pencil-thin, streamlined *Blériot XXXVI.** In Paris a Baron Odkolok had built a seat that would use explosives to eject a pilot from a stricken craft. In Germany, the gossamer and stable Etrich Taube was be-ginning to be built by a handful of indigenous manufacturers. In England A. V. Roe had built a midwing monoplane shaped like a guppy because its cockpit fully enclosed its pilot. Even Russia had become an outpost of aviation. After experimenting with heli-copters, engineer Igor Sikorsky turned to something easy and built the first successful four-motored aeroplane—the eight-passenger, 9,000-pound *Le Grand;* its immediate descendant had a promenade deck on the spine of the fuselage so passengers could stretch their legs in flight.

By the end of 1912, France would have almost a thousand pi-lots, compared with under 400 in England and 350 in Germany. But in America, birthplace of the aeroplane, there were fewer than 200

---

*Yet it was his classic, simple, infinitely adaptable XI that kept showing up everywhere, in both manufactured and homebuilt versions. One of the latter category even sprang up in as remote a place as tiny Wichita, Kansas, shaped by the hands of a young Clyde Cessna.

pilots. The environment was simply too harsh. If a man wanted to build an aeroplane himself for his own private, uncommercial use, that was fine with the Wright Company; it just levied a modest, one-time licensing fee, now usually around five percent of the machine's value. When one pilot named Glenn Martin built his first machine, he contacted the company and said that he probably could not pay the full fee and asked what they would accept. Because he was of upstanding moral character—Martin never dated and revered his mother—Orville waived the fee. For most manufacturers, though, any fee at all was prohibitive, and so only a few companies sprouted, and they survived only weakly.

Even air meets had begun to loose their novelty. While hundreds of thousands showed up for the first two Gordon Bennett races, the crowd for the third measured in the mere thousands. (Though the cup was won by America that year, both pilot and machine were French, hired by the Aero Club of America.)

Fans had grown a little jaded about stunt pilots flying the same old circuits around a pylon, and the aeroplane-versus-automobile races featuring the famous stunt pilot Lincoln Beachey* flying his primordial, exoskeletal Curtiss machine against famous Indy racers like Barney Oldfield and Eddie Rickenbacker. At the third annual Los Angeles aerial exhibition in 1912, though, spectators were in for a treat, for the promoters had come up with something new: a "mimic aerial battle" at nighttime. Around three thousand people showed up, and two aviators participated: Lincoln Beachey with his Curtiss machine; and the same Glenn Martin just mentioned, known as the Flying Dude for his foppish black leather costume, with a machine pretty much copied from Glenn Curtiss's after his 1910 visit. There was noise and the fireworks and searchlights from

---

*Robert Frost was so impressed by Beachey that he wrote a short poem about the aviator—not Frost's best work, however.

naval ships in the harbor bearing down and following the roaring, whining aeroplanes, while the aviators tossed their bombs onto a miniature fortress on the ground, utterly destroying it, and likewise throwing bombs on "enemy" warships with quite some accuracy, or so the naval observers said. It behooved them to have a successful show if they wanted to keep the newly organized naval air service organized, well funded, and well equipped with renegade Glenn Curtiss's new hydroaeroplanes. Soldiers on the ground fired round after round at the pair of heroes in the black sky, but to no avail; their rifles were loaded with blanks, naturally. The crowd was delighted nonetheless by the flash, smoke, and deep, loud percussions—by the thrill of its own bombardment.

What a show it was.

More than a year after the Los Angeles meet, the Flying Dude boldly formed a manufacturing company and sold a machine to Mexican rebels, who five times that year tried dropping homemade bombs on a government gunship in Guamas Harbor. Five times they failed. Perhaps the rebels should have purchased the Flying Dude's services as well: Aside from being an accomplished nighttime bomber, during daytime exhibitions Martin could hit a toy balloon with a rifle while flying his machine.

The Moisant team, by the way, had long before been to Mexico for a purpose similar to that of the Martin machine, only for the opposite side. Right after the death of Johnny Moisant, the team flew reconnaissance for the Mexican government. French Blériot pilot Roland Garros was touring with them then, and during missions he liked to toss oranges at the rebels below. Garros would go on to fly many landmark flights: from Paris to Rome (and before a papal audience); and then across the Mediterranean nonstop in a new Morane-Saulnier monoplane, 470 miles in just under eight hours. At home his puppy-dog eyes and overbite became much adored. In America he was just another unwelcome patent-infringer.

Orville Takes Over with a Vengeance

The day of the funeral, twenty-five thousand mourners filed past Wilbur Wright's casket. At 3:30 P.M. the entire city of Dayton stopped to observe three minutes' silence. Even the telephone company shut off service at that time.

While closing the business of Wilbur's life, Orville Wright became convinced that the patent-infringement suits had been responsible for Wilbur's death; that Glenn Curtiss had, in effect, killed his brother. Orville took over as president of the company and continued prosecuting the infringement suits to the fullest, refusing to back down one inch. He would make Curtiss pay.

The trial was postponed until November 1912, and the decision handed down the following February was once again in favor of the Wrights: their broad wingwarping patent was indeed valid. Curtiss would not be allowed to build, sell, or exhibit aeroplanes. He could, however, appeal one more time—and did.

Orville and Katharine sailed for Britain that month, finally organizing a Wright company there, which helped them collect a £15,000 lump-sum payment from the British government for their patents. They then headed to Germany and heard the German Supreme Court uphold its decision that through Chanute's 1903 Aéro-Club speech, the brothers had committed prior disclosure. The court would, however, allow them to prosecute those who used wingwarping in conjunction with the vertical rudder. In France they had their patents upheld again, only to face another appeal from the French manufacturers.

Dismayed, the two arrived back in Dayton that March, in time for the worst flood in the city's history. They evacuated 7 Hawthorne and watched from a distance while fire broke out around their home and the bicycle shop, where lay the awards, their aeronautical data, all the glass plate negatives, and the 1903 machine—of all their machines, the only one that they had thought to save—still packed in its crate. The fires burned out, the water receded, and somehow the artifacts of their early experiments came through safe—buried beneath a layer of mud. On many negatives the emulsion had started peeling, and the lower left corner had broken off of the negative that recorded the first powered, controlled flight.

All of it belonged in a museum. While Wilbur was still alive, they had looked into having the 1903 flyer displayed at the Smithsonian. But when they saw how the Institution wanted to word the displays, they thought it portrayed Langley's work as more groundbreaking and successful than it had actually been, thus implying that their work was neither as original nor as consequential. Unable to agree on the wording to be used on both the Langley and Wright displays, the Smithsonian proudly displayed the 1896 *Aerodrome No. 5* as the first successful, powered, heavier-than-air craft, and the Wrights kept the 1903 machine in its crate.

In 1911, however, the U.S. Army had been glad to turn over to the Smithsonian the machine that had taught it to fly, the 1909 Signal Corps flyer, tattered and patched and oilstained below the motor. Most of the Wright aeroplanes flying now belonged in a museum as well, including the new Model Cs. In the Model C, the pilot was still fully exposed to the skies, and it had the confusing, unnatural two-lever control system—most builders preferred to copy Blériot's (who had had patent troubles of his own from copying it from Robert Esnault-Pelterie), or even Curtiss's shoulder-yoke system. Most of all, what made the C obsolete was the very thing the Wrights had fought so hard to protect: wingwarping, which required a degree of flexibility from the wing, which in turn limited the safe flying speed of a substantially sized biplane. While the Curtiss suit was still in court, switching to ailerons like Curtiss would be turned against the Wright Company.

Worse, though, Army pilots seemed to be falling out of the sky in them with alarming frequency: Eight out of fourteen pilots died in early 1914. After an official investigation into the accidents, former

Wright factory manager Grover Loening, now with the Army, determined that the cause was the tail-heavy pusher configuration. He ordered that all pusher machines were to be grounded—Wright and Curtiss alike. Curtiss answered this latest threat by hiring a British designer who was familiar with the single-engine tractor configuration.

Bitter over what he saw as Loening's betrayal, Orville thought the machines were really stalling, and so while publicly announcing that as his diagnosis, he privately concentrated on finishing his automatic control system, which would prevent stalls. The system consisted of a pendulum and vanes, and with it Orville flew past the judges with his hands off the controls and snatched away the third Collier Trophy. It was somewhat of a personal victory for Orville: the first two Colliers (underwritten by Wright Company investor and personal friend Robert Collier) had been won by Curtiss hydroaeroplanes.

The following year, though, young Lawrence Sperry flew his Curtiss hydroaeroplane before the Aéro Club de France and while he held his hands in the air, his passenger crawled out on the wingtip—without throwing the machine out of balance. Sperry was the son of the founder of the Sperry Gyroscope Company, which manufactured stabilization systems for ships, and he designed the gyroscope device that kept the machine stable. The first modern autopilot—in a Curtiss machine, yet—rendered Orville's automatic stability system obsolete in under a year.

Finally, though, in February 1914 the U.S. Court of Appeals sustained the patent decision once and for all. Curtiss and all the rest were guilty as charged. There could be no more appeals.

In America at least, the Wright Company, with its grossly outdated machines, now held a virtual monopoly on aeroplanes and was now free to exact its percentage from everyone. It ordered every infringer to pay up to twenty percent of the value of their craft. It ordered everyone except Glenn Curtiss.

Curtiss would have to fold his business.

Curtiss Sowing Seeds

Glenn Curtiss had already lost one company. Now Wright was going to force the second under, too. What Curtiss needed was a loop-
hole, and right away. He found one, and started working on another.

For the first, he developed a mechanism that worked the ailerons
separately instead of in conjunction. Even though that was covered
in the Wright patent it wasn't covered in the litigation. Now the
whole process would begin anew. Next, he was going to convince
those horse-and-buggy-brained judges that someone had been capable of manned, powered flight before the Wrights.

Curtiss went to the new secretary of the Smithsonian Institution,
Charles Wolcott, and made a proposition: Lend him the Langley
Great Aerodrome, now gathering a coat of dust in the Langley Laboratory's workshop. In return he, Curtiss, would get the aerodrome to
fly, which would then prove that Secretary Langley had been on the
right track all along, that he had been on the verge of achieving
powered, controlled, sustained *manned* heavier-than-air flight before
he simply ran out of money. Both parties had a lot to gain. A successful flight would force the courts to reconsider how broadly the
Wrights should be allowed to protect their "pioneering" work.
Success would also help the Smithsonian regain lost integrity, and
allow the late Secretary Langley to be elevated to the position of
True Father of the Aeroplane. No great supporter of the Wrights,
Wolcott agreed, and so in April 1914 the old *Great Aerodrome* was secretly shipped and reassembled in a concealed part of the Hammondsport factory.

Over the next two months Curtiss and his engineers subtly recast
the machine into a modern aeroplane: they rebuilt the wings and
made them stronger, with a more efficient aspect ratio and camber;
they gave the old 52-horse Manly engine a modern and reliable ignition, carburetor, and radiator and changed the propellers for

greater efficiency; they also radically altered the control surfaces, re- placing the cruciform rudder with a vertical one, adding a seat about amidships with a Curtiss-style steering yoke to control it as well as an elevator. To top it all off, Curtiss did away with the cata- pult launch, and with significant alterations in its wire bracing (which further strengthened the flimsy machine), he mounted the reconditioned aerodome on floats. On the water, Curtiss felt his own hydroaeroplane patents would protect him as he tried to de- stroy the Wrights'.

From Lake Keuka in late May and early June, he managed to hop the machine twice for less than five seconds. That was long enough to get a couple of photographs, and it was long enough for the offi- cial impartial observer—and a paid technical witness for Curtiss— Dr. A. F. Zahm of the Smithsonian to, well, observe. In the 1914 Smithsonian *Annual Report* Zahm wrote, "It has demonstrated that with its original structure and power, it is capable of flying with a pilot and several hundred pounds of useful load. It is the first aero- plane in the history of the world of which this can truthfully be said."

Reporting that the machine was in its original condition except for the floats, *The New York Times* said with Epimethian hindsight, "'Langley's Folly' flew over Lake Keuka today—approximately eleven years since it caused the country to laugh at its inventor when on its trial flight it fell into the Potomac."

Curtiss then restored the *Great Aerodrome* to its original condition, and it was placed proudly on display in the Smithsonian Institution as the very first powered, controlled, sustained, manned, heavier- than-air flying machine. He succeeded in casting doubt on the Wrights' claim of having invented the aeroplane, in the courts (for the time being) and, for as long as there were pictures, in the mind of an American public that is forever sympathetic to the underdog, and suspicious of the victor: Just look at the photo, boys, here's your proof that Langley was capable of flight before the Wrights!

Swept up in the wave of favorable sentiment, Curtiss announced that he had built a huge, modern, twin-engine, enclosed-cockpit hydroaeroplane, patriotically christened *America,* that, in August 1914, would attempt to become the first to fly across the Atlantic Ocean—and win for America the £10,000 prize Lord Northcliffe had just offered for the feat.

Hawthorn Hill

All this business was too much for Orville. Wilbur had been the businessman, he was the tinkerer. Orville let the company decline and bought up all the outstanding shares, then he sold the company and the patent rights, too, for a pretty hefty sum—probably more than a million dollars—and got out from under the mess completely. Financially, he was set for life. He built a giant pink mansion on Dayton's Hawthorn Hill for himself, Katharine, and the bishop and filled it with strange and wonderful complex gadgets he made himself. The place was an eccentric mix of opulence and sensibility: Between the bedrooms of Orville and Katharine was their huge shared bathroom and its room-size all-around shower that Orville designed, with its curtain of muslin from the 1903 machine. Why let such perfectly good material go to waste?

He stayed in the public eye, accepting awards and medals to remind the world that the Wright brothers were first, but never, ever spoke except through letters typed and issued by Miss Mabel Beck. He worked in his laboratory in town, mostly building elaborate toys there for his nieces and nephews.

But he would never again design another flying machine.

CHAPTER ELEVEN

1914 to 1918

All This and World War, Too

One week after Curtiss's *America* announcement, on June 28, 1914, a Bosnian Serb high school student named Gavrilo Princip sat down in a Sarajevo café and ordered a drink to calm his jangled nerves.

Princip was one of seven men a Serbian terrorist group sent to assassinate Archduke Francis Ferdinand of Austria while he was on a state visit to a recently annexed Bosnian territory. During the parade Princip heard a bomb explode, assumed the deed was done, and headed to the café. A few minutes later he looked up and was shocked to see the archduke and his wife, Sofie, very much alive and backing their automobile down the narrow street facing the café. Princip jumped up and pulled out his revolver and fired a shot at the archduke, then at Sophie. Both bled to death within the quarter-hour.

It was just the kind of act that gives belligerent countries an excuse to start a war. Within one month of the archduke's assassination, Austria-Hungary declared war on Serbia. Serbia's ally, Russia, began mobilizing on its border with Austria-Hungary. For years, since the Franco-Prussian War, Germany had been building its army and navy and planning for the speedy conquest and domination of

Europe. Not wanting to miss its chance, Germany declared war against Russia on August 1, citing its alliance with Austria-Hungary. The next day, German troops marched in the opposite direction and swept over Luxembourg. The day after that, Germany declared war on Russia's ally, France, and sent troops into Belgium hoping to take Paris through France's undefended northern border. That breach of Belgian sanctity forced England to declare war on Germany the following day. Just to take care of loose ends, Austria-Hungary declared war on Russia, Serbia declared on Germany, and France and England declared on Austria-Hungary.

So far, so good.

Told they would be home by Christmas, a million and a half German soldiers plowed through the border countries on the west and slammed straight into a million Frenchmen dug in behind machine guns (courtesy the late Sir Hiram Maxim) waiting for them along the Marne River. The Germans kept trying to flank, and the line kept unrolling and unrolling until it stretched from the English Channel to the Swiss Alps. The German advance ground to a halt, and soon its troops were dug in as well. Assault followed counter-assault, in which large groups of men on either side would clamber out of their trenches and stand up and walk slowly forward as if the machine guns would spray water and not bullets. Casualties were astronomical, but still the lines held.

"When one sees the wasting, burning villages and towns," wrote one soldier, Rudolph Binding, "plundered cellars and attics in which troops have pulled everything to pieces in the blind instinct of self-preservation, dead or half-starved animals, cattle bellowing in the sugar-beet fields, and then corpses, corpses, and corpses, streams of wounded one after another—then everything becomes senseless, a lunacy, a horrible bad joke of peoples and their history, and endless reproach to mankind, a negation of all civilization, killing all belief in the capacity of mankind and men for progress, a desecration of what is holy, so that one feels that all human beings are doomed in this war."

Synchronicity

It was over more or less the same front the following June, during the spring offensive at Verdun, that the famous stunt pilot Tony Fokker found himself floating in his small monoplane, searching the sky for an enemy aeroplane, and praying he wouldn't find one. Though Fokker, twenty-four, was from neutral Holland and officially a noncombatant, he had sold Germany production versions of his small monoplane and would do almost anything to sell more. That meant his enemy at the moment was France and Britain.

The French military had begun the war with some 138 flying machines of various shapes and sizes. Though all were pressed immediately into observation duties and proved their worth when they helped warn of the flanking Germans, the machines fell into two general configurations. There were the small, clean wingwarping tractor racing monoplanes of Blériot, Morane-Saulnier, Déperdussin, and Nieuport, all powered by the 80-horsepower version of the Gnome rotary, and (except the Blériot) all having a covered fuselage. And there were the larger Farman and Voisin pusher biplanes, with partially enclosed fuselage for pilot and passenger, but otherwise bristling lumber aft like the old Wright machines. Both configurations were capable of speeds of around 70 miles per hour, though the monoplanes had a slight edge there and were more agile. As a trade-off, the biplanes could fly longer and carry a load—an observer to sketch the battle lines, which relieved the pilot to concentrate on flying a machine whose engine might explode from the strain; or whose wings might shed their fabric, ripped away by the high pressure caused by flying too fast in a steep dive.

Britain had mobilized a 113-machine air force, the Royal Flying Corps—a grander name than perhaps it deserved. Its pilots flew their motley of frail crafts across the Channel and quartered them a safe twenty-five miles behind the front like their counterparts, friend and foe. The British crafts also consisted of two general types, each of which combined the characteristics of the two classes of French ships. There were enclosed-fuselage, tractor-engine, two-seat biplanes capable of 70 mph: the Royal Aircraft Factory's B.E.2a and B.E.8, for example.* The factory's R.E.5 could get up to 78 mph, and A.V. Roe's Avro 504 was good for 82 mph. The second type was the single-seat, enclosed-fuselage Gnome-rotary-powered biplane, like the Martinsyde S.1 or Tom Sopwith's Tabloid, the last powered by a 100-horse Gnome to reach speeds of up to 92 mph.

Germany had 180 craft. Aside from a handful of tiny Fokkers, the majority type was the beautiful Taube, or dove, the two-seated monoplane with a swept-tip wing, swallow tail, and a Mercedes 100-horse inline six-cylinder engine. It was held together with so many bracing wires that it looked like a bird caught in a spider's web. Almost a dozen companies had built the machine before the war, including the manufacturers Gotha, Albatross, and Aviatik. These companies now began building designs of their own, mostly 70 mph two-seated biplanes with sharp noses—a configuration made possible by the coveted water-cooled Mercedes 100-horse-power inline.

No matter the nation, all the machines had been built for the pre-war endurance and racing contests, and many of the first combat pilots had flown exhibition. They clung tenaciously to its mock-circus chivalry, bringing the theatrics of aerial exhibition to the theater of war. Civilian pilots quickly took to wearing uniforms and were naturally issued sidearms. The observer might tuck a rifle in his compartment as well—there was, after all, a war on. But aircrews

---

*A note on the company's designations. "B.E." indicated "Blériot Experimental," Blériot being recognized as having originated the tractor configuration. "F.E." stood for "Farman Experimental," Farman receiving credit for the pusher configuration. "R.E." and "S.E." stood for "Reconnaissance Experimental" and "Scouting Experimental" respectively.

disregarded the iron cross or tricolor roundel or Union Jack painted on another pilot's machine, reluctant to accept the unfamiliar feeling of hostility toward men who fly. They found themselves waving at their brother in the air while he took note of one's brothers-in-arms below. The greatest danger of flying during war seemed to be that ground troops might riddle a machine with small-arms fire if it wandered within range of the trenches.

"I got tremendously excited whenever I saw an aviator," recalled a young cavalry lieutenant, Manfred von Richthofen. "Of course I had not the slightest idea whether it was a German airplane or an enemy. . . . The consequence was that every aeroplane we saw was fired upon." The main duty of the cavalry being reconnaissance also, von Richthofen made his scouting missions as he had been taught as a cadet. He probed the front lines and drew enemy fire, or climbed the steeple of the church closest to the enemy, then reported back to headquarters with the news. During such missions, cavalry scouts might be gone for days.* But from the beginning the reconnaissance information brought back by aeroplanes could cover much more area than a lieutenant gripping a church steeple, and in a couple of hours instead of days. Early on, British pilots were credited with warning ground troops of a lightning-speed German flanking maneuver and keeping the Huns from celebrating Christmas in Paris. With the observation aeroplane's usefulness readily apparent, innovations happened rapidly. Machines were outfitted with wireless radios to direct ground fire. Then armies on both sides began equipping their two-seaters with cameras, which brought back more precise information and, since photography worked best at high altitudes—10,000 feet—took the ship out of the range of ground fire. Von Richthofen and his ilk found themselves relieved of horse and assigned to scavenging food or carrying

---

*Von Richthofen once billeted with French monks and commented favorably on their hospitality; yet he hung a couple of them days later to set an example.

messages on foot in the muddy trenches. It was not a gallant way to fight a war.

Field commanders quickly realized that with their aeroplanes the enemy could see his trenches and gun emplacements just as well as he could theirs. To make matters worse, early in the war a flight of British Avro 504s dropped specially finned artillery shells on the Zeppelin sheds at Metz in Germany, destroying several of the big airships on the ground. Dropping bombs on soldiers was only a matter of time.

And so the official word went out: Knock the enemy from the skies.

Pilots were issued hand grenades and steel-tipped darts and told to try dropping them on enemy flying machines from above, but usually the brunt of the punishment fell on the infantrymen even farther below. Then pilots and mechanics tried mounting guns on aircraft as well as they could. The best way seemed to be to fix one on the nose of the aeroplane and aim the gun with the flying machine. It worked well—so long as the propeller wasn't turning. When it was, bullets would blast the prop into splinters.

Thus the small, single-seat monoplane quickly fell from favor: it could not hold an observer, and the less powerful ones could barely lift a camera or a machine gun mounted to fire over the propeller. Guns were, however, installed on the observer's cockpit of a tandem-seat biplane, the one behind the pilot; or in the nose of a pusher biplane, to allow the pilot to see what his observer was aiming toward and help as best he could.

Just a couple of months into the war, two such disparately equipped machines from opposite sides came together above the lines over Reims, birthplace of the international aerial meet. One was a German Aviatik with its observer-fired rifle behind the pilot, the other a French Voisin with its observer firing the machine gun mounted on the nose. While thousands of muddy soldiers on both sides stared on, the two flying machines twisted and turned for untold minutes while each observer tried to hold on and take aim at the other machine long enough to fire a burst of lead. After the Voisin observer emptied one drum of bullets and most of another at the Aviatik, the German machine rolled over and slammed into the earth from 600 feet. The French troops cheered at the top of their lungs.

Thus, the first aerial combat ended in death for the Germans. The French crew received medals.

As the war's unanticipated spring came around, German pilots had learned to be on the lookout for frontal attacks from such pusher machines and side attacks from the tractor biplanes. Monoplanes posed no threat, especially at high altitude.

Then early one April morning, a flight of four German two-seaters were photographing the lines from 10,000 feet, when a small Morane-Saulnier monoplane with a big nose spinner approached head-on. The Germans continued going about their business. What could happen?

Suddenly flame sprouted through the monoplane's propeller—a lead slug slammed into the pilot of the closest machine. As it began a long, tight spiral toward the ground, the monoplane pointed its nose at the next German machine and fired. This time he hit a fuel line, and the other machine caught fire and left a trail of black smoke leading to earth.

The other two Germans got away as fast as they could and spread word of the small death machine along the front. Over the next three weeks it appeared again and again, destroying three more observation machines in the air. Germans began to flee when approached head-on by the enemy.

Not long after, a Morane-Saulnier was forced down behind German lines with engine trouble. Its pilot set it on fire to prevent its capture, but alert infantrymen doused the flames and turned the pilot and his machine over to a nearby aerial squadron. They saw that the Morane had a lightweight Hotchkiss eight-millimeter machine gun mounted on the cowling to fire through its propeller. The pilot was unharmed, and under the articles of warfare he politely refused to offer any information except his name:

Roland Garros.

The famous Roland Garros! He dined as an honored guest with the flying officers that night, delighted to have at their table the world-famous aviator. The next day they turned him over to a prison camp and immediately turned their attention toward his half-charred machine. They found it was just a machine gun bolted on the cowling. Garros had installed steel wedges on the propeller, though, intended to deflect bullets without splintering the propeller.

And that was how Tony Fokker came to be flying one of his own machines over the front.

Fokker was the young and only son of a Dutch merchant who had made a fortune growing coffee in Java. Retiring to Holland, the elder Fokker was determined to give his son the finest education money could buy. Tony would have nothing of formal education, and so to avoid mandatory conscription in the army, he bribed a doctor to sign him off as medically unfit—he lacked a stomach for war. Having seen Hubert Latham fly in Belgium and Orville Wright over Berlin, Tony knew what kind of education he wanted. Instead of funding a diploma, his father found himself financing a small exhibition company centered upon his son's simple steel-tubing-framed monoplane, the *Spider*. At first Tony arrogantly shunned Wright-style control surfaces ("Birds, as everyone knows, have neither rudder nor ailerons"), then just as arrogantly reinvented the wheel. ("It took some time for us early designers to learn that we couldn't build airplanes by copying birds.") In no time at all, Tony had followed Frenchman Adolphe Pégoud and American Lincoln Beachey in flying the loop the loop; at exhibitions across Europe, they called him the Flying Dutchman. He was only slightly more interested in fortune than fame, so he soon began attempting to mass-manufacture his machines. He tried peddling them to Russia, Britain, France, and Italy, but with no luck. In Germany, however, Fokker entered his new monoplane in a procurement contest, the main objective of which was to find the aeroplane most transportable by ground. Fokker's won, and before the outbreak of the war he began supplying the Germans with copies of his Eindecker, essentially a steel-tubing-framed replica of the French Morane-Saulnier.

Thus, when the Germans hauled what was left of Garros's Morane to Berlin, they logically called Fokker in from his factory at Schwerin, ordered him to duplicate the mechanism on one of his Eindeckers, and handed him an air-cooled Parabellum machine gun capable of firing 600 rounds a minute. He had forty-eight hours, they told him as they put him the train back to Schwerin.

Fokker had gone to extraordinary lengths to keep from carrying a weapon. But now his future depended on what he could do with a machine gun. He took it apart to see how it worked, then he took it outside the factory and blasted away at some targets. He decided the Garros solution was too dangerous; bullets such as these could hit with enough force to break a propeller, steel wedges or not. Worse, they might ricochet and hit the pilot. He remembered hurling stones at the slow-moving blades of a windmill as a child, and how hard it was to hit those blades. Then it came to him. "The technical problem was to shoot between the propeller blades," he wrote later. ". . . This meant that the pilot must not pull the trigger or shoot the gun as long as one of the blades was directly in front of the muzzle. Once the problem was stated, its solution came to me in a flash.

"The obvious thing to do was to make the propeller shoot the gun, instead of trying to shoot the bullets through the propeller."

He attached a small knob on one blade of an Eindecker's propeller, which, as it revolved, would hit a cam attached to the firing hammer of the Parabellum. Turning the propeller over slowly—and carefully—by hand, Fokker saw that the machine gun would indeed fire between the blades. He added a simple rod and spring control system to let the pilot fire at will, then lashed the Eindecker by the tailskid to his touring car and roared off to Berlin, 220 miles away.

Fokker arrived within his deadline, but the officers were not happy after they took over the machine. Where were the steel wedges on the propeller that they'd asked for?

It didn't need the wedges, Fokker explained, since its synchronization mechanism allowed the bullets to fire between the propeller blades.

Well, okay. But they wanted to see it work.

Fokker set the machine up on a firing range, its nose aimed toward targets shoved into the dirt at the far end of the range. He started the engine and fired short bursts, which turned the butts into splinters. Then he shut off the engine. The officers gathered around to inspect the propeller and found it unscratched.

The Dutchman fired short bursts. There must be some trick.

Fokker slapped a fresh 100-round magazine into the Parabellum, and with the propeller spinning he emptied the gun without pause.

Now the officers were satisfied. It worked—on the ground. Seeing it work in the air was completely different, of course.

"I decided to teach them a lesson which would make them think twice before being skeptical again," Fokker wrote, and had some old wings placed on the field's stoniest ground. Encouraging the officers to stand close for a good view of the bullets striking, Fokker took off. He climbed to 900 feet, shoved the Eindecker's nose over, and fired away. Bullets and Germans flew in every direction. Only after Fokker landed did the officers slink out from the safety of nearby hangars to look over the riddled wings.

They had to admit, the synchronized machine gun worked in the air. On stationary wings sitting on the ground.

"Still they were not satisfied, contending that the only certain test of the gun was to shoot an airplane down," Fokker said. "The suggestion was made that I, a foreigner and a civilian, go to the Front, find a French or British flyer and demonstrate by actually bringing down an enemy plane that my gun was practical."

Of course, if he were forced down and captured, he would be shot as a spy, so the Germans supplied him with papers identifying him as a lieutenant in the signal corps. Now if he were captured, he would spend the rest of the war cooling his heels in a prison camp. With that, the officers told him happy hunting and had him escorted to forward headquarters, eventually ending up at the airfield at Douai. After several days patrolling the skies, "Lieutenant" Fokker spotted a two-seated Farman pusher biplane emerging from the clouds some 2,000 feet below him. He dived for it.

"While approaching, I thought of what a deadly accurate stream of lead I could send into the plane," he wrote.

"As the distance between us narrowed the plane grew larger in my sights. My imagination could vision my shots puncturing the gasoline tanks in front of the engine. The tank would catch fire. Even if my bullets failed to kill the pilot and observer, the ship would fall down in flames. I had my finger on the trigger. What I imagined recalled my own narrow escapes; [the] time the gasoline tank burst; the breaking . . . wing at Johannisthal when my passenger was killed. I had no personal animosity towards the French. I was flying merely to prove that a certain mechanism I had invented would work. By this time I was near enough to open fire, and the French pilots were watching me curiously, wondering, no doubt, why I was flying up behind them. In another instant, it would be all over for them.

"Suddenly, I decided that the whole job could go to hell. It was too much like 'cold meat' to suit me. I had no stomach for the whole business, nor any wish to kill Frenchmen for Germans. Let them do their own killing."

He broke off the attack and turned back to base and heatedly told the field commander to find himself another pilot. Then he left for Berlin.

But before departing, Fokker went over the machine gun's operation with his assigned substitute, Lieutenant Oswald Boelcke, a pilot on the field who had some experience flying the Fokker Eindecker and had no compunction about killing the enemy. After hunting for three days, Lieutenant Boelcke came up behind an unsuspecting French machine, fired into its tail, and sent it spinning down in flames. One day later, Lieutenant Max Immelmann did the same.

As for Tony Fokker, he arrived back at his factory half-expecting retribution—he was, after all, dealing with Germans. But as it turned out, the high command was elated and wanted more of his Eindecker scouts: as many as he could build. Supplies would not be a problem. And every last one would come equipped with his synchronized machine gun, of course.

The Fokker Scourge was on.

Lead Zeppelins

And then the lights went out all over London.

The Fokker Scourge wasn't all the Entente Allies had to reckon with, but it had a lot to do with the rest of it. To complete one reconnaissance mission, the Allies now had to send two observation machines—guarded by six more—in the hope that one would get through and come back home. As long as German machines controlled the skies over the front, German reconnaissance aeroplanes could always get through, and so could their bombers. For now, those machines lacked the range to carry themselves across the Channel and carry the war home to the English. The Germans had something else, though, that could.

Count Ferdinand von Zeppelin's passenger carriers, nearly a dozen aluminum-framed airships, were pressed into service by the army and formed the core of its wartime fleet. Each was nearly 700 feet long and capable of carrying more than two tons of artillery shells up to an altitude of 13,000 feet. Powered by between four and six engines, the most powerful could reach speeds of 65 mph over the ground and remain aloft 21 hours—ample time to reach any of Britain's great industrial cities. They were protected from aerial attack by little machine-gun nests placed fore and aft, and worse yet, their highly volatile hydrogen cells were thought (by the British) to be surrounded by an inert gas that made them impervious to gunfire. Unless a pilot could get high enough to drop a bomb on a Zeppelin, they were unstoppable.

Aiming for military targets, the Zeppelins hit Dover first, then small towns in Suffolk, but the Germans really wanted London to feel the bombs. On the night of May 31, 1915, less than six weeks after Roland Garros single-handedly lost the Allies' air superiority, a Zeppelin halfheartedly aiming for military warehouses dropped its bombshells on a small London pub. Seven died, and fourteen were injured.

Now and forever, enemy civilians would become subject to random death from the air.

More raids followed, and a few more people died; by popular demand Britain was forced to withdraw flying squadrons from the front, ring its cities with gun batteries, and reposition its ships on the coast. Of course, defense against Zeppelin raids could begin on European soil and did: In a daring nighttime raid that June, British pilots again got through and laid bombs on the Zeppelin sheds. As one fleeing Zeppelin was climbing through 11,000 feet, Flight Sublieutenant R.A.J. Warneford managed to push his loaded Morane to just 70 feet above the immense gasbag. Flying its length, Warneford laid three of his six bombs on it in sequence. He heard a terrific explosion from the first bomb, and then his machine was blown high into the air and tossed upside down. While Warneford recovered control of his Morane, flames lit the night and then streamed down to the ground two miles below.

Those Zeppelins really burned.

Not long after, Lieutenant Leefe Robinson climbed up after a Zeppelin raider and let loose with a stream of incendiary bullets into the machine's belly, and it promptly exploded in flames. If there was an inert gas, it didn't work.

Still, the Zeppelins somehow kept getting through well into 1916, dropping tons of bombs and killing indiscriminately. The secretary of war allocated more money to develop pursuit squadrons and new aeroplanes and began buying the newest French single-seat pursuits in the interim: the Nieuport and the Spad—the first a production version of the racer scheduled to compete in the canceled 1914 Gordon Bennett, and the second a biplane derivative of the Déperdussin monoplane. The English also put up great steel nets of cables held with balloons, and they put aeroplanes on the deck of a converted collier, *Ark Royal*. But the Zeppelins kept coming.

That October, Second Lieutenant W. J. Tempest pursued a Zeppelin through a barrage of exploding shells from London's gun batteries and dived on it from 15,000 feet, hammering away with his machine guns.

"As I was firing," he reported, "I noticed her begin to go red inside like an enormous Chinese lantern, and then a flame shot out of the front part of her and I realized she was on fire. She then . . . came roaring down straight on to me before I had time to get out of the way. I nose-dived for all I was worth, with the Zepp tearing after me, and expecting every minute to be engulfed in the flames. I put my machine into a spin and just managed to corkscrew out of the way and she shot past me roaring like a furnace."

Inside was Heinrich Mathy, the most experienced airship commander. Left without his guidance, that month almost the entire Zeppelin corps, a flight of eleven airships, was blown away by gale-force winds like a latter-day Spanish Armada. Some were never heard from again. The Zeppelin Terror was over.

Much worse was on its way from the Fatherland, though. Already huge two- and four-engine Gotha bombers had dropped their eggs on Dover. Then a flight of Gothas hit the London docks in broad daylight, killing 162 and injuring nearly five hundred. More British squadrons were taken off duty in France to defend London.

During the Battle of the Somme that year, there were more than one million casualties—57,000 in one day. In the Battle of Verdun, there were 700,000 casualties. Neither clash changed the lines appreciably. And so the stalemate continued.

The First of the Chasers

Cavalry Lieutenant Manfred von Richthofen demanded a transfer and received orders to report to the air service, which he did immediately. Instead of piloting school, he was assigned to be an observer. His experience in reconnoitering in the cavalry had something to do with it, plus the fact that as a nobleman—he was a titled Prussian baron—von Richthofen could be trusted with command of the machine, as all observers were.

Though von Richthofen was a born hunter, he gladly accepted the observer's assignment. Pilot training took three months, and by then the war would be over. After two weeks' training he was assigned to the Russian Front; then after the war's first anniversary, he was transferred to Ostend, an aerodrome* on the English Channel north of Dunkirk, for patrol and bombing duties. Reassigned to a *Grossflugzeug,* a huge twin-engine pusher biplane, Von Richthofen thought it resembled a lumbering apple cart.

"The title of our barge alone gave us so much courage that we thought it impossible for any opponent to escape us," he wrote sar-

---

*Thus Langley's "air runner" had come to mean a landing field.

castically, adding that in this machine he first gave blood for the Fatherland, accidentally losing a fingertip by getting it in the way of the spinning propeller next to his seat. "Only my beauty was slightly damaged," he said, "but after all I can say with pride that I also have been wounded in the War."

The next blood he drew was more substantial.

His squadron moved south during the Battle of Champagne, near Reims, and one day he and his pilot took up a small two-seater. Three miles behind the lines, he spotted a Farman two-seater, and while his pilot flew alongside it, von Richthofen emptied a 100-round cartridge belt at the French. "I thought I could not trust my eyes when I suddenly noticed that my opponent was going down in curious spirals," he wrote. ". . . Our opponent fell and fell and dropped at last into a large crater. There he was standing on his head, the tail pointing towards the sky." Since it crashed behind enemy lines, he could receive no confirmation for shooting down the machine and thus no official credit.

But he began to yearn for more kills. During yet another transfer along the front, he happened to meet Oswald Boelcke, who by now had shot down four machines with his Fokker.

"Tell me, how do you manage it?" von Richthofen asked.

"Well, it is quite simple," Boelcke said. "I fly close to my man, aim well, and then of course he falls down."

There was more to it than that, von Richthofen thought. While he flew as a passenger in a huge packing crate, Boelcke piloted a small Fokker.

"At last I formed the resolution that I also would learn to fly a Fokker," he said. "Perhaps then my chances would improve."

In Champagne he began to learn piloting "on an old box," and after twenty-five flights and one crash he went for his certification flight that October, consisting of figure eights and a few landings before an examiner. He failed. He tried again at a flying school outside of Berlin, and again he failed. He was transferred to Tony Fokker's own school at Schwerin, and on Christmas Day 1915 he took the test a third time. It was the charm.

In March 1916 he was assigned to pilot a two-seat observation craft in time for the Battle of Verdun. It already came equipped with a machine gun for the observer, but von Richthofen wanted one for himself. Lacking the interrupter device, he ordered his mechanic to mount a machine gun on the top wing so it fired over the propeller arc. While flying an observation mission over enemy lines that April, he came upon a single-seat Nieuport. He got as close as possible and aimed well.

"The Nieuport reared up in the air and turned over and over," he said, and he and his observer thought it was a French evasive maneuver. "However, his tricks did not cease. Turning over and over, the machine went lower and lower. At last my observer patted me on the head and called out to me: 'I congratulate you. He is falling.' "

He liked the way it felt to hunt and kill a man.

Von Richthofen again received no official credit, but he was given a chance to learn to fly Fokkers and promptly crashed one after its motor failed. He was transferred to the Eastern Front to fly bombers in the June offensive, which stretched into August. There being no Russian aeroplanes to shoot at, von Richthofen grew restless.

Then the great Boelcke came by the squadron one evening to visit his brother. He mentioned to von Richthofen that he was charged with organizing a fighting squadron, a Jagdstaffel, from handpicked men in the German air service. They would fight, led by Boelcke himself, in the 1916 spring offensive at the Somme.

"I did not dare ask to be taken on," von Richthofen said, but early the next morning there was a knock at the door. Boelcke stood before him like a Teutonic warrior-god—but flat-nosed and toothy—and wearing the Blue Max, the coveted medal conferred upon great warriors in the past, now conferred upon himself and Immelmann once each had downed his eighth enemy machine.

"I almost fell on his neck when he inquired whether I cared to go with him to the Somme," Richthofen said, and in three days he left Russia on a train heading west.

"See that you do not come back without the Blue Max," a former colleague shouted after him.

In classes on the ground over the next month, Boelcke trained his young pilots in all that his sixteen kills had taught him. They learned to attack from superior altitude, from behind and out of the sun if possible; to always keep the enemy in sight, and fire at close range with the enemy in their gunsights. And above all they learned to always attack in groups covering one another—never attack alone or be drawn away from the main skirmish. They learned the maneuvers of a dogfight like the Immelmann Turn, which combined a half-loop with a half-roll to level, good for gaining altitude and switching directions on one's opponent. Boelcke would fly patrols in his Fokker every morning; his cubs knew that if he returned with gunpowder on his face, Boelcke had had another Englishman for breakfast. He did not waste bullets.

The Jagdstaffel would not be equipped with Fokkers. True, Anthony Fokker had designed a superior single-seat biplane to replace his aging, wingwarping Eindecker. But the German army had intercepted a telegram from the British, asking Fokker to build machines for England. Suspicious, the high command told Fokker he must become a German citizen. Fokker refused.

So instead Boelcke's cubs had a different single-seat chase machine: the Albatross, a streamlined biplane that seemed modeled on the Le Bris *Albatross* monoplane glider of more innocent times, but that was built especially for fighting. The Albatross company received priority on delivery of the new 180-horsepower Mercedes water-cooled six-cylinder, which weighed less than four pounds per horsepower. Though not a Fokker, the new Albatross fighting machine was still first-rate. With its monocoque plywood fuselage and rugged biplane wings, it was sturdier and more maneuverable than the old Fokker or any monoplane for that matter, since two wings generate twice as much lift. And at 110 mph, it was much faster than the Fokkers, too. Its nose, like later Eindeckers, held twin synchronized Spandau machine guns.

The Jagdstaffel had one day to get used to its Albatrosses. Then they joined the battle.

Boelcke led four of his cubs—von Richthofen among them—in a dawn patrol of the front. In the distance Boelcke saw a formation of British aeroplanes crossing over the lines: a couple of bombing machines surrounded for protection by five two-seat pusher fighting machines. Boelcke motioned to the others to swoop behind and cut off the British retreat. Then he ordered the attack.

Von Richthofen picked one of the pushers and dived on its tail. It twisted and turned; its pilot lost sight of the Albatross and straightened. That was all von Richthofen needed. Pulling up from below, he sent a burst into its engine and up the belly of the fuselage.

"The English machine was swinging curiously to and fro," he said, and he saw the two crewmen slumped in their seats. He followed it down and watched it make a perfect landing behind the German lines while he nearly crashed his own machine landing beside it.

Infantrymen pulled the observer from the wreckage, and von Richthofen watched him die. The pilot died on the way to a dressing station.

After cutting the serial numbers off the side of the British machine for purposes of official confirmation (he later sent the swatch home to his beloved mama), von Richthofen arrived back at the squadron late for breakfast. All the other cubs had scored confirmed kills as well.

That night he wrote a Berlin silversmith and ordered a two-inch-high sterling trophy cup. On its side he wished to have engraved *1. Vickers 2. 17.9.16.*

In reverse order: a date, a type of flying machine, and a sequential number, for he anticipated there would be other kills, and there were. Over the following weeks he placed more orders for more silver trophy cups, for he hunted most eagerly.

"I would like to be the first of the chasers," he decided. "That must be very nice."

His fellow air officers began dying.

First was the great Max Immelmann, who had brought down fifteen enemy machines. He was found dead in 1916 in his crashed Eindecker, its propeller shot away. Was it the synchronizer malfunctioning or a lucky shot from an opponent? No one could tell, but Fokker and his Eindeckers lost further favor among pilots. Then Boelcke died after forty kills, his top plane torn off in a midair collision with a squadron mate.

It was God's will, said von Richthofen.

At the moment of Boelcke's death, von Richthofen became the first of Germany's chasers. He had sixteen tiny silver trophy cups.

The German high command awarded him with the Blue Max and gave him a Jagdstaffel to make in his own image with promising, handpicked men, among them Werner Voss, Ernest Udet, Hermann Goering, and his own brother, Lothar von Richthofen, whom even Manfred called a butcher. With the exception of Goering, each would go on to shoot down forty or more machines.

To taunt the enemy, von Richthofen ordered his Albatross painted red, except for the black crosses on white squares that marked his nationality. His cubs followed and shunned the factory's safe green-and-brown camouflage patterns for bright colors and bold designs—but only von Richthofen's machine was totally red. The squadron moved where they were needed along the front in a special train, and they lived and worked in tents when they couldn't commandeer a suitable chalet. To the enemy they became known as the Flying Circus. Interrogating two uninjured French fliers, von Richthofen was delighted to find that his machine was known up and down the front: they called it *le Petit Rouge*. The English had a more personal name based upon his titled nobility: they called him the Red Baron.

Escadrille Les Cigognes

Increasingly, the red German chasers found themselves up against a flock of red storks.

Roland Garros had left behind a squadron of Morane-Saulnier pilots grasping for a sense of tradition in an infant service, foundering and now dying under the guns of a better-equipped and more organized foe. Garros had four victories; so the *pilote de chasse* who first topped that number, Eugène Gilbert, was called an *as,* after the highest card in the deck. Others who managed to destroy five enemy machines would soon also call themselves an ace.

In the beginning of the Fokker Scourge, the slower Morane-Saulniers gave way to the new Nieuport 11 *Bébé avion de chasse* biplane. Its diminutive 26-foot wings were braced together with V-shaped struts; the lower plane had seemingly half the chord of the upper and added more structural integrity to the main wing rather than lift to the entire machine. The Nieuport *Bébé* was capable of almost 100 mph—10 mph faster than the fastest Fokker Eindecker—and was equipped with a machine gun firing over the top wing. If chase pilots couldn't outgun the Fokker, they could at least try to outmaneuver it, outclimb it, or outrun it.

The red stork was a good-luck symbol that Escadrille No. 3 had painted on the sides of every one of the safely camouflaged Nieuports. *Escadrille Les Cigognes,* the squadron was called. And soon, among fliers and the general population, the Stork Squadron found its tradition: it was France's elite squadron for chase pilots, their Flying Circus.

Its first real hero was Georges Guynemer, a slight man with sad, dark eyes who talked his way into the air service after being rejected as physically unfit for the army and navy. As an observation pilot in his two-place, high-wing Morane-Saulnier L and finally flying alone in Nieuport 11's, Guynemer shot down eight German machines.

Then after many months of the Fokker Scourge, an Eindecker pilot got lost and landed behind French lines. His machine was captured intact—with the synchronized Parabellum mounted on its engine cowling. French engineers dissected the mechanism with interest, improved upon it by adding a hydraulic actuator mounted on the control stick—which allowed the pilot to fly and shoot with the same hand—then installed the finished product on the production run of the new improved Nieuport, model 17. Its souped-up nine-cylinder le Rhone rotary pulled it along at just under 110 mph, and it was lighter and smaller than its German adversary in chase, the Albatross, though the Nieuport 17 had less power and less of an edge on speed. In a steep dive the Nieuport would shed fabric from its top wing, and when that happened there was no place to go but down.

The Storks received the new machines in May 1916, and Guynemer continued to shoot down *boches* at a methodical pace. But that September the escadrille received entirely new machines: the first Spad 7s. Built around the Hispano-Suiza 125-horsepower V-8, the Spad was streamlined, solid, and nimble, and it could fly 127 miles per hour. Flying Spads during the Battle of the Somme, Guynemer's tally reached twenty-two kills. He called a favorite machine *Le Vieux Charles.* When landing at the airfield after gunning down another enemy machine, he liked to pass low overhead first, killing and starting the engine.*To Guynemer, it sounded like *I got one . . . I got one.* Other pilots started doing the same when *they* got one, and again a tradition was born.

Another aggressive observation pilot, René Fonck, joined the Storks that spring.

"I received a really comforting welcome from . . . my new comrades," he wrote. "Every day of the war was marked by heroic acts, and if a chart were created where only the exploits of the Storks were reckoned, there would not be any difficulty in filling it.

"I was happy to find myself in this atmosphere. In a fighter squadron the spirit is quite liberal, and one finds characters there completely unconcerned about danger, types who would risk their lives for the sake of a *beau jeste.*

"A little exalted, perhaps; not military enough in the eyes of the General Staff, no doubt; but magnificent soul, nevertheless—these fighter pilots."

In single engagements Fonck would twice come to shoot down six enemy machines. While his kill tally crept up behind Guynemer's, his unconfirmed kills averaged roughly one-third more than his confirmed total. And so the squadron began a new tradition: Anyone claiming kills that were unconfirmed had to pay a fine to the officer's mess.

The traditions spread to and from other units and helped hold them together. In a war where men were led to the slaughter like muddy anonymous cattle, the romance of what from afar appeared to be knightlike jousting in the air—a cleaner version of war than that found in the trenches—also helped give the people back home individual heroes to worship. This was soon realized by the military

---

*The early machines had only two throttle settings anyway: on full blast, and off. Pilots had to control speed by killing the engine, so that while flying the machine went *braaat . . . braaat . . . braaat . . .* ad nauseum. Speaking of which: After two hours on patrol, the castor oil fumes from the engine had the same effect on the pilot as a couple of tablespoonsful of the liquid taken orally.

leaders, who shot their own soldiers to keep them from retreating, who needed popular support to feed the war machine, who needed to keep supplying their armies with young men to die horribly by the tens of thousands in the wasteful strategy of forward assault.

But the knightly individual heroes had also been flying in combat straight through since getting their wings, flying to the physical limit in frail machines that could and would fall apart at any minute—all while surrounded by other pilots who were trying to kill them. Though cleaner, they were as shell-shocked as any man in the trenchwork.

On both sides of the line, combat pilots were cracking from the strain.

If not one of the first, Georges Guynemer was one of the best known. The other pilots noticed his behavior grew increasingly erratic: he talked to himself and heard voices. In September 1917, after shooting down fifty-four machines, Guynemer flew into a cloud bank over the lines and simply disappeared. His Spad was never found.

Fighting the Flying Circus

In Great Britain the Royal Flying Corps needed relief in more ways than simply rest. The English had begun the war barely out of the Wright Age; as the fighting progressed, its machines had grown dangerously outdated, and the nation only sluggishly developed better. Tactically, its approach to air warfare was the same as to ground warfare: try to overcome the enemy with superior numbers. The pilots called themselves Fokker Fodder.

While France and Germany publicized the exploits of their pilots—even American mercenaries received adulatory coverage in the U.S. press, to the delight of the nation's hawks—the official word from the War Office was that aviators were no better than the average Johnny in the trenches, and so both would be treated the same in the press as on the battlefield. RFC pilots felt unappreciated.

They had their moments, however. In July 1915 Major Lanoe Hawker miraculously shot down three Germans in a single day, flying a Bristol Scout armed only with a single-shot carbine rifle mounted to fire outside the Bristol's propeller arc. Sixteen months later, in a fierce dogfight, Hawker became Manfred von Richthofen's eleventh silver trophy cup.

The loss was deeper than simply one soldier; his combat experience was irreplaceable.

"To be able to fight well," wrote Canadian ace William Bishop, flying for the RFC, "a pilot must be able to have absolute control over his machine. He must know by the 'feel' of it exactly how the machine is, what position it is in, and how it is flying, so that he may maneuver rapidly, and at the same time watch his opponent or opponents. He must be able to loop, turn his machine over on its back, and do various other flying 'stunts'—not that these are actually necessary during a combat, but from the fact that he has done these things several times he gets absolute confidence, and when the fight comes along he is not worrying about how the machine will act. He can devote all his time to fighting the other fellow, the flying part of it coming instinctively."

Without better machines and equipment, however, Britain would continue to lose its best fighters. The Flying Corps' most effective pursuits at this time, Nieuports built under license at the Royal Aircraft Factory, were armed with the upper-wing-mounted Lewis. The Lewis had a tendency to jam at inopportune moments—which was just about anytime a pilot was firing a machine gun in combat.

The RFC reorganized, and by spring 1917, in time for the Second Battle of the Somme, it was able to get better pursuit machines in the air. The first came from the hopelessly bureaucratic Royal Aircraft Factory, the clean and angular S.E.5A. It was the production version of a machine that had set the world speed record of 134.54 mph—less than three months before the war. The pitiful delay was due to engine problems: problems in mass-producing adequate numbers of the license-built 150-horsepower Hispano-Suiza V-8 water-cooled engine. The eventual compromise was adequate: the 200-horse V-8 Wolseley Viper, which gave the S.E.5A its long rectangular nose, its superior ceiling of 19,500 feet, and its production in serious numbers. The S.E.5 came armed with a Lewis gun on a swivel mount on the top wing (for stitching Hun aeroplanes in the belly) and a single synchronized Vickers firing through the propeller.

It was joined in the skies by the Sopwith Camel, so called for the hump on its nose that housed twin synchronized machine guns. Driven by a simple air-cooled radial, the 130-horse, nine-cylinder Clerget, the Camel had a speed of 115 and a ceiling of 19,000. The gyroscopic effect from the big radial also made it brutal for novice pilots to handle, especially taking off and landing. But in exchange the machine would turn in a blink—which an experienced dogfighter appreciated. The novice had only to live long enough to appreciate it.

At the beginning of the Somme, the British were able to amass nearly 800 machines against just over 250 German machines, a three-to-one numerical superiority. As Bloody April wore on, the Germans were blasting them out of the skies at the same rate, and the Brits lost three machines for each German that went down: 316 to 119. But the British navy had an effective blockade of German ports and thus on raw materials. So the RFC just had to keep on building more new machines and sending more new pilots into the clutches of von Richthofen's Flying Circus, and sooner or later the Huns wouldn't be able to shoot them down fast enough.

The War Office finally recognized the propaganda value of its pilots and started allowing some to quietly become heroes, notably the men of No. 56 Squadron. The anointment came honestly; the country's leading ace, Albert Ball, flew his S.E. with the 56th. He liked to fly into battle alone and had a suicidal maneuver that worked for him: He'd let the enemy get on his tail, then he'd loop his machine quickly and pull out right under the German's belly in time to let loose with a burst from the Lewis gun. Ball had forty-four kills when he disappeared over the lines, at the age of nineteen. But the 56th also had Mick Mannock, a poor, angry socialist who once happened upon a squadron of new German students and shot them all down; and James McCudden, who liked to soup up the engine in his S.E.; and A. P. Rhys-Davis, who hoped to live as recklessly as Ball.

Late that summer attrition turned the tide in the Allies' favor, but a new machine—and a concept as old as Stringfellow—appeared from beyond the German lines: It was a triplane, painted green, with a white-mustached face drawn on the cowling. Its exposed 110-horse radial engine cylinders looked like a row of buck teeth. It was stubby and slow compared with the new British machines, but it was remarkably maneuverable and deadly in the hands of an experienced pilot. Flying his new triplane, Werner Voss of von Richthofen's Flying Circus shot down twenty-one British aeroplanes in three weeks. With its comma-shaped tail and the lines of its fuselage, the machine was unmistakably Fokker.

Still unable to get superior engines, Tony Fokker built a superior machine with the engine he had. The Dreidecker's three short wings gave it the maneuverability. They were cantilevered—so strong and cunningly braced internally that they, in fact, needed no external bracing at all, though Fokker built the triplane with a single strut on each side because he now understood suspicious German minds.

One day seven pilots from the 56th pounced Voss as he was flying alone; after a ten-minute dogfight a burst of lead from Rhys-Davis killed the German.

That autumn, after Bloody Spring had segued into a bloody summer, Rhys-Davis was awarded the Distinguished Service Order. At a boozy celebration in the mess hall that evening, McCudden egged him to give a speech. Rhys-Davis stood up.

"I'm very happy to receive this decoration," he said, "but I'm not going to talk about that. I've been thinking about the great bravery of the men we fight, men like Werner Voss. We are fighting against men of magnificent courage, and I'm going to ask you to rise and drink a toast."

The men stood, and held their glasses high.

"Gentlemen," he said, "I drink to Manfred von Richthofen, our most worthy enemy."

Hat in the Ring

"He kept us out of war" was Woodrow Wilson's reelection slogan in 1916, which was what the American public wanted to hear about the bloodbath everyone called the Great War more for its size than its popularity. The sinking of the *Lusitania* in 1915 had done little to change American sentiment, even though 128 of the 1,198 dead were Americans: All the passengers had been warned they were sailing into a war zone.

But more unrestricted U-boat action followed, and then there was the Zimmerman telegram proposing a German-Mexican alliance against the United States, which was intercepted by England. Hostile posturings from Congress followed, and in June 1917 General John J. Pershing of the American Expeditionary Force led the first shipload of Americans ashore in France.

"Lafayette, we are here," he said.

He was talking to a dead man; Lafayette was a French general who had led troops in the American Revolution and swayed France to ally with the colonies against Britain. Recently it had been popular to invoke his name when someone wanted to stimulate a little down-home public sentiment for France or a little guilt about

American neutrality. In fact, a volunteer aerial squadron originally named *Escadrille Américaine,* which had been flying combat equipped with shiny new French Nieuport 17 chase machines, had only months before changed its name to *Escadrille Lafayette.*

The squadron's exploits made headlines back home: Everyone read about Kiffin Rockwell downing a German over Alsace and mourned when Victor Chapman died in a dogfight over Verdun— he was the most popular man in the squadron, too. With America joining the War to End All Wars to Make the World Safe for Democracy, the *Lafayette Escadrille* would form the core of its combat air service.

When the United States declared war, its armed services had fewer than four hundred aircraft;* most owed more to the ancient Wright and Curtiss machines than to those of Sopwith, Spad, and Fokker. The U.S. aircraft industry was still shrunken from lack of government funding, its technology strangled by the withering grasp of the Wright patents and every other piddling patent guarding every minor innovation.

That July, in its largest single expenditure to date, Congress appropriated $640 million for military aviation. Thousands of pilots and thousands of airplanes would be needed: 3,000 machines—no, 20,000, including orders from France and Britain. Only the automobile industry had the know-how to mass-manufacture machines and engines in those numbers. There were fortunes to be made—if only it weren't for those patents. The automakers said they wouldn't think about starting until everyone got everything settled. So the members of an aviation trade group, the Manufacturers Aircraft Association, came together in 1917 and in two weeks hashed out its Cross-License Agreement. The solution was simple: to avoid litigation, a company only had to pay the MAA membership fee, pool its patents with the other manufacturers for set royalties paid out

---

*When hostilities opened in 1914, the armed forces had but ten flying machines.

through the MAA, and agree to the findings of an arbitration board in case of conflict. The manufacturers agreed to the Agreement, and a truce was finally declared: The patent war was officially over.

Boomtime was now officially on.

America had no combat-tested airplane designs of its own, naturally, but the automobile industry got started building the engines anyway. They didn't want to copy battle-hardened foreign engines, however, so they designed and built their own from scratch in five months: the huge, 400-horse, 12-cylinder Liberty engine, liquid-cooled, heavy, and temperamental. Now any flying machine that the airplane manufacturers built would simply be adapted to the Liberty. After searching the Aircraft Production Board found one English airplane that could be adapted, the D.H.4, a sturdy two-seat observation machine designed by Geoffrey de Havilland. And since the nation needed to train its thousands of new pilots, the board searched for a training machine and found the large, slow, and forgiving Curtiss JN-4, the two-place Jenny, powered by Curtiss's own temperamental 250-horse OX-5 engine. Huge orders for the two aircraft were doled out to the handful of U.S. airplane manufacturers at a cost-plus-ten-percent basis ("the more the cost, the more the plus," smiled the manufacturers), while the board for the time being entrusted the construction of pursuit ships to French manufacturers.

Lafayette, here we are.

The American industry itself was perhaps still too adolescent to be so entrusted. In the space of two years, Glenn Martin had bought the Wright Company from Orville and renamed it Wright-Martin; then Martin got out of it and it became the Wright-Dayton Aircraft Company, except for one factory in New Jersey that went independent and kept on calling itself Wright-Martin. Not to confuse matters, right away Glenn Martin formed the Glenn L. Martin Company. And now that there was lots of money to go around, more manufacturers popped up overnight: Vought, Thomas-Morse,

Standard, and Boeing. All you needed, it seems, was a designer and a dream.

Of all the U.S. manufacturers, only Glenn Curtiss had experience building warplanes, having supplied the U.S. Army with some early JNs which flew observation in the recent campaign against Mexican rebels. Curtiss also sold Great Britain flying boats for spotting U-boats. One of those was, ironically, the *America,* which indeed crossed the Atlantic—inside a supply ship. Curtiss, too, had more orders than his company could fill. It wasn't lost on him, however, that after years of legal battles the Wright Company—companies—were building *his* machines.

Officially Orville Wright was a consultant to Wright-Dayton, whose war-engorged plant soon sprawled over and so consumed Huffman Prairie that the exact location of the brothers' original hangar became in dispute.

But Wright-Dayton didn't need Orville to tell them how to manufacture D.H.4's and JN-4's, nor did he care to. His only contribution to the war effort was scientific; he went about designing and building the era's most advanced wind tunnel, itself a work of art.

With a few thousand machines on order, the Air Service needed pilots to fly them and many times more mechanics to work on them. The famous race-car driver Eddie Rickenbacker knew this, and while he toured the country speaking about Money, Munitions, Men, he also talked to the Army about forming a pursuit squadron of racing drivers. Who else would be as comfortable under the stress of speed and as knowledgeable about mechanics? The Army turned him down.

"We don't believe that it would be wise for a pilot to have any knowledge of engines and mechanics," an officer told him. "Airplane engines are always breaking down, and a man who knew a great deal about engines would know if his engine wasn't functioning correctly and be hesitant about going into combat."

Rickenbacker joined up anyway. Of course he knew a lot about engines and was uneducated except in the school of hard knocks, so he was assigned to be a staff driver with the rank of sergeant and made it over to France on the same boat with Black Jack Pershing. Though the newspapers thought it made a good story to say he was Pershing's chauffeur, Rickenbacker made himself the favorite driver of Colonel Billy Mitchell, the head of the Air Service, who saw to it that Rick was transferred to work at the French flying school at Tours. Seventeen days and twenty-five hours later (in a Morane-Saulnier with clipped wings, and then a Caudron pusher), Rickenbacker became a pilot and a lieutenant, and was placed in charge of organizing the mechanical end of the advanced American flying school at Issoudun. There, on the sly, he learned to fly the French-built and American-bought Nieuports and trained himself to fly the more complex combat maneuvers like the tailspin.

"It was a good stunt to know, as in combat a plane in a tailspin is hard to hit," he said, and by constant practice he mastered it and the other important maneuvers originated by Pégoud. He had himself transferred to gunnery school, where they rowed him out into a lake and handed him a 30-caliber rifle and told him to shoot, standing, at a target in another boat. Once he got used to that they let him take up a Nieuport equipped with a machine gun and let him fire at a ten-foot-long sock towed behind a Caudron, and after he could hit that too, he was officially a combat pilot, so they had no choice but assign him to the 94th Aero Pursuit Squadron, the first all-American squadron of the AEF. It was now March 1918.

The 94th was equipped with some twenty ratty old unarmed French Nieuports; on the side of each the men painted a hat tossed in a ring—the traditional symbol for accepting a challenge—only the hat was Uncle Sam's stovepipe. The squadron was led by Major John Huffer, formerly of the *Lafayette Escadrille.* Other seasoned Lafayette veterans fleshed out the staff, including Major Raoul Lufbery, who, with seventeen kills, was America's Ace of Aces. Like his German predecessor, Oswald Boeckle, Luf led the raw pilots into combat, showed them how to fly formation in a corkscrew path, and taught how to scan the skies for the enemy systematically. Of all the new American pilots, Luf chose to initiate Rickenbacker to combat first. "All the boys [tried] to look as though they were not half mad with envy over my chance to get my head blown off first," Rick said. Then like Boeckle, Lufbury died in a freakish accident: With his ship going down in flames, he chose to jump instead of being roasted to death. Of course, he had no parachute. No one except balloon observers and a few Germans were equipped with para-chutes; the Allied commanders believed that having a parachute would only encourage pilots to abandon their machines when things got a little warm in battle.

In late April, Rickenbacker engaged a German in combat for the first time. "My heart started pounding," he wrote. "The image of a Liberty Bond poster popped into my mind. It was of a beautiful girl with outstretched arms. In big black letters were the words 'Fight or Buy Bonds.' Well, I did not have much of a choice."

He dived out of the sun and got on the tail of a Pfalz machine, aimed his sights on the back of the pilot's seat, and pulled his Nieu-port's two triggers. "Every fourth shell was a tracer, and I could see two streaks of fire pouring into the Pfalz's tail assembly. I held the triggers down and pulled back on the stick slightly, lifting the nose of the plane. It was like raising a garden hose. I could see the stream of fire climbing up on the fuselage and into the pilot's seat. The plane swerved. It was no longer being flown. I pulled out of the dive and watched the Pfalz curve down and crash. I had brought down my first enemy airplane. . . .

"I had no regrets over killing a fellow human being. I do not be-lieve that at that moment I even considered the matter. Like nearly all air fighters, I was an automaton behind the gun barrels of my plane. I never thought of killing an individual but of shooting down an enemy plane."

In the following month Rickenbacker would shoot down five more Germans and become an ace. Then, following a mastoid operation, he was grounded.

Milk and Brandy

With the fresh spring offensive came a fresh wave of French and British and now American men and machines—and that meant fresh kills for von Richthofen. In the previous year, 1917, his number of confirmed kills had shot up to sixty, and he kept ordering silver cups and cutting the serial numbers off the downed machines as if they were animal skins. He sent the canvas scrap—and sometimes a propeller or a gun or whatever piece of the plane caught his fancy—back home to mama. Then he was hit in the head by a bullet and injured badly enough to be sent home himself to recover. He spent some time arranging his trophies in his room and having intimations of mortality. Now he was back, it was spring, and he had a new red Fokker Dreidecker with black iron crosses on it, and in no time his total shot up to eighty confirmed kills. His new bus had no range and less speed, but that did not matter to von Richthofen. He would take off from the Doubai airfield and climb high into the sky, which the machine did well, and wait for the Englishmen to come to him, which they always did in numbers. He did not care that just twenty percent of aerial combat reached the dogfight stage at which his machine excelled, that the majority of engagements began with a surprise high-speed pass and ended in the quick death of the opponent.

And so one cold Sunday morning in late April 1918, von Richthofen led his Jagdstaffel into the air and waited for the English. They did not disappoint him: Coming over the line were three flights of five aeroplanes flying in V-formations like ducks, all of them new Sopwith Camels. Though von Richthofen could not know it, the pilot in the lead was Captain Roy Brown, a Canadian who had learned to fly at the Wrights' Dayton school back in 1912. In combat continuously for a year and a half, Brown had twelve confirmed kills and stomach ulcers from the stress. He drank milk mixed with brandy; one kept the pain from his stomach long enough for the other to take the pain from his head.

Von Richthofen signaled for his Circus triplanes to block the Camels' retreat, and while dogfights broke out over the Somme, von Richthofen spotted a fledgling on the edge of the battle trying to sneak away. The novice, "Wop" May, had gotten excited and fired until his gun had heated and jammed, and now he was hoping to run for home. Von Richthofen rolled over and jumped May from behind, firing his twin Spandaus into the Camel's back. May dived toward the river trying to lose the triplane, pulled up 50 feet above its surface and whipped his pursuit machine back and forth, following the river's meanders. When he turned his head to look back, the red triplane was still swerving with him.

Brown saw the attack and immediately dived after Richthofen. He let go with a burst into the triplane's fuselage and watched the machine right itself and glide until it touched down and rolled to a stop in the no man's land, just beyond a line of Allied trenches filled with Australians. Risking death, the Aussies rushed out, crouching, to capture the pilot. He was sitting in the cockpit with his hand still on the stick. A single bullet hole passed through his chest.

"He's dead," said one soldier, and so they tied a rope to the red machine and pulled it to their side of the line. Word quickly spread along the front that the Red Baron had been killed.

Brown and May landed safely back at the airfield. When he learned the identity of the red Fokker's pilot, Roy Brown downed a bicarbonate of soda.

And so the war ended for Baron Manfred von Richthofen, twenty-five. He was buried the next day with full military honors. His own machine was stripped of its skin and cut up for souvenirs.

Safe for Democracy

Hermann Goering took over the renamed Jagdstaffel Richthofen, and the Dreidecker was withdrawn from service after the loss of von Richthofen. Still, its ascendance had allowed Tony Fokker to get a commitment for the coveted 160-horse Mercedes in-line V-8 without having to pledge allegiance to the Fatherland, and around this engine the Fokker company built the sleek new Fokker D-VII biplane, faster, stronger, and better than any machines the Allies had. It was rushed to the front, and during August 1918 alone, D-VII pilots shot down 565 Allied machines. Still, they kept coming.

But by July, the German advance had ground to a halt again. "The Yanks are coming," said the popular song, and in fact they had finally arrived in full force only that summer, just in time for the Allied assault on Saint-Mihiel salient. While the doughboys helped slowly shove the German infantry back, an air armada of fifteen hundred Allied machines—six hundred of them flown by Americans—went after the Huns with a vengeance. Who knew how long such hunting would last?

Most had learned to fly in Curtiss Jennies back home, and in France they were given the Allied machines that the Army said was most like it: the new and inadequate Nieuport 28 and the new and exceptional Spad 13. And then they were sent out to fight or die trying like everyone else.

The first American to gain notice after Rickenbacker was a young blond second lieutenant from Arizona named Frank Luke, and that recognition was not all positive. He was considered a braggart and a coward because he was never seen in the thick of a dog fight and his kills always seemed to fall behind enemy lines, and as such, were unconfirmed. So Luke's specialty became shooting down tethered observation balloons, which were usually held in plain sight but low to the ground and as such were protected by murderous, accurate ground fire. Somewhat murderous and accurate himself, in just seventeen days Luke destroyed fifteen such balloons and four German airplanes with his incendiary bullets and his swift Spad. He did not care for orders and insisted on fighting on his own terms, which meant flying mostly alone and mostly against balloons. Though officially grounded for misconduct, on his last day alive Luke shot down three balloons. Hit by gunfire, he landed behind enemy lines and died in a shootout with German infantry. If he had lived, he would have been court-martialed. Instead, he was awarded the Medal of Honor.

Rickenbacker recovered from his mastoid operation, and at age twenty-nine, ancient for a combat pilot, he was put in command of his old squadron, the 94th. Now also piloting the new Spad, over the next few weeks he surpassed Luke's number of kills and reached twenty-six. Who knew how long such hunting would last?

In truth, not long. After four years, with the front having been shoved back fifty miles—and now only fifty miles from their own border—the German people had grown weary of being bled dry. They rose up against the Kaiser and forced the royal family to flee to Holland. That October the new government sued for peace. In the same sort of calloused homage to numbers with which they had fought the war, the generals agreed to cease firing on November 11, at eleven in the morning. It sounded neat and clean on paper, so until that moment the numbers on both sides continued falling along a line that had no intention of moving.

The Great War had taken a total of ten million human lives. The people who compile such things figured that the average life expectancy of a pilot alone was three weeks in combat. In their few months above the front the American pilots had suffered a thirty-six percent casualty rate, and that was considered good.

The war forced the airplane to branch into different types with differing capabilities, and it helped develop mass manufacturing and training techniques. But besides new varieties of machines and the new tactics, and a whole new level of destructive capability, the war in the air also created a lasting paradox: It forever utterly and completely dehumanized war, while glorifying it with the gallant, boyish face of the daring individual pilot.

What a show it was.

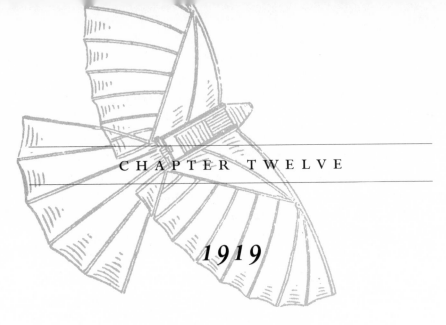

CHAPTER TWELVE

1919

Graduation Day, 1919

It was a scene that Wilbur would have enjoyed—might have even been the distinguished guest speaker: the Manufacturers Aircraft Association's banquet at New York's Waldorf-Astoria Hotel, on the cold evening of January 7, 1919. The Grand Ballroom was decked out in red-white-and-blue star-spangled bunting, patriotic eagle banners, real Liberty engine radiators complete with real propellers, and the national flags of all the Allies and their standard roundel insignias to boot—so many of those, it started to look like von Richthofen's personal collection on display. Everybody came dressed to the nines in black tie and tails, except every now and then there was an officer in dress uniform at the table with a small pair of wings pinned to his breast. And not a woman in sight. Both of the Wright brothers would have appreciated that.

But the remaining brother had sent his regrets, for he seldom attended such functions. Also begging off was Wright's nemesis, the Smithsonian Institution's Dr. Charles Wolcott.*

---

* After his part in the Curtiss-Langley Aerodrome affair, Wolcott had gone on to lead the National Advisory Committee for Aeronautics, or NACA, starting from Langley's old aerodromics laboratory in the Smithsonian castle. After around a half-century of

Still, the banquet managed to fill the night with remembrances of the association's humble beginnings and the dark days when America, Birthplace of the Airplane, had joined the forces of freedom and liberty with only a few machines, its can-do pluck, bottomless wealth, and manufacturing might, and after a brief pause to get wound up, had managed to crank out 13,943 airplanes and thousands more Liberty engines, a handful of which actually made it to the front before the War was over.

And now, the Peace.

Of course the businessmen had prospered and were thankful for it, but now they wanted more: They wanted to stay in business and keep on making more money, and they needed to find a way to do that pretty quick.

The same sentiment held true for mass manufacturers of airplanes the world over. Uniforms had been seen in the unemployment lines.

Unfortunately for business, while airplanes weren't the war's most effective swords, they were one of the easiest to beat into plowshares. More than 200,000 warplanes had been manufactured worldwide during the war, and everywhere enterprising folks were buying up the more than 100,000 machines left and modifying the biggest ones to carry passengers and the mail. It seemed lucklessly appropriate. At the outbreak of hostilities, the mass of airplanes were civilian machines adapted to military use; conversely, in the postwar period the majority of flying machines would be military adapted to civilian use.

Perhaps there was a market for flying machines out there somewhere. Britain would need aeroplanes to keep its presence felt around its global Empire; America would need airplanes to patrol and defend its huge coastal border from attack by the sea. As for the other major nations, well, France was nearly broke but was busy setting up air service between its major cities using converted wartime

---

valuable aeronautic research, NACA changed its name to National Aeronautics and Space Administration.

bombers. So was Germany. Still, there wasn't much of a market for new machines over there. Tony Fokker had managed to smuggle to Holland millions in foreign currencies, a trainload of frames, bolts of silk, and spare parts of many of his airplanes including the hot new D-VII, the only airplane to be banned under the Treaty of Versailles. He would start all over again—and maybe even join the MAA in the near future.

He was, after all, a neutral.

But back to our dinner party. Toastmaster and MAA President Frank Russell introduced numerous guest speakers, including a real live war hero, Canada's Colonel William Bishop. The All-American Ace with seventy-two kills and twenty-three more probables, Bishop was the second-highest ranking Allied ace behind René Fonck, with his seventy-five kills. Speaking on the future of aviation—even an All-American Ace has to make a living—Colonel Bishop quickly told the audience that the future was not in warfare but in commerce. "I think that the wonderful record the science of flying has had will be equalled and surpassed in the next few years by the development of commercial aviation," he said, adding that the era would begin with the first flight across the Atlantic—which, now with the war over, was only a matter of time.

Truthfully, the members were more interested in what H. Snowden Marshall had to say. Marshall had led the committee investigating charges that the manufacturers had gouged the Aircraft Production Board of millions of dollars.

"I think I will be violating no confidence at all," said Marshall, "if I say that every member of our committee, after going up and down and all over the country and looking at all of the people and discussing things with the manufacturers, and with the Signal Corps, and with everybody concerned, unanimously formed the opinion that there was no truth whatever in the false and libelous charges that has been made against the body of the people who were working on this, but that we had been in contact with an able, a patriotic, and an honest body of men who were striving, under the great handicaps to accomplish a great good for the country."

Well, that was a relief. But as Marshall went on to add, "The only customer, the only present customer is Uncle Sam. The commercial or other uses of aircraft have not yet developed, but it seems to me it would be an awful pity if we slumped back into the state in which we were before, and left to other countries, left to countries across the water the development of that industry that belongs to the United States by right of discovery."

There was dinner, and drinks, and finally, the members of the association and the committee wished to thank the celebrants for their being there, for their patience, and for their enthusiasm.

Good night!

(Applause.)

Would Someone Silence that Man?

As if Lord Northcliffe hadn't learned his lesson about muddling with progress in aviation—Blériot's 1909 Channel crossing was followed in seven years by daylight Gotha air raids over London—the guns on the Western Front had barely grown cold when he republished in the London *Daily Mail* his £10,000 prize for the first to fly nonstop across the Atlantic.

There was no shortage of serious indigenous contenders this time: Britain had quietly amassed the largest aerial fleet in the world: 22,000 machines, including, finally, swift, strong fighters like the Camel and S.E.5A and the new 120 mph Sopwith Snipe. The country had also learned something from Germany's Gothas, and its major aircraft manufacturers had all begun to turn out long-range bombers by the armistice.

One of the latest was the Sopwith B.1; in six weeks Tom Sopwith's company had modified a B.1 to carry enough extra fuel to fly two men nearly 1,800 miles. The biplane, called *Atlantic,* had a 46-foot wing and a length of 32 feet; on the spine of its fuselage the engineers had incorporated an inverted wooden dinghy, which the crew could use in case of a water landing. For the long journey it would rely solely on one Rolls-Royce Eagle VIII, a 350-horsepower liquid-cooled V-12 engine. More promising perhaps was the Vimy bomber manufactured by Vickers, also built too late to join the war, though the company now hoped it might sell as a civil transport. With two Rolls-Royce Eagle VIII's for power, the slightly larger Vimy could fly two tons of payload an estimated 2,400 miles. And more promising still, there was the mammoth Handley Page V/1500, a four-engine bomber. When flying over long stretches of water, there is safety in numbers—the number of engines onboard, that is.

All three manufacturers hoped winning a race across the Atlantic would be just the thing to impress civilian buyers.

Clearly the best route to officially cross the Atlantic was the 1,900-mile gap between Newfoundland and Ireland—to take advantage of the prevailing winds. By April, the three competing machines were ready; now all the participants needed was to ship the aeroplanes across the ocean and set them on their way.

There was, however, a fourth serious contender, and it was already in position to depart.

The More the Cost

NC stood for Navy Curtiss, and it was a wartime plan begun by the U.S. Navy. Wanting a fleet of long-range flying boats to fly above and protect convoys crossing the Atlantic, the Navy went to its most experienced hydroplane manufacturer, Curtiss, and in December 1917 it ordered four huge flying boats, with the option of ordering many, many, more.

A gaggle of engineers from both the Navy and Curtiss set to work designing the NC—or Nancy—and perhaps because of it the flying boat was spared the smooth aerodynamic looks of the a modern combat airplane for something more classical, like the first flying machines, for example. In other words, there was no fuselage, other than the long, cavernous, dark gray boatlike hull (which housed the crews' several cockpits and passenger and cargo compartment), upon which the machine bobbed in the water. Most of the NC's skeleton was on the outside, like those prewar machines. It was a biplane 24 feet tall, with six sets of uprights, and a monstrous biplane elevator and triple-vaned rudder, all held on aft by tubular steel framework exposed to the wind. It would be powered by several 360-horse Liberty engines, of course, since pretty much all government-ordered aircraft had to make do with the centerpiece of its manufacturing effort: to carry its 15,000-plus-pound empty weight, plus a cargo of 5,000 pounds, it would need three of the liquid-cooled 12-cylinder Libertys. To sustain it in the air, a wingspan of 126 feet was necessary.

That was six feet longer than that first flight made by Orville Wright back in 1903.

Initially estimated to cost between $50,000 and $75,000 (without engines), design changes forced the first NC's price to run above $100,000—with Curtiss, the main contractor, to make the standard cost plus ten percent like all armament suppliers. By September 1918, its parts had arrived at a special hangar on Long Island's Rockaway Beach built to house all four Nancys. As *NC-1* came together, it became painfully obvious that someone had designed a hangar half as large as needed. Somehow, though, the flying boat lifted off the water and flew.

The Navy tested it for a month, then in early November a crew of nine officers flew it down to Washington for an official presentation, with only one emergency stop to fill a leaky radiator.

Then peace broke out and ruined the whole thing.

Washington shut down the money fountain; without a war going on, the government didn't need huge fleets of trainers, fighters, observation craft, and bombers, and it certainly didn't need huge escort flying boats, and it didn't need to support a large Army Air Corps or a useless naval air service. The government began auctioning off its huge surplus fleet of Jennies and D.H.4s, still crated for shipping, to anyone with a hundred dollars or so. Aviation had at last come to the common man.

But as a result the unsinkable Glenn Curtiss was being put out of business again—not by the Wrights but by his own airplanes.

And while the Army Air Corps maneuvered its way into the air mail business in its surplus D.H.4's, the career Naval Air Service officers realized they had to have a purpose, too. They flew the *NC-1* for publicity's sake, setting a record by flying 51 passengers—although briefly, just under one minute—in late November. Now Commander John Towers, a Glenn Curtiss–trained aviator and would-be co-pilot of the ill-starred Curtiss *America,* came up with another idea: They would assemble the other three Nancys and, like the Great White Fleet of the Air Age, fly softly with a big stick across the Atlantic. Curtiss liked the idea—the other three $100,000 Nancys, after all, remained only blueprints on the drawing tables instead of as checks deposited in his bank account. And so they both went to the assistant secretary of the navy, a New Yorker and a savvy career politician named Franklin D. Roosevelt, who got the attempt approved. Within days the veins of Curtiss Aircraft and the arteries of the naval air service once again felt the warm rush of money.

The More the Plus

Though Towers and Curtiss promised delivery by March 1919, it was late April before the *NC-2, NC-3,* and *NC-4* were resting comfortably—outside—at the naval air station at Rockaway. Along the way they had modified the design somewhat, too. Each now had a fourth 400-horse Liberty bolted as a pusher behind the center tractor engine, adding a little more power to lift enough fuel for the journey's longest leg. Each also now had two wireless radio sets: a short-beam transmitter for sending messages among the other NCs and to surface ships, and for that occasional important message from Washington, a long-distance transmitter that used a 250-foot wire antenna unreeled in flight.

During flight tests *NC-2*'s engines were badly damaged in an accident involving a depth charge, so from then on engineers cannibalized the *-2* for spare parts. And then there were three.

The plan was this: They would fly north and east in easy stages from New York, to Halifax, Nova Scotia, then finally to Trepassey Bay, Newfoundland. There, instead of flying the 1,900 miles to Ireland, they would fly the 1,200 miles to the Azores, then 800 more to Lisbon, Portugal, and finally up the coast of Europe to England. To prevent the English from grousing over the size of the American attempt, they would refuse the *Daily Mail* prize should they be the first to cross.

Their longest flight leg was shorter than the nonstop route, true. But to hit a group of islands after flying for nearly fifteen hours straight over water, and in the stormy spring Atlantic weather yet— well, that would take some fancy navigating. Lieutenant Commander Richard Byrd had designed an aerial sextant, used like an ordinary sextant to shoot the sun or the moon and triangulate one's position—only Byrd's had a bubble, as in a carpenter's level, to find the horizon, assuming it was lost in a layer of clouds. More important to this attempt at aerial navigation, the Navy positioned its destroyer fleet along the flight's intended route, to act as giant markers, weather-reporting stations, or rescue craft.

Each NC would have a crew of six: a radio operator; two engineers or mechanics, with stations near the rear engine; the two pilots, seated in tiny cockpits just ahead and below the three forward propellers; and the air navigator-commander, crouched inside a turret in the nose. Each open cockpit would have access to the hull. Over the noise of four loud Libertys and the wind in the wires, the crew could remain in contact with one another through the airplane's intercom system.

Concocted by career officers, the whole affair took on all the trappings of a formal naval ceremony. Commander Towers would lead the flight, in command of the flagship, *NC-3*. Lieutenant Commander Patrick Bellenger, the eighth U.S. Navy pilot, would be in charge of *NC-1*. *NC-4* went to Lieutenant Commander A. C. Read, a short, hawklike navigator nicknamed Putty for having returned to work from summer vacation with a pasty complexion.

Normally, Commander Byrd would have been a shoo-in for such a role. He had commanded a small naval air station in Nova Scotia during the war and thus had intimate knowledge of Atlantic weather. He also had the most experience with that aerial sextant he had designed, which the navigators would be using. Both areas of expertise would be vital to the mission's success. But to help spread a little glory around, only officers who had fought on the home front were assigned to the trip. To the U.S. Navy, Nova Scotia was overseas. Byrd, however, could and would go along with Tower as far as his old overseas post at Halifax.

And so it was that on the gray morning of May 8, 1919, after the requisite oration opportunity for Roosevelt and other dignitaries and with flashbulbs popping, the three NCs took off in a neat V-formation with Towers in the lead. Climbing slowly, they flew toward the northern tip of Long Island and then turned toward Halifax. Over Montauk by noon, they took up a heading for Cape Cod. Towers ordered every ship to proceed at will.

Right away the *NC-4* fell behind. In the first long overwater stretch, between the Cape and Nova Scotia, the *-4* lost its aft-center engine and then blew its forward-center engine, and the machine settled down into the sea. While the *NC-1* and *-3* flew on to Halifax, the *NC-4* taxied on its two faltering engines back to Cape Cod's naval air station, as ships searched for it in closing darkness. The Libertys died for good less than a mile from shore.

In Halifax, meanwhile, Towers and Bellenger were grounded briefly by cracked props, but they scrounged replacements and took off. After another day's flying, both landed at Trepassey Bay in worsening weather.

The *NC-4*'s mechanics spent the next two days rebuilding one Liberty and replacing the other with the only engine available at the base, a 300-horse Liberty. A bad starter kept the *NC-4* on the ground long enough for a gale to move in to Newfoundland, but on May 14, after a week, Read and his crew took off and flew to Halifax in under four hours. His mechanics had to clean the new Liberty there, but the *NC-4* took off again successfully the next morning for Trepassey, only to be forced down into the sea eighteen miles out by more engine trouble. In the middle of the ocean, the mechanics cleaned all the carburetors on the bobbing *NC-4* and plucked an errant chunk of rubber from a fuel line. They took off once again, arriving at Trepassey Bay just as the others were trying to depart for the Azores—with little luck.

Fully fueled *in the water* for the first time, the NCs took on extra gas: some 200 pounds extra, which placed them over their maximum weight limit. Something had to go overboard, so Bellenger and Towers were draining off a few gallons of fuel when Read landed beside them. All together now for the first time, Towers decided they should take off in formation together, too, fly through the night, and arrive in the vicinity of the Azores with plenty of light left in case they had to search around for the islands. Read's crew needed time to change an engine, so Towers rescheduled takeoff for late afternoon the next day.

Time, now, was of the essence for the Navy. In nearby St. John's, the three British machines and their pilots needed only a storm to pass between them and Ireland before setting off.

May 16 was clear and cold, and the British were still grounded by that Irish storm; just before five P.M. the U.S. Navy's commanders and their crews formally marched off to their ships in their baggy leather flightsuits and started the engines before the good-size crowd that assembled in small craft and along the bay. After one attempt at formation takeoff, the *NC-3* still refused to rise, forcing Towers to chuck his long-range radio, his heaviest mechanic, and a bag of mail taken along to quell any sentiment back home that this big expensive project might only be a frivolous and risky publicity stunt for the Navy.

With the plane lightened enough, Towers finally took off. The trio of biplanes flew out into the sea, barely scraping the waves, with nothing between them and the Azores but twenty-five destroyers and a lot of open water. It was now six P.M.

They passed the first destroyer without incident. Gradually gaining altitude as they burned off fuel, the NCs droned on into the enveloping darkness; their crews settled in and capitulated to the boredom of a long flight. When the second destroyer radioed and asked for a souvenir, the *NC-4*'s men all took turns urinating in a weather balloon—the only head these new ships came equipped with—and the pilots set up for a bomb run. A mechanic launched the balloon overboard, square onto the destroyer's deck.

As night fell the crews found that the luminous dials of their instrument panels refused to glow; the position lights on the *NC-3* were out as well. Then clouds rolled in, and around three A.M. the *NC-1* nearly collided with the *-3*. Once again Towers ordered each ship for itself. When dawn broke, the *NC-4* was ahead of the pack.

But by ten A.M., now within a few hundred miles of the Azores, all three were firmly enmeshed in rain and fog and were worried about being blown off course and running out of fuel. Too low for the radio and unable to use the aerial sextant or see the destroyers marking the course below, both Bellenger and Towers separately decided to land on the water long enough to calculate their positions. Just minutes apart, both came down through thick fog and ran into sixty-foot waves dead-on. Wires and struts snapped as the sea pounded both machines. They'd never fly again—but somehow they managed to stay afloat.

Though he had lost contact with the other two, Read had been able to contact three destroyers ahead; while things looked bad now, the weather seemed to clear around the Azores. Flying at 3,400 feet between layers of clouds, he saw a break in the layer below. On the ocean's surface he spotted a surf line; he figured they were near the southern coast of Flores, the westernmost island. They flew past, hoping to make São Miguel and the capital, Ponta Delgada. Soon they hit fog again, so Read backtracked and circled the island of Horta until he found the destroyer station offshore. There the *NC-4* landed, 14 hours and 18 minutes after leaving Trepassey Bay.

That evening they learned that Bellenger and his crew had been rescued—after five hours at sea—first by a radioless Greek ship that just happened upon them in the fog, then by one of the destroyers that was actually searching for them. Unable to tow the flying boat, the destroyer's captain declared it a hazard to shipping and rammed it, sending the *NC-1* to the bottom.

Next morning there was still no word of Towers. The *NC-4* was socked in by fog and couldn't yet attempt the leg to Portugal. Read learned that the single-engine Sopwith *Atlantic,* flown by Harry Hawker with K. Mackenzie-Grieve as navigator, had taken off successfully from St. John's in Newfoundland but without a radio onboard. Only time would tell. Hawker grew well overdue, but thinking he may have landed in a remote section of Ireland or even Scotland with word not yet arrived back in civilization, no one gave up hope right away.

Meanwhile, Towers and the crew of the *NC-3* spent a harrowing two nights and three days in the storm-tossed Atlantic, shedding parts as it blew them ever closer to Ponta Delgada. After having flown a record overseas flight of 1,220 miles and then sailing for 60 hours at sea, and with crewmen balancing the wing to make up for a pontoon that had been torn away, the *NC-3* taxied into its intended port under the power of its two remaining engines. It received a twenty-one-gun salute.

Read was grounded by squalls for a couple of days, then flew to Ponta Delgada, where tradition dictated he turn the *NC-4* over to the fleet's flag officer, Commander Towers. But from Washington, the secretary of the navy ordered that Read continue the flight. The old traditions didn't apply to the air age. Read was the hero—he wasn't the one who landed in sixty-foot waves and wrecked his ship.

People who knew them said that afterward it was never the same between Read and Towers.

London radio now reported that Hawker and Grieve had had engine trouble after flying 1,200 miles and were lucky enough to ditch in front of a radioless Liverpool-bound tramp freighter. "[The captain] thought we were Americans," Hawker told a reporter, "and we were struck by the manner in which he took the whole business, as if it were an everyday affair to take airmen out of the Atlantic."

The crews of the Vickers Vimy and the Handley Page were now only waiting for the weather to clear before they tried the flight.

But foul weather continued to hold the *NC-4* on the ground until May 27. Finally the big airplane took off and blandly followed thirteen repositioned destroyers straight into Portugal, landing nine uneventful hours later at a full formal reception in Lisbon's harbor.

After 3,322 miles, 19 days, and nearly 42 hours of flying time at an average speed of under 90 miles per hour, with two airplanes lost, a fortune spent, and a dramatic military presence involving more than two dozen ships and their crews and countless other men and women in industry and all the resources that the American government could with good conscience bring to bear, the first flight across the Atlantic was completed. By Americans.

Look on our works, ye mighty, and despair.

Alcock and Brown

Only eighteen days later, John Alcock and Arthur Brown put on their heated flying suits and climbed into the nose of the Vickers Vimy at a 900-foot field they had scraped out of sand and rock with the help of locals. Alcock started the two Rolls-Royce Eagle engines and poured the power on. Though Ireland lay 1,890 miles away, the Vimy carried fuel for 2,440 miles just in case—there wasn't going to be a string of destroyers to mark their way—and the extra petrol pushed its weight to 13,285 pounds. At 4:19 P.M. it started rolling, and kept rolling, and picked up speed, and went off the end of the field, dipping out of sight.

Onlookers held their breath, waiting for the sound of the explosion to reach them—but they only saw the Vimy slowly rise into view and chug low and sluggish out to sea.

Unlike the Americans, the crew were experienced wartime airmen. Captain John Alcock, twenty-seven, was the testing pilot for Vickers; a flier since he was seventeen, Alcock had been an instructor before ending up flying bombers in the Turkish theater during the war, and he had finished it a guest of the Turks. Lieutenant Arthur Brown, the thirty-three-year-old navigator, had spent his early days of the war in the infantry. After his nerves had had enough of the constant bombardment, crouching to make himself smaller when he heard the whine of shells and—worse—waiting for poison gas to float silently over and settle in the trenches, he managed a transfer to the Flying Corps and the clean war as an observer. But Brown got shot down twice, ending up a German prisoner of war the second time. He learned a trade during his two years in a POW camp: navigation. After the armistice he met Alcock and signed up for the transatlantic attempt.

The bomber they were flying now had itself been only briefly tested twice since being reassembled in the new world. Its bomb racks were removed and extra fuel tanks installed in the bay; to hold up the all the weight, the Vimy rested on two sets of double-wheeled undercarriages, one under each engine. There would be no intentional sea landings for this flying machine.

As if to make up for it, instead of being open to the elements like on the production Vimy, the cockpit was crammed mercifully inside what was normally the bomb dropper's position in the machine's nose.

After an hour enough fuel had burned off to let the machine climb to 1,500 feet, where it was pinched between a layer of cloud and sea fog. Brown couldn't get a sextant shot of the sun, and so they flew along by compass; then, trying to send a wireless back to base, he discovered that the external generator's propeller had blown off into the slipstream. No radio. Otherwise the machine held together wonderfully, its engines droning on perfectly monotonously, so they decided they should continue.

Now a series of pops shook the starboard Eagle, and it started a staccato whine. Part of the exhaust manifold had been blown off, they realized, but that was no reason to turn back. They continued on.

Night fell.

Through the clouds, Brown managed to get a couple of quick shots at some stars: They were a bit south of course and flying over the ground at a speed of 122 mph, which meant they had a good wind at their tail. They flew onward—and into rain, which changed to ice, which began sticking to the Vimy's wings. Then they hit clouds, and turbulence.

Without a horizon and with his airspeed indicator around one hundred, ignoring the propellers overspeeding as he knew they did in a dive, Alcock gradually banked the bomber over into a tight spiral; mistrusting all the signs, he and Brown watched while the altimeter unwound from five thousand, four thousand, three thousand, two thousand, one thousand . . . five hundred . . .

They plowed through the bottom of the clouds, and ocean filled the windscreen. Alcock barely had time enough to straighten the wings and pull up—but he did, and they breathed, and once again he swang the Vimy's nose toward Ireland. And finally into the sunlight.

At 8:40 that morning, less than 17 hours after leaving Newfoundland, Alcock and Brown crossed the coast of Ireland and crash-landed in a bog at Clifden rather than face more clouds farther ahead.

The Atlantic Ocean had been breached, nonstop, by an aeroplane.

The English-speaking world happily embraced the pair, even America. The English were, after all, our allies, and as it turned out, Brown was born of American parents in Glasgow and had even carried the U.S. flag across in his pocket.

He would never get into another flying machine as long as he lived, which was a ripe old age. Less than six months after the flight, Alcock crashed in fog and was killed.

As quick as that, both crossings were forgotten, lost among the armistice negotiations and women's suffrage and rising persecution of Jews in Eastern Europe and, of course, the deadly influenza epidemic, which spread as fast as the troops could return home, killing more people, quicker, than had the Great War.

On both sides of the Atlantic, the aircraft industry steeled itself for the bumpy ride ahead.

Wright behind You, Orville

Alcock and Brown's Atlantic flight was exactly 83,160 times the distance of that first flight at Kitty Hawk.

To think Wilbur Wright himself once said, "Not within fifty years will man ever fly." But a fellow American inventor had seen the flyer's progenitor and answered, "Of what use is a newborn baby?" At age sixteen, the airplane was barely a teenager.

Born as an intellectual exercise for two bicycle mechanics from Ohio, the airplane had reached adolescence; nourished by war, it had grown at a terrifying pace. It was a swift bridge between distant continents, capable of raining destruction in between.

"What a dream it was, what a nightmare it had become," someone once quoted Orville saying, not knowing he preferred to keep quiet in public. He did write, "The aeroplane has made war so terrible that I do not believe any country will again care to start a war; but I hope that the Allies will make another war absolutely impossible as part of the peace terms." He said little else on the subject. Wilbur had been the writer, and he did all the talking, too.

Orville rested heavier on his laurels with each passing day, turning grayer and grayer. His final record, for longest time in a glide, fell to a German in 1919, and after that the Wright name left the record books, except for their numerous firsts. After taking to the air one last time to fly formation with a D.H.4 in an old Wright machine— by that time he was one of the few pilots who could fly with the Wright control system—Orville gave up flying for good. All that vibrating hurt his bad leg, he said.

From then on he was Aviation's reclusive elder statesman and was content with that role. He abhorred public speaking so violently that there is no known recording of his voice, though he lived almost to the century's halfway point. He gladly researched and relived early aeronautical history for almost anyone who wrote, helping to insure that he and his brother forever retained their hard-fought, elevated place in it. He accepted honorary degrees and doctorates and seemed to make a cottage industry of neatly autographing artifacts of his and Wilbur's experiments with flyers—a chunk of wood here, a scrap of canvas there:

I authenticate the above pieces as genuine parts of the original "Kitty Hawk" plane, flown on December 17, 1903. They are parts broken when the plane, while standing on the ground, was overturned on the fourth flight of the day
                                                                          —Orville Wright.

The brothers' remote Kitty Hawk was eventually overrun with tourists, and overbuilt with their vacation homes.

One company that bore his name eventually merged with the company that bore Curtiss's name, business not understanding irony. But Orville wasn't out of airplane manufacturing yet: He would go on to make millions of gliders—balsawood with WRIGHT FLYER stamped on the wing, found in each specially marked box of Quaker Oats.

He lived on at the pink columned mansion at Hawthorn Hill, accepting visits from presidents and dignitaries and celebrities. He sold the old white house at 7 Hawthorne Street and the bicycle shop to Henry Ford, who moved every last plank and brick to his personal theme-park-style homage to industry, Greenfield Village, in Dearborn, Michigan, hiring Charlie Taylor to make sure everything came back together just the way it had been.

Orville sent the 1903 flyer to the Science Museum in London, to return to the States only when the Smithsonian finally recognized it as the first true powered, controlled, sustained, manned, heavier-than-air flying machine—which after long decades it finally did, offering a gracious, humble apology for the 1914 aerodrome incident.

He still refused to date or marry, and when his beloved sister Katharine eventually did, Orville did not speak to her again until she lay on her deathbed.

And to his final day, Orville was proud that he and his brother had made something of themselves, and had used their wits and their modest resources to change the future: that of all the giants who had come before, he and Wilbur alone had gumption and the know-how to succeed with their frail machine of sticks and canvas on the remote stretch of sand at Kitty Hawk.

BIBLIOGRAPHY

For source material I relied heavily on the papers and the published works of the principal characters, fleshed out with contemporaneous newspaper, magazine, and journal articles. As a general rule, I tried to reference those materials within the text and thus avoid cluttering up the book with footnotes. Some of the more important articles, however, are listed below (perhaps redundantly), along with texts that readers might find helpful should they wish to learn more specifics on any particular area covered in this work.

Ader, Clement. *Là Premièr Etape de l'Aviation Militaire en France.* Paris: 1906.

Aircraft Year Book. New York: Manufacturers Aircraft Association, 1919.

Archibald, Norman. *Heaven High, Hell Deep: 1917–1918.* New York: Albert and Charles Boni, 1935.

Anonymous. *The Air Balloon.* 1784.

Bishop, Lt. Col. William A. *Winged Warfare.* New York: Arco Publishing, 1967.

Boelcke, Oswald, Capt. *An Aviator's Field Book.* Nashville: The Battery Press, 1917.

Bordeaux, Henry. *Guynemer: Knight of the Air.* New Haven: Yale University Press, 1918.

Borelli, Giovanni Alphonso. *The Flight of Birds.* London: Newcomen Society, 1911.

Casey, Louis S. *Curtiss: The Hammondsport Era 1907–1915.* New York: Crown Publishers, 1981.

Cayley, Elizabeth, and Gerard Fairlie. *The Life of a Genius.* London: Hodder and Stoughton, 1965.

Cayley, Sir George. *Aerial Navigation.* London: Newcomen Society, 1910.

Cayley, Sir George. *Aeronautical and Miscellaneous Note-book (ca. 1799–1826).* Cambridge: W. Heffer & Sons, 1933.

Chanute, Octave. *Progress in Flying Machines.* New York: 1894.

Cole, Christopher, Ed. *Royal Air Force Communiques, 1915–1916.* London: Tom Donovan, 1990.

Cole, Christopher, Ed. *Royal Air Force Communiques, 1918.* London: Tom Donovan, 1990.

Crouch, Tom D. *Blériot XI: The Story of a Classic Aircraft.* Washington: Smithsonian Institution Press, 1982.

Curtiss, Glenn H. *The Curtiss Aviation Book.* New York: F.A. Stokes, 1912.

Da Vinci, Leonardo. *Codex Atlanticus.*

Davy, M.J.P. *Henson and Stringfellow.* London: His Majesty's Stationery Office, 1931.

de Terzi, Francisco Lana. *The Aerial Ship.* London: Newcomen Society, 1911.

Fisk, Fred C., and Marlin W. Todd. *The Wright Brothers from Bicycle to Biplane: An Illustrated History of the Wright Brothers.* West Milton, Ohio: Miami Graphics Services, 1993.

Fokker, Anthony G., and Bruce Gould. *Flying Dutchman: The Life of Anthony Fokker.* New York: Henry Holt & Co., 1931.

Fonck, Capt. René. *Ace of Aces.* New York: Doubleday & Co., 1967.

Geibert, Ronald R., and Patrick B. Nolan. *Kitty Hawk and Beyond: The Wright Brothers and the Early Years of Aviation, A Photographic History.* Dayton, Ohio: Wright State University Press, 1990.

Geoffrey of Monmouth. *The History of the Kings of Britain.* Translated by Lewis Thorpe. New York: Viking Penguin, 1986.

Gibbs-Smith, Charles H. *Sir George Cayley's Aeronautics: 1796–1855.* London: Her Majesty's Stationery Office, 1962.

Gibbs-Smith, Charles H. *A Directory and Nomenclature of the First Aeroplanes.* London: Her Majesty's Stationery Office, 1966.

Gray, Peter, and Owen Thetford. *German Aircraft of the First World War.* London: Putnam & Co., 1962.

Hall, James Norman. *High Adventure: A Narrative of Air Fighting in France.* Boston: Houghton-Mifflin, 1929.

Harris, Sherwood. *The First to Fly.* New York: Simon and Schuster, 1970.

Hatfield, D.D. *Dominiquez Air Meet, 1910.* Inglewood, CA: Northrop University Press, 1976.

Jane's Fighting Aircraft of World War I. London: Studio Editions, 1990.

Kelly, Fred C. *Miracle at Kitty Hawk: The Letters of Wilbur and Orville Wright.* New York: Farrar, Straus, and Young, 1951.

Kelly, Fred C. *The Wright Brothers: A Biography Authorized by Orville Wright.* New York: Harcourt, Brace & Co., 1943.

Langley, Samuel P. *Experiments with the Langley Aerodrome.* Washington: Smithsonian Annual Report, 1904.

Langley, Samuel P. "The 'Flying-Machine.' " *McClure's Magazine,* vol. 9, no. 2, June 1897.

Langley, Samuel P. *Langley Memoir on Mechanical Flight.* Washington: Smithsonian Institution, 1911.

Lawson, Alfred W. *Fly: The National Aeronautic Magazine, Vol. 1–10.* Philadelphia, 1908–1909.

Lilienthal, Otto. *Birdflight as the Basis of Aviation.* London: Longmans, Green & Co., 1911.

Loening, Grover C. *Military Aeroplanes.* Boston: W.S. Best Printing Co., 1918.

Loening, Grover C. *Our Wings Grow Faster.* New York: Doubleday, 1935.

McFarland, Marvin W., ed. *The Papers of Wilbur and Orville Wright.* New York: McGraw-Hill, 1953.

Means, James. *The Aeronautical Annual, 1895, 1896, 1897.*

Miller, Ivonette Wright. *Wright Reminiscences.* Wright-Patterson AFB, Ohio: Air Force Museum Foundation, 1978.

Penrose, Harald. *An Ancient Air: a Biography of John Stringfellow of Chard, the Victorian Aeronautical Pioneer.* Shrewsbury: Airlife Publishing, 1988.

Randers-Pehrson, N.H. and A.G., Renstrom. *Aeronautic Americana: A Bibliography.* New York, 1943.

Renstrom, Arthur G. *Wilbur and Orville Wright: A Bibliography.* Washington, Library of Congress, 1968.

Reynolds, Francis J. Ed. *World's War Events.* New York: Collier & Son, 1919.

Rickenbacker, Edward V. *Fighting the Flying Circus.* New York: Frederick A. Stokes Co. 1919.

Rickenbacker, Edward V. *Rickenbacker: An Autobiography.* Engelwood Cliffs, N.J.: Prentice-Hall, 1967.

Roseberry, C.R. *Glenn Curtiss: Pioneer of Flight.* Syracuse, NY: Syracuse University Press, 1991.

Steirman, Hy, and Glenn D. Kittler. *The First Transatlantic Flight, 1919.* New York: Richardson & Steirman, 1986.

Studer, Clara. *Sky Storming Yankee: The Life of Glenn Curtiss.* Stackpole & Sons, 1937.

Tanner, John., gen. ed. *Fighting in the Air: The Official Combat Technique Instructions for British Fighter Pilots 1916–1945*. London: Arms and Armour Press, 1978.

Taylor, Charles E. "My Story of the Wright Brothers." *Collier's Weekly*, Dec. 25, 1948.

Vasari, Giorgio. *Lives of the Artists*. Translated by George Bull. New York:Viking Penguin, 1965.

Villard, Henry Serrano. *Blue Ribbon of the Air: The Gordon Bennett Races*. Washington: Smithsonian Institution Press, 1987.

Villard, Henry Serrano. *Contact! The Story of the Early Birds*. Washington, Smithsonian Institution Press. 1987.

Voisin, Gabriel. *Men, Women, and 10,000 Kites*. London; Putnam, 1961.

von Kármán, Theodore. *Aerodynamics: Selected Topics in the Light of their Historical Development*. New York: Cornell University Press, 1954.

von Richthofen, Manfred. *The Red Air Fighter*. London: The "Aeroplane" & General Publishing Co., 1918.

Wenham, Francis H. *Aerial Locomotion*. London, 1866.

Wescott, Lynanne, and Paula Degen. *Wind and Sand: The Story of the Wright Brothers at Kitty Hawk, Told Through Their Own Words and Photographs*. New York: Harry N. Abrams, 1983.

Wolco, Howard S. *The Wright Flyer: An Engineering Perspective*. Washington: Smithsonian Institution Press, 1987.

Wright, Orville, and Wilbur Wright, "The Wright Brothers' Aëroplane." *Century Magazine,* 1908.

Wright Company. *Wright Co. vs. Herring-Curtiss: Brief for Complaint, Abstract*. Springfield, Ohio:Young & Bennett, 1909.

Young, Pearl I. *Alphonse Pénaud's Letters on Aeronautics*. Self-published, 1943.

Zahm, A. F. *Early Powerplane Fathers*. South Bend, In: Notre Dame University Press, 1951.

INDEX